KS2 MATHS

REVISION AND PRACTICE

David Rayner

Co-authors
David Allman
Laurence Campbell

Elmwood Press

© David Rayner
Reprinted 2000, 2001, 2002, 2005, 2006, 2008

First published 1998 by
Elmwood Press
80 Attimore Road
Welwyn Garden City
Herts. AL8 6LP
Tel. 01707 333232

British Library Cataloguing in Publication Data

Rayner, David

   1. Mathematics – 1961 –
   I. Title

   ISBN 978 1 902 214 00 9

Homework sheets (photocopiable) are published separately.

Numerical answers are published in a separate book

Artwork by Stephen Hill

Typeset and illustrated by Tech-Set, Gateshead, Tyne and Wear
Printed and bound in Great Britain by CPI Antony Rowe, Chippenham, Wilshire

PREFACE

KS2 Maths is written for pupils in year 6. Most classrooms contain children with a range of abilities in mathematics. This book has been written to cater for this situation.

The authors believe that children learn mathematics most effectively by *doing* mathematics. Many youngsters who find mathematics difficult derive much more pleasure and enjoyment from the subject when they are doing questions which help them build up their confidence. Pupils feel a greater sense of satisfaction when they work in a systematic way and when they can appreciate the purpose and the power of the mathematics they are studying.

The authors, who are all experienced teachers, emphasise a thorough grounding in the fundamentals of number when working in year 6. In particular the recommendations of the National Centre for Numeracy lie behind the approach adopted to mental arithmetic and calculations performed without calculators.

There is no set path through the books and it is anticipated that most teachers will prefer to take sections in the order of their own choice. No text book will have the 'right' amount of material for every class and the authors believe that it is better to have too much material rather than too little. Consequently teachers should judge for themselves which sections or exercises can be studied later. On a practical note, the authors recommend the use of exercise books consisting of 7 mm squares

Many activities, investigations, games and puzzles are included to provide a healthy variety of learning experiences. The authors are aware of the difficulties of teaching on 'Friday afternoons' or on the last few days of term, when both pupils and teachers are tired, and suitable activities are included. Photocopiable homework sheets are available from the publisher separately.

The authors are indebted to the many students and colleagues who have assisted them in this work. They are particularly grateful to Steve Pearce for his invaluable advice and encouragement.

David Rayner
David Allman
Laurence Campbell

CONTENTS

Part 1

1.1 Place value

- Whole numbers are made up from units, tens, hundreds, thousands and so on. The value of a figure depends on the position it occupies in the number.

thousands	hundreds	tens	units
5	3	8	7

- In the number 5387:

  the digit 5 means 5 thousands
  the digit 3 means 3 hundreds
  the digit 8 means 8 tens
  the digit 7 means 7 units (ones)

  In words we write 'five thousand, three hundred and eighty-seven'.

- Each of the figures that make up a number is called a *digit*
  The number 2 is a single digit number.
  The number 792 is a three digit number.

Exercise 1 [Oral]

State the value of the figure underlined.

1. 3<u>5</u>	**2.** 1<u>2</u>6	**3.** <u>1</u>04	**4.** <u>9</u>7	**5.** 6<u>9</u>
6. 347<u>8</u>	**7.** <u>1</u>28	**8.** 4<u>6</u>3	**9.** <u>2</u>116	**10.** <u>3</u>00
11. 2<u>1</u>6	**12.** 74<u>3</u>11	**13.** <u>8</u>5109	**14.** 29<u>3</u>	**15.** <u>4</u>12405
16. <u>3</u>5714	**17.** <u>6</u>500000	**18.** <u>4</u>09	**19.** <u>9</u>491111	**20.** 6<u>5</u>10123

Exercise 2

In Questions **1** to **10** write down the number which goes in each box.

1. $375 = \square + 70 + 5$

2. $418 = 400 + \square + 8$

3. $562 = \square + 60 + 2$

4. $4329 = 4000 + \square + 20 + 9$

5. $37\,413 = \square + 7000 + 400 + 10 + 3$

6. $48\,607 = 40\,000 + \square + 600 + 7$

7. $5117 = 5000 + 100 + \square + 7$

8. $65\,409 = \square + 5000 + 400 + 9$

9. $207\,425 = 200\,000 + 7000 + 400 + 20 + \square$

10. $99\,999 = \square + 9000 + 900 + 90 + 9$

In Questions **11** to **20** write the numbers in figures.

11. Eight hundred and ten.
12. One thousand two hundred and sixty-four.
13. One thousand five hundred.
14. Two thousand six hundred and ten.
15. Three thousand and twenty.
16. Four thousand and six.
17. Six thousand and fifty-eight.
18. Seven thousand and eighty-nine.
19. Eight thousand five hundred and twenty-six.
20. Nine thousand and ninety-nine.
20. The Romans used: X for ten,
                         V for five,
                         I for one.
   Find out what these numbers are

(a) XX   (b) VI   (c) XV   (d) XXVII

When you write a cheque to pay for something you have to write the amount in figures *and* in words.

Here is a cheque to pay 'Grange Motors' for a car.

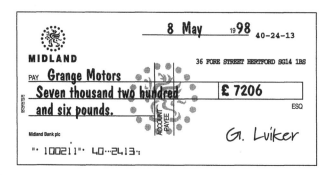

Exercise 3

1. Write the number 327 in words.

Write the following numbers in words

2. 101	**3.** 123	**4.** 150	**5.** 1200	**6.** 3270
7. 4031	**8.** 5009	**9.** 1356	**10.** 67300	**11.** 107 326
12. 970 001	**13.** 1 000 001	**14.** 180 000 000	**15.** 7 654 321	**16.** 900 019

17. Here are three number cards

One number that can be made with the three cards is 583.
(a) Use the three cards to make a number which is more than 583.
(b) Use the three cards to make a number which is less than 583.
(c) Use the three cards to make an even number.

18. Here are four number cards

(a) Use all the cards to make the largest possible number.
(b) Use all the cards to make the smallest possible number.

19. You are looking for a mystery number.
Use the clues to find it.

- the sum of the digits is 10
- the number reads the same forwards as backwards
- the number is less than 2000
- the number has no zeros
- the number has four digits

20. Here are three number cards

Make a list of all the different three figure numbers you can make.

21. Write down the number that is ten more than
(a) 3645   (b) 471   (c) 53 408   (d) 5005

22. Write down the number that is one hundred more than
(a) 5341   (b) 8094   (c) 2941   (d) 6666

23. Write down the number that is one thousand *less* than
(a) 56 985   (b) 2389   (c) 62 540   (d) 50 458

24. Write down the numbers in order, from the smallest to the largest

    (a) 2010,   2645,   2045,   2654

    (b) 5124,   5099,   5322,   5119,   5085

    (c) 63 414,   62 495,   63 411,   62 455,   63 407

25. Draw a picture of a cheque like the one shown. Pay yourself £10 304 and write the amount in figures and in words. Ask your teacher to sign the cheque! (But don't be too surprised if he/she declines.)

And finally ...

A taxi driver who spent six years writing out every number from one to a million in an attempt to win a place in the Guinness Book of records has been told he may have to start again.

The compilers have a rule that the numbers should be in words rather than digits!

1.2 Addition

- Method 1: Using 'carrying'

    (a) 54 + 281 + 3052   (b) 40514 + 24 + 3216

    line up the units digits

```
        54                      40514
       281                         24
     + 3052                    +  3216
     ------                    -------
      3387                      43754
        1                          1
```

- Method 2: Work from the left [add the most significant digits first.]

(a)	374	(b)	432	(c)	5327	(d)	6529
	+ 27		+ 265		+ 824		+ 3782
	300		600		5000		9000
	90		90		1100		1200
	11		7		40		100
	401		697		11		11
					6151		10 311

Notes: A. In (c) $300 + 800 = 1100$ and $7 + 4 = 11$. Work 'in your head'.

       B. Many people prefer this method. Give it a try!

Exercise 1

Copy and complete the following addition problems.

1.　　7　　　**2.**　　17　　　**3.**　　9　　　**4.**　　47
　　　　8　　　　　　+ 14　　　　　+ 13　　　　　+ 34
　　　+ 9

5.　　6　　　**6.**　　19　　　**7.**　　67　　　**8.**　　32
　　　38　　　　　　27　　　　　　44　　　　　　49
　　+ 44　　　　　+ 3　　　　　+ 5　　　　　+ 51

9.　126　　　**10.**　48　　　**11.**　　9　　　**12.**　28
　　+ 37　　　　+ 173　　　　　17　　　　　63
　　　　　　　　　　　　　　+ 193　　　　+ 205

13.　355　　　**14.**　573　　　**15.**　301　　　**16.**　114
　　+ 278　　　　+ 209　　　　　99　　　　　9
　　　　　　　　　　　　　　+ 257　　　　+ 867

17.　501　　　**18.**　634　　　**19.**　389　　　**20.**　371
　　397　　　　　769　　　　　193　　　　　567
　　+ 124　　　　+ 127　　　　+ 624　　　　+ 462

In Questions **21** to **40** set the problems out correctly in columns.

21. $3 + 12 + 109$
24. $39 + 357$
27. $201 + 76 + 40$
30. $2030 + 69 + 5$
33. $1089 + 891 + 19 + 9$
36. $873 + 2316 + 473$
39. $45\,609 + 20\,047$

22. $27 + 260$
25. $3 + 109 + 61$
28. $679 + 63 + 4$
31. $6006 + 708 + 99$
34. $5867 + 321 + 45 + 9$
37. $2644 + 55685$
40. $67\,508 + 95\,607 + 436$

23. $584 + 617$
26. $5034 + 69$
29. $54 + 507 + 2704$
32. $842 + 67 + 2011$
35. $8647 + 198$
38. $26\,514 + 749$

41. Find the missing digits.

$5\,\boxed{} + \boxed{}\,4 = 78$

$4\,\boxed{} + \boxed{}\,8 = 110$

$3\,\boxed{} + \boxed{}\,5 = 82$

42. Write the numbers 1 to 9 in the circles so that each side of the square adds up to 12.

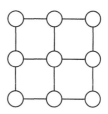

43. Here are three eggs. Arrange the numbers 1, 2, 3, ... 9 so that the numbers in each egg add up to 15.
Try to find different ways of doing it.

44. Choose 3 digits from 2, 3, 5, 7.   ☐☐ + ☐ = 32

Put them in the boxes to make a true statement.

Addition – Keywords

The following words are all associated with addition.

'Add'   Two *add* two?

'Plus'   Two *plus* two?

'Greater than'   What number is two *greater than* two?

'Count on'   *Count on* two from two, where are you?

'And'   What is two *and* two?

'Sum'   What is the *sum* of two and two?

'More than'   What is two *more than* two?

'Total'   What is the *total* of two and two?

'Altogether'   What is two and two *altogether*?

All these statements are saying ... $2 + 2 = 4$

```
2 GOOD
2 BE
_____
4 GOTTEN
```

What is the *sum of* nine hundred and eighty-one and one hundred and eighty-nine?

```
              981
            + 189
            _____
The answer is ...   1170
            _____
              1  1
```

Exercise 2

Do these questions without a calculator.

1. Sixteen add twenty-seven.

2. What is the sum of forty-eight and ninety-seven?

3. What is seventy-five plus sixty-nine?

4. What number is sixty-six greater than fifty-nine?

5. What number is thirty-nine more than eighty-seven?

6. What is the total of one hundred and twenty-four and two hundred and seventy-eight?

7. If you count on thirty-seven from sixty-five, what number will you reach?

8. How much do seventy-seven and eighty-nine make altogether?

9. What is sixty-eight and forty-seven?

10. What is the sum of one hundred and sixty-four and eight hundred and thirty-seven?

11. Jack was playing cricket, he scored 124 in his first innings and 38 in his second innings. What was the total number of runs he scored?

12. There are 30 days in September, 31 in October, 30 in November and 31 in December. How many days altogether in these four months?

13. Kathy and Jenny were playing darts. Jenny scored 59. Kathy scored 28 more than Jenny. What did Kathy score?

14. Tina scored 55 marks in her maths test. Mary scored 18 more. What was Mary's mark in the test?

15. Eddie had 27 pence, Jim had 34 pence and Joe had 49 pence. How much money did they have altogether?

16. Add together 142 and 759.

17. Karen has three dogs. 'Amy' is aged 12, 'Jody' is 15 and 'Foxy' is 9. What is the total of their combined ages?

18. Roy has 148 conkers and Dave has 79. How many conkers do they have altogether?

19. Billy needs to add together 327 and 609. What answer should he get?

20. Find the sum of the three numbers: two and a half million, eighty-eight thousand and three and a half thousand.

Cross number puzzles 1

Copy the following cross number puzzles onto squared paper. Complete the puzzles.

1.

Clues across	Clues down
1. $37 + 38$	1. $57 + 15$
3. $55 + 49$	2. $20 + 27$
5. $71 + 6$	3. $24 + 86$
6. $89 + 20$	4. $29 + 11$
7. $39 + 11$	5. $33 + 46$
8. $34 + 51$	6. $49 + 62$
9. $17 + 24$	7. $17 + 38$
10. $23 + 95$	8. $12 + 68$
12. $41 + 15$	9. $15 + 31$
13. $13 + 56$	10. $27 + 88$
15. $69 + 9$	11. $53 + 33$
17. $49 + 9$	12. $16 + 42$
18. $86 + 80$	14. $20 + 71$
19. $46 + 46$	15. $65 + 11$
	16. $15 + 17$

2.

Clues across	Clues down
1. $19 + 38$	1. $163 + 419$
3. $871 + 105$	2. $36 + 34$
5. $67 + 24$	4. $257 + 387$
6. $261 + 548$	5. $822 + 92$
7. $356 + 55$	8. $518 + 67$
8. $314 + 250$	10. $746 + 201$
9. $17 + 26$	11. $354 + 579$
12. $288 + 471$	12. $703 + 66$
14. $143 + 274$	13. $899 + 79$
16. $213 + 504$	15. $162 + 567$
17. $210 + 109$	
18. $62 + 27$	

Magic squares

Look at this numbered square ...

8	1	6
3	5	7
4	9	2

Add the numbers across in rows ←——→

$8 + 1 + 6 = 15$
$3 + 5 + 7 = 15$
$4 + 9 + 2 = 15$

Add the numbers in the columns ↕

$8 + 3 + 4 = 15$
$1 + 5 + 9 = 15$
$6 + 7 + 2 = 15$

Add the numbers diagonally ↘ ↗

$8 + 5 + 2 = 15$
$4 + 5 + 6 = 15$

All the answers are the same. In this case 15.

When a set of numbers is arranged to do this it is called a 'magic square'.

Here is another magic square ...

6	13	8
11	9	7
11	5	12

Exercise 3

Copy and complete the following magic squares

1.

4	3	
	5	
		6

2.

		3
	6	
9		4

3.

	10	8
	7	
	4	

4.

		11
5	12	7

5.

6		2
	5	
8		

6.

6	7	
13	8	
	9	

7.

	6	10	15
16		5	4
	12	8	
		11	

8.

9	14		
		16	7
12	3	15	8
6			

9.

11			10
2	13	16	
		4	
7	12		6

1.3 Two dimensional shapes

Lines and angles

- Lines that meet at a point ...

  ... or cross each other ...

  ... create angles.

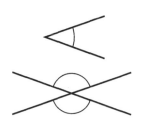

- Lines which are at right angles are *perpendicular* to each other.

- Lines like these which never meet are called *parallel*. To show that lines are parallel we draw arrows.

- A *horizontal* line is parallel to the horizon.

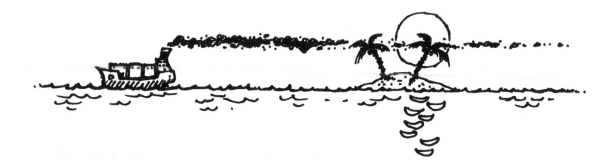

- A *vertical* line is perpendicular to the surface of the earth.

Look around the classroom. Where can you see parallel lines? Where can you see *perpendicular* lines?

Can you see anything which is *vertical*? Is there anything which is *horizontal*?

Builders sometimes use a plumb line or a spirit level.
What is a plumb line?
What is a spirit level?

For each of the letters of the word 'LINES' use the following 'key' to indicate ...

1. perpendicular lines ⟶

2. parallel vertical lines ⟶

3. parallel horizontal lines ⟶

4. angles ⟶

... like this:-

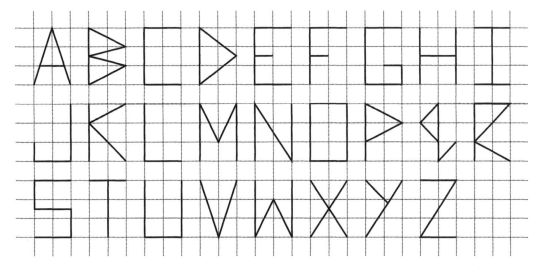

Exercise 1

Copy out the key given in the above example and colour the stencil of the alphabet below onto squared paper. Use the key to show on all the letters any:

(a) perpendicular lines   (b) parallel lines   (c) horizontal lines (in green)
(d) vertical lines (in red)   (e) angles

Exercise 2

In Questions **1** to **3** write the sentence choosing the correct word.

1. 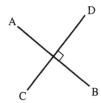   AB is (parallel/perpendicular) to CD.

2.   LM is (parallel/perpendicular) to MN.
ON is (parallel/perpendicular) to LM.
OL is (parallel/perpendicular) to MN.

3. CD is _____ to EF.

AB is _____ to CD.

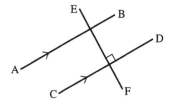

4. In the rectangle PQRS, RQ is perpendicular to SR.
(a) Which other line is perpendicular to PQ?
(b) Which line is parallel to PQ?

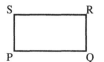

5. Find out which lines are perpendicular.

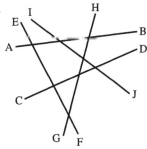

6. Can you see any parallel lines in the diagram?

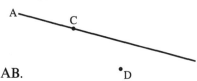

7. Copy the diagram on the right.
(a) Draw a line through C which is perpendicular to AB
(b) Draw a line through D which is parallel to AB
(c) Draw a line through D which is perpendicular to the line AB.

8.

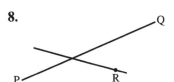

Copy the diagram on the left.
(a) Draw a line through R which is parallel to PQ.
(b) Draw a line through R which is perpendicular to PQ.

9.* Answer true or false (Think carefully).
(a) Two vertical lines are always parallel.
(b) Two horizontal lines are always parallel.

Triangles

- A plane figure with three sides and angles is a triangle.

- A triangle with three different sides and three different angles is a *scalene* triangle.

- A triangle with two sides the same length and two angles the same is an *isosceles* triangle.

- A triangle with three sides the same length and three equal angles is an *equilateral* triangle.

- A triangle which contains a right angle is a *right angled* triangle.

- *Congruent* triangles are the same shape and size

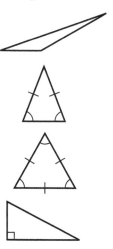

Exercise 3

For each of the following triangles state whether it is scalene, isosceles, equilateral or right angled. (Lines of the same length are indicated by dashes and equal angles are marked.)

1. 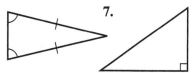 **2.** 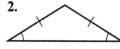 **3.**  **4.**   **5.**

6. 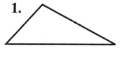 **7.** **8.**   **9.**   **10.**

Quadrilaterals

● A plane figure with four sides and angles is a *quadrilateral*

Here are some special types of quadrilaterals:

1. A *square* has all its sides equal in length and all its angles are right angles.

2. A *rectangle* has pairs of opposite sides equal in length and all its angles are right angles.

3. A *parallelogram* has its opposite sides equal in length and parallel. Its opposite angles are equal.

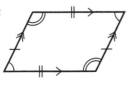

4. A *rhombus* is a parallelogram with all its sides equal.

5. A *trapezium* has one pair of opposite sides parallel.

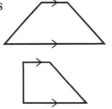

6. A *kite* is a quadrilateral with two pairs of adjacent sides equal in length. (Adjacent means 'next to'.)

Polygons

A polygon is a plane figure with straight sides. A polygon can have any number of sides from 3 upwards.

Here is a five-sided polygon or pentagon.

If a polygon is described as *regular*, then all its sides and angles are equal. Here is a regular pentagon.

Here are the names of other common polygons:
Hexagon = 6 sides; Heptagon = 7 sides; Octagon = 8 sides;
Nonagon = 9 sides; Decagon = 10 sides.

Exercise 4

Write down the name for each shape. If the shape has a special name like 'parallelogram' or 'kite' write that name. Otherwise write 'quadrilateral', 'hexagon', 'regular pentagon' and so on.

1.

2.

3.

4.

5.

6.

7.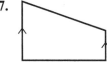

8.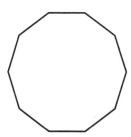

9.

10.

11.

12.

13.

14.

15.

16.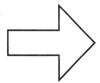

17.

18.

19.

20.

21. Draw any rectangle and any rhombus. Copy and complete:

    (a) The diagonals of a rectangle are _____.

    (b) The diagonals of a rhombus cut each other in _____ and the angle between the diagonals is_____.

Shapes investigation

On a square grid of 9 dots it is possible to draw several different triangles with vertices on dots. A vertex (plural vertices) is where two lines meet. Look at the three examples below:

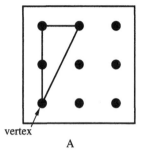

vertex

A

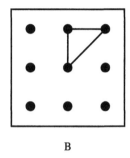

B

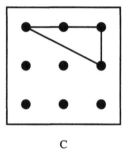

C

A and B are different triangles but C is the same as A. If a triangle could be cut out and placed exactly over another triangle then the two triangles are the same. The two triangles are called *congruent*.

1. Copy A and B above and then draw as many different triangles as you can. Check carefully that you have not repeated the same triangle.

2. On a grid of 9 dots it is also possible to draw several different *quadrilaterals*.

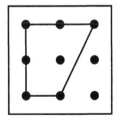
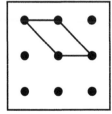
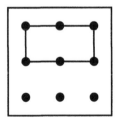

Copy the three shapes above and then draw as many other different quadrilaterals as possible. You are doing well if you can find 12 shapes but there are a few more!

Check carefully that you have not repeated the same quadrilateral. (Congruent shapes are not allowed.)

Circles

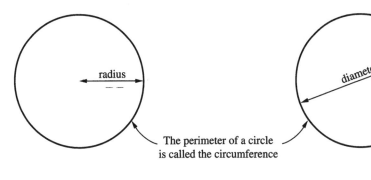

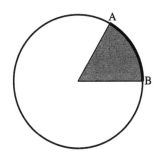

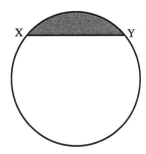

AB is an *arc* of the circle
A *sector* of the circle is shaded.

XY is a *chord* of the circle
A *segment* of the circle is shaded.

Exercise 5

1. Copy and complete these sentences

    (a) The straight line PQ is a _____.

    (b) The shaded region is a _____ of the circle.

    (c) The perimeter of the whole circle is the _____.

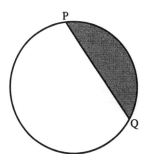

2. (a) Line AC is a _____ of the circle.

    (b) Line AB is a _____ of the circle.

    (c) The shaded region is a _____ of the circle.

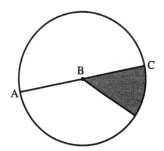

Bisecting lines and angles

Bisecting a line

Take a pair of compasses and set the radius
at more than half the length AB. With centre
A draw two arcs. With the same radius and
centre B draw two more arcs. Draw a
straight line through the points where the
arcs cut. This is the line which bisects the line
AB. (shown with a broken line).

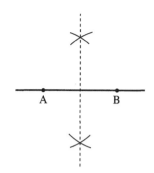

Bisecting an angle

(a) With a pair of compasses and centre
    at A, draw two arcs to cut the lines
    at P and Q.
(b) With centres P and Q draw two
    more arcs to intersect at X.
(c) Draw a straight line through
    A and X.

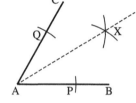

The broken line bisects (cuts exactly in half) the
angle between AB and AC.

Exercise 6   [Teachers note: see also homework sheet 00.]

1. Draw a line AB which is 6 cm long.
   Use a pair of compasses to construct
   the line which bisects AB.

2. Draw an angle like the one shown.
   Construct the line which bisects the
   angle

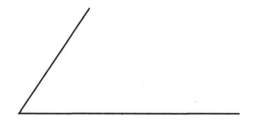

1.4 Subtraction

● Method 1: 'Exchanging'

(a)
```
   5 8 3
 −1 4 7
```

(b)
```
   6 7 4 3
 −3 9 2 7
```

Exchange ten from 80 to make 13

```
   5 ⁷8̸ ¹3
 −1 4  7
   4 3  6
```

Exchange in two places.

```
   ⁵6̸ ¹7 ³4̸ ¹3
 − 3  9  2  7
   2  8  1  6
```

● Method 2: 'Look at the numbers.'

The calculation 205 − 97 can be done by exchanging but there is an easier way.
From 97 to 200 = 103
From 205 to 200 = 5
So the answer is 108

Do these subtractions using this method

(a) 302 − 84

(b) 5005 − 4997

Copy each of the following problems and perform the calculation. (No calculators.)

1.
```
   49
 − 15
```

2.
```
   76
 −  7
```

3.
```
   83
 − 67
```

4.
```
   92
 −17
```

5.
```
   50
 − 26
```

6.
```
   421
 −  59
```

7.
```
   368
 − 274
```

8.
```
   573
 −  94
```

9.
```
   900
 − 487
```

10.
```
   1001
 −  697
```

In Questions **11** to **30** write the numbers in columns and then subtract.

11. 33 − 16   **12.** 24 − 7   **13.** 57 − 19   **14.** 40 − 13   **15.** 167 − 78
16. 319 − 234 **17.** 743 − 517 **18.** 800 − 342 **19.** 965 − 877 **20.** 2001 − 416

21. Two hundred and four take away forty-eight.
22. Five hundred and thirteen take away one hundred and twenty-five.
23. Two hundred and eight take away thirty-one.
24. Six hundred and nineteen take away two hundred and twenty-seven.
25. Seven hundred and fifty take away three hundred and ninety-one.

26. $213 - 50$	**27.** $452 - 172$	**28.** $95 - 18$	**29.** $200 - 35$	**30.** $601 - 150$
31. $412 - 108$	**32.** $563 - 185$	**33.** $692 - 119$	**34.** $504 - 167$	**35.** $230 - 66$
36. $516 - 219$	**37.** $300 - 24$	**38.** $700 - 585$	**39.** $901 - 896$	**40.** $234 - 78$

Subtraction – Keywords

The following words are all associated with subtraction.

'Subtract'   Three *subtract* two equals?
'Take away'   Three *take away* two equals?
'Difference between'   What is the *difference*
    between three and two?
'Minus'   What is three *minus* two?

'Less than'   What is two *less than* three?
'Fewer than'   What number is two *fewer*
    than three?
'From'   What is two *from* three?

All these statements are saying $3 - 2 = 1$

Exercise 2

1. What is seventeen subtract nine?

2. Thirty-four take away nineteen equals?

3. What is the difference between ninety-three and sixty-seven?

4. What is one hundred and seven minus twenty-nine?

5. What is sixty-eight less than two hundred and four?

6. What number is eighty-three fewer than three hundred?

7. If you count sixty-nine back from one hundred and thirty-eight, what number do you reach?

8. What is seventy-five from one hundred and sixty-four?

9. There were one hundred and eighty-six crisps in a bag. Forty-nine were eaten. How many crisps were left over?

10. There are eight hundred and one pupils in a school. If there are three hundred and eighty-three boys, how many girls are in the school?

11. There are 365 days in a year, 176 days have passed. How many days are left in the year?

12. What is the difference between £431 and £134?

13. There were 100 biscuits in a tin. Jackie ate 29, how many biscuits were left?

14. An apple tree had 189 apples growing on it. After a windy night, 93 apples had fallen off the tree. How many apples were still on the tree?

15. Bob needs to work out 743 minus 529. What answer should he get?

16. Julie needs to take £123 from £321. What answer should she get?

17. Dawn's tennis racket cost £78. Mark's cricket bat cost £127. What is the difference in the two costs?

18. Vicky's book was 900 pages long. She had read 529 pages. How many pages does she still have to read to finish the book?

19. What is 303 subtracted from 3001?

20. A monster bouncy castle can hold a maximum of 1000 children. There are 223 children bouncing around inside. How many fewer than the maximum is this?

21. John says '26 + 39 = 65'   Graham says   'So I know three facts:
$$39 + 26 = 65$$
$$65 - 26 = 39$$
$$65 - 39 = 26$$

In each question write down the number fact given and then write down the three related number facts.

(a) $24 + 7 = 31$, $\square + \square = 31$

   $31 - \square = \square$, $31 - \square = \square$

(b) $47 + 19 = 66$, $\square + \square = \square$,

   $66 - \square = \square$, $\square - \square = \square$

(c) $85 + 47 = 132$, $\square + \square = \square$

   $\square - \square = \square$, $\square - \square = \square$

(d) $429 + 85 = 514$, $\square + \square = \square$,

   $\square - \square = \square$, $\square - \square = \square$

22. Work out the calculation stated and then write down the three other related facts

    (a) $14 + 39$ (b) $44 + 72$ (c) $115 - 81$

Cross number puzzles 2

Copy the following cross number puzzles onto squared paper. Complete the puzzles using the clues given.

1.

Clues across	**Clues down**
1. $501 - 26$	1. $501 - 78$
3. $231 - 147$	2. $118 - 67$
4. $189 - 68$	3. $1000 - 182$
6. $70 - 40$	5. $301 - 75$
7. $471 - 190$	8. $613 - 286$
8. $83 - 47$	9. $31 - 19$
11. $425 - 350$	10. $42 - 28$
12. $200 - 143$	

2.

Clues across	**Clues down**
1. $586 - 330$	1. $2503 - 187$
4. $231 - 152$	2. $101 - 45$
5. $1154 - 789$	3. $1000 - 349$
6. $2010 - 921$	4. $811 - 23$
8. $420 - 359$	7. $9999 - 978$
10. $918 - 397$	9. $580 - 423$
11. $821 - 648$	
12. $615 - 574$	

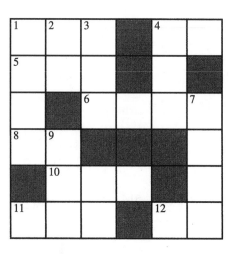

1.5 Coordinates

- To get to the point P on this grid we go **across** 1 and **up** 3 from the bottom corner.
  The position of P is (1, 3).
  The numbers 1 and 3 are called the **coordinates** of P.
  The coordinates of Q are (4, 2).
  The *origin* is at (0, 0).

- The *across* coordinate is always *first* and the *up* coordinate is *second*.
  Remember: 'Along the corridor and up the stairs'.

- Notice also that the *lines* are numbered, *not* the squares.

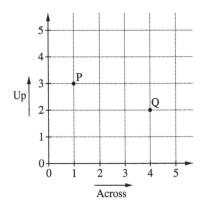

Exercise 1

1. Write down the coordinates of all the points marked like this: A(5, 1) B(1,4)

   Don't forget the brackets.

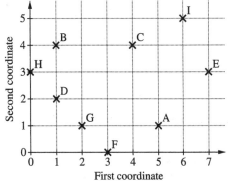

2. The map below shows a remote Scottish island used for training by the S.A.S.

   Write down the coordinates of the following places:
   (a) Rocket launcher
   (b) H.Q.
   (c) Hospital A
   (d) Rifle range
   (e) Officers' mess
   (f) Radar control

3. Make a list of the places which are at the following points:
   (a) (2, 8)   (b) (7, 8)
   (c) (3, 3)   (d) (6, 4)
   (e) (2, 6)   (f) (6, 2)
   (g) (2, 4)   (h) (9, 1)

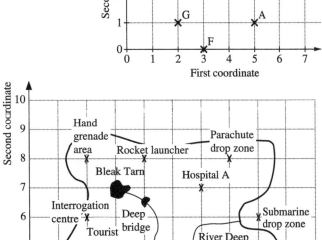

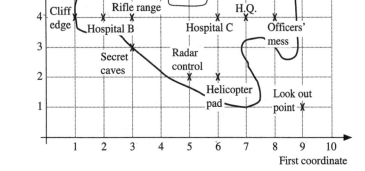

4. The map below shows the first two holes on a rather hazardous golf course. What is at the following points?
   (a) (6, 3)   (b) (4, 2)   (c) (2, 6)
   (d) (6, 4)   (e) (3, 3)   (f) (7, 3)

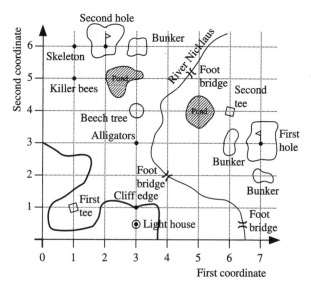

5. (a) Write down the positions in which the ball might land if *you* played the first hole.
   (b) Where would you like the ball to go if your maths teacher was playing the hole?

6. Make up your own map. Mark some interesting points and make a list, giving the coordinates of eight points.

x and *y* coordinates (*x*, *y*)

We call the first coordinate of a point the *x*-coordinate and the second coordinate the *y*-coordinate. So for the point (1, 4) the *x*-coordinate is 1 and the *y*-coordinate is 4.

The line across the page at the bottom is called the *x* axis and the line up the page at the side is called the *y* axis.

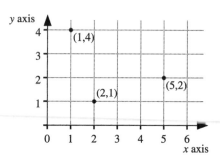

Coordinate messages

Example:- Write down the letters situated at these coordinates:-

     (3, 2),   (0, 0),   (0, 3),   (2, 1),   (1, 2)
       ↓   ↓   ↓   ↓   ↓
       M   A   T   H   S

Note 'T' is at (0, 3) meaning zero across, three up, but 'D' is at (3, 0) meaning three across, zero up.

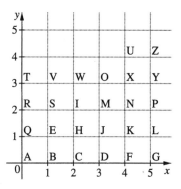

Exercise 2

Use the grid opposite to decode these messages:-

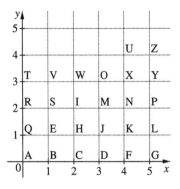

1. (5, 2), (5, 1), (3, 3), (0, 3), (0, 3), (2, 2), (4, 2), (5, 0),
   (5, 2), (3, 3), (2, 2), (4, 2), (0, 3), (1, 2). (two words).

2. (3, 0), (0, 2), (0, 0), (2, 3),
   (0, 0)
   (5, 0), (0, 2), (2, 2), (3, 0). (three words).

3. (4, 2), (4, 4), (3, 2), (1, 0), (1, 1), 0, 2).
   (5, 1), (2, 2), (4, 2), (1, 1), (1, 2).
   (4, 2), (3, 3), (0, 3).
   (1, 2), (0, 1), (4, 4), (0, 0), (0, 2), (1, 1), (1, 2). (four words).

4. (5, 0), (3, 3).
   (0, 0), (2, 0), (0, 2), (3, 3), (1, 2), (1, 2).
   (1, 0), (1, 1), (4, 0), (3, 3), (0, 2), (1, 1).
   (5, 0), (3, 3), (2, 2), (4, 2), (5, 0).
   (4, 4), (5, 2). (five words).

5. Write your own coded message from the grid.

Coordinate pictures

Plot the points below and join them up in order.
(a) (2, 4), (8, 1), (6, 3), (4, 4),
    (2, 6), (2, 4), (0, 3), (6, 2).
(b) (5, 3½), (4, 5).

N.B.   You must join up the points
           in the order given.

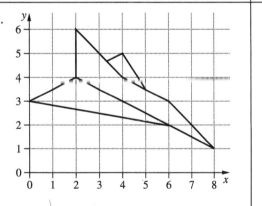

Exercise 3

Plot the points given and *join them up in order*.
Write on the grid what the picture is.

1. Draw *x* and *y* axes with values from 0 to 14.
   (a) (6, 13), (1, 3), (2, 1), (12, 1), (8, 9), (6, 5),
       (4, 5), (8, 13), (6, 13), (8, 13), (13, 3), (12, 1).

   (b) (1, 3), (9, 3), (7, 7), (6, 5), (8, 5).
       Now colour in the shape.

2. Draw x and y axes with values from 0 to 10.
  (a) (3, 2), (4, 2), (5, 3), (3, 5), (3, 6), (2, 7), (1, 6),
      (1, 8), (2, 9), (3, 9), (5, 7), (4, 6), (4, 5), (6, 4)
      (8, 4), (8, 5), (6, 7), (5, 7).
  (b) (7, 4), (9, 2), (8, 1), (7, 3), (5, 3).
  (c) (1, 6), (2, 8), (2, 9), (2, 7).
  (d) Draw a dot at (3, 8).
      Colour in the shape.

3. Draw x and y axes with values from 0 to 16
  (a) (4, 9), (1, 11), (3, 8), (1, 5), (4, 7), (6, 5), (7, 5), (8, 3),
      (9, 5), (11, 5), (12, 7), (15, 9), (15, 10), (12, 11), (9, 11),
      (8, 14), (7, 11), (6, 11), (4, 9).
  (b) (15, 12), (16, 12), (16, 13), (15, 13), (15, 12).
  (c) (14, 14), (13, 14), (13, 15), (14, 15), (14, 14).
  (d) (12, 8), (13, 8).
  (e) Draw a dot at (13, 10).
      Colour in the shape.

4. Draw axes with both x and y from 0 to 17.
  (a) (5, 1), (6, 6), (6, 3), (7, 2), (6, 2), (5, 1).
  (b) (8, 11), (8, 8), (10, 10), (11, 12), (11, 15).
  (c) (2, 14), (1, 14), (1, 15), (2, 15).
  (d) (12, 1), (11, 2), (10, 2), (10, 4), (9, 6), (8, 7), (7, 10),
      (8, 11), (9, 13), (11, 15), (10, 17), (8, 17), (7, 16), (4, 16),
      (2, 15), (2, 14), (3, 13), (5, 13), (6, 12), (4, 7), (4, 2),
      (3, 2), (2, 1), (12, 1).
  (e) (7, 16), (7, 15).
  (f) (5, 13), (6, 13).

5. Draw axes with both x and y from 0 to 11.
  (a) (7, 1), (3, 1), (1, 10), (2, 11), (3, 10), (4, 11), (5, 10),
      (6, 11), (7, 10), (8, 6), (8, 5), (9, $4\frac{1}{2}$), (9, 4), (8, 4), (9, 3),
      (5, 3), (5, 2), (7, 1).
  (b) (5, 5), (4, 6), (5, 7), (6, 6), (7, 7), (8, 6), (7, 5), (6, 6), (5, 5).
  (c) (5, 2), (6, 2), (6, $1\frac{1}{2}$).
  (d) (7, 5), (8, 5).
  (e) (7, 4), (8, 4).
  (f) (3, 7), (2, $6\frac{1}{2}$), (3, 6).
  (g) Put dots at (5, 6) and (7, 6).

6. Draw axes with both x and y from 0 to 18.
  (a) (0, 3), (1, 4), (2, 6), (4, 8), (6, 8), (8, 9), (12, 9), (13, 11),
      (12, 12), (12, 14), (14, 12), (15, 12), (17, 14), (17, 12),
      (16, 11), (17, 10), (17, 9), (16, 9), (15, 8), (14, 9), (13, 9).
  (b) (16, 9), (16, 7), (14, 5), (14, 1), (15, 1), (15, 6), (13, 4),
      (13, 1), (12, 1), (12, 4), (11, 5), (9, 5), (9, $6\frac{1}{2}$), (9, 4), (8, 3),
      (8, 1), (7, 1), (7, 4), (6, 6), (6, 4), (5, 3), (5, 1), (6, 1), (6, 3),
      (7, 4), (6, 6), (6, 7), (3, 2), (1, 2), (0, 3).

7. Design your own coordinates picture.

Exercise 4

1. The graph shows several
   incomplete quadrilaterals.
   Copy the diagram and
   complete the shapes.
   (a) Write down the
       coordinates of the fourth
       vertex of each shape.
       (A *vertex* is the
       mathematical word for a
       'corner')
   (b) Write down the
       coordinates of the centre
       of each shape.

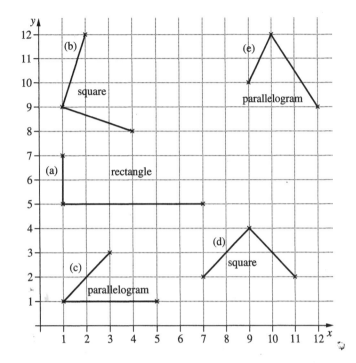

2. Copy the graph shown.
   (a) A, B and F are three corners of a square.
       Write down the coordinates of the other
       corner.
   (b) B, C and D are three corners of another
       square. Write down the coordinates of the
       other corner.
   (c) D, E and F are three corners of a
       rectangle. Write down the coordinates of
       the other corner.

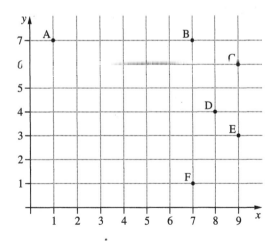

3. Draw a grid with values from 0 to 10. Plot the three points given
   and then find the coordinates of the point which makes a square
   when the points are joined up.
   (a) (1, 2) (1, 5) (4, 5)
   (b) (5, 6) (7, 3) (10, 5)
   (c) (0, 9) (1, 6) (4, 7)

4. You are given the vertices but not the sides of two parallelograms P and Q.

For each parallelogram find *three* possible positions for the fourth vertex.

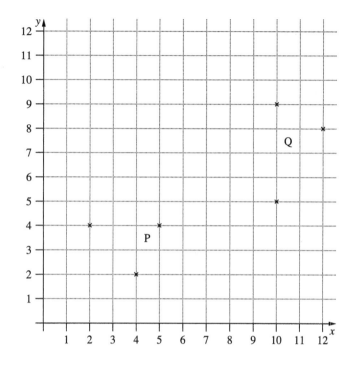

Negative coordinates

The letters from A to Z are shown on the grid.
Coded messages can be sent using coordinates.

For example (−5, −5) (−4, 2)
          (2, 5) (5, −2)
          reads 'LOTS'.

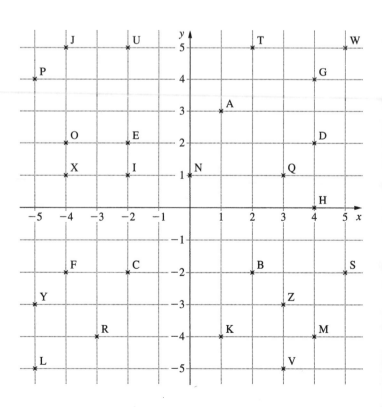

Decode the following messages:

1. (5, 5) (4, 0) (1, 3) (2, 5) □ (4, 2) (−4, 2) □ (−5, −3)
(−4, 2) (−2, 5) □ (−2, −2) (1, 3) (−5, −5) (−5, −5) □
(1, 3) □ (5, 5) (−4, 2) (4, −4) (1, 3) (0, 1) □ (−2, 1) (0, 1) □
(1, 3) □ (2, −2) (−4, 2) (−4, 2) (1, −4) (4, −4) (1, 3)
(1, −4) (−2, 2) (−3, −4) (5, −2) ? □ (2, −2) (−2, 2) (2, 5) !

2. Change the sixth word to: (4, −4) (1, 3) (0, 1) □
Change the seventh word to: (−2, 5) (0, 1) (4, 2) (−2, 2)
(−3, −4) □
then (1, 3) □ (−2, −2) (1, 3) (−3, −4) ? □ (−4, 5) (1, 3)
(−2, −2) (1, −4) !

3. (5, 5) (4, 0) (1, 3) (2, 5) □ (4, 2) (−4, 2) □ (−5, −3)
(−4, 2) (−2, 5) □ (−2, −2) (1, 3) (−5, −5) (−5, −5) #
(1, 3) □ (4, 2) (−2, 2) (1, 3) (4, 2) □ (−5, 4) (1, 3) (−3, −4)
(−3, −4) (−4, 2) (2, 5) ? □ (−5, 4) (−4, 2) (−5, −5) (−5, −3)
(4, 4) (−4, 2) (0, 1) !

4. (5, 5) (−2, 1) (2, 5) (4, 0) □ (5, 5) (4, 0) (1, 3) (2, 5) □
(4, 2) (−4, 2) □ (−5, −3) (−4, 2) (−2, 5) □ (5, −2) (2, 5)
(−2, 5) (−4, −2) (−4, −2) □ (1, 3) □ (4, 2) (−2, 2) (1, 3)
(4, 2) □ (−5, 4) (1, 3) (−3, −4) (−3, −4) (−4, 2)
(2, 5) ? □ (−5, 4) (−4, 2) (−5, −5) (−5, −3) (−4, −2) (−2, 1)
(−5, −5) (−5, −5) (1, 3) !

5. (5, 5) (4, 0) (1, 3) (2, 5) □ (4, 2) (−4, 2) □ (3, −5) (−2, 2)
(4, 4) (−2, 2) (2, 5) (1, 3) (−3, −4) (−2, 1) (1, 3) (0, 1) □
(4, −4) (−4, 2) (0, 1) (5, −2) (2, 5) (−2, 2) (−3, −4)
(5, 2) □ (2, 2) (1, 3) (2, 5) ? (5, −2) (5, 5) (−2, 2) (4, 2)
(−2, 2) (5, −2).

6. Write a message or joke of your own using coordinates. Ask a
friend to decode your words.

7. Write down the coordinates of the
points which will produce this picture.

Start at (3, 1) and follow the arrows.

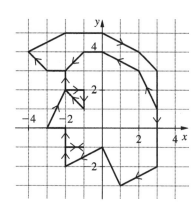

8. Design a coordinates picture of your own and write down the
points needed to produce the shape.

Part 2

2.1 Multiplication

- Multiplication is a quick method of adding together the same number ...
  $7+7+7+7+7+7+7+7+7$ is the same as 9×7 and $9 \times 7 = 63$.

- Your ability to solve multiplication problems will be greatly improved if you learn your multiplication tables up to 10×10 thoroughly.

Exercise 1

Copy each multiplication and insert the correct answer.

1. $10 \times 5 = ?$	**2.** $6 \times 6 = ?$	**3.** $9 \times 5 = ?$	**4.** $7 \times 6 = ?$
5. $8 \times 5 = ?$	**6.** $8 \times 6 = ?$	**7.** $7 \times 5 = ?$	**8.** $9 \times 6 = ?$
9. $6 \times 5 = ?$	**10.** $10 \times 6 = ?$	**11.** $5 \times 5 = ?$	**12.** $7 \times 7 = ?$
13. $11 \times 4 = ?$	**14.** $8 \times 7 = ?$	**15.** $9 \times 4 = ?$	**16.** $9 \times 7 = ?$
17. $8 \times 4 = ?$	**18.** $10 \times 7 = ?$	**19.** $7 \times 4 = ?$	**20.** $8 \times 8 = ?$
21. $6 \times 4 = ?$	**22.** $9 \times 8 = ?$	**23.** $5 \times 4 = ?$	**24.** $10 \times 8 = ?$
25. $4 \times 4 = ?$	**26.** $9 \times 9 = ?$	**27.** $12 \times 3 = ?$	**28.** $0 \times 9 = ?$
29. $9 \times 3 = ?$	**30.** $1 \times 10 = ?$	**31.** $8 \times 3 = ?$	**32.** $5 \times 11 = ?$
33. $7 \times 3 = ?$	**34.** $7 \times 11 = ?$	**35.** $6 \times 3 = ?$	**36.** $10 \times 11 = ?$
37. $5 \times 3 = ?$	**38.** $3 \times 3 = ?$	**39.** $10 \times 10 = ?$	**40.** $4 \times 3 = ?$

Exercise 2

Speed Test 1.
Copy and complete the grids opposite. Time yourself on grid 1. Try to improve your time on grid 2.

×	7	2	10	8	6	3	1	9	4	5
7	49									
2										
10										
8										
6				48						
3						9				
1										
9										
4										
5										

×	2	9	6	3	5	11	10	8	7	4
2										
9										
6										
3										
5										
11										
10										
8										
7										
4										

Multiplication by 10, 100 and 1000

$2 \times 10 = 20$
$6 \times 10 = 60$
$13 \times 10 = 130$

- When multiplying whole numbers by 10, just add a zero to the number being multiplied.

$3 \times 100 = 300$
$12 \times 100 = 1200$
$40 \times 100 = 4000$

- When multiplying whole numbers by 100, just add on two zeros to the number being multiplied.

$4 \times 1000 = 4000$
$10 \times 1000 = 10\,000$
$39 \times 1000 = 39\,000$

- When multiplying whole numbers by 1000, just add on three zeros to the number being multiplied.

Exercise 3

Copy and complete the following multiplications.

1. $5 \times 10 = ?$
2. $7 \times 100 = ?$
3. $3 \times 1000 = ?$
4. $12 \times 10 = ?$
5. $40 \times 10 = ?$
6. $137 \times 100 = ?$
7. $19 \times 100 = ?$
8. $30 \times 100 = ?$
9. $314 \times 100 = ?$
10. $13 \times 1000 = ?$
11. $67 \times 1000 = ?$
12. $80 \times 1000 = ?$

13. $601 \times 10 = ?$ **14.** $302 \times 100 = ?$ **15.** $901 \times 100 = ?$ **16.** $300 \times 10 = ?$
17. $21 \times 1000 = ?$ **18.** $100 \times 61 = ?$ **19.** $2170 \times 10 = ?$ **20.** $1000 \times 43 = ?$
21. $10 \times 27 = ?$ **22.** $304 \times 100 = ?$ **23.** $1000 \times 50 = ?$ **24.** $0 \times 10 = ?$
25. $10 \times 10 = ?$ **26.** $10 \times 100 = ?$ **27.** $100 \times 1000 = ?$ **28.** $10 \times 1000 = ?$
29. $100 \times 100 = ?$ **30.** $1000 \times 1000 = ?$ **31.** $21 \times 10 \times 100 = ?$ **32.** $7 \times 1000 \times 100 = ?$

33. How many £10 notes are in (a) £1000, (b) £2500, (c) £140 000?

34. How many £100 notes are in (a) £1800, (b) £200 000, (c) £5 million?

35. How many 1p coins are in (a) £10, (b) £500, (c) £2700?

36. Copy and complete these two sentences:
  (a) Multiplying by 100 is the same as multiplying by ⬚ and
   again by ⬚.

  (b) Multiplying by 1000 is the same as multiplying by ⬚,
   again by ⬚ and again by ⬚

37. Cans of coke at 55p each are put in packs of 10.
  Ten packs are put in a box.
  One hundred boxes are put in a container.
  Find the cost of:
  (a) 1 pack
  (b) 1 box
  (c) 1 container
  (d) 100 containers.

38. Magazines costing £2 each are wrapped in packs of 10.
  Ten packs are put in a box.
  Ten boxes are put in a van.
  Find the cost of:
  (a) 1 pack
  (b) 1 box
  (c) 1 van load
  (d) 1000 van loads.

Short multiplication

- The order in which you multiply numbers is not important. For example 7×35 is the same as 35×7.
- Here is a 'pencil and paper' method using carrying.

(a) $\begin{array}{r} 52 \\ \times\ 3 \\ \hline 156 \\ \hline \end{array}$ (b) $\begin{array}{r} 49 \\ \times\ 8 \\ \hline 392 \\ \hline {\scriptstyle 7} \end{array}$ (c) $\begin{array}{r} 231 \\ \times\ 6 \\ \hline 1386 \\ \hline {\scriptstyle 1} \end{array}$

Exercise 4

Work out

1.	$\begin{array}{r} 32 \\ \times\ 5 \\ \hline \end{array}$	**2.**	$\begin{array}{r} 61 \\ \times\ 4 \\ \hline \end{array}$	**3.**	$\begin{array}{r} 35 \\ \times\ 3 \\ \hline \end{array}$	**4.**	$\begin{array}{r} 48 \\ \times\ 2 \\ \hline \end{array}$
5.	$\begin{array}{r} 26 \\ \times\ 6 \\ \hline \end{array}$	**6.**	$\begin{array}{r} 51 \\ \times\ 8 \\ \hline \end{array}$	**7.**	$\begin{array}{r} 62 \\ \times\ 9 \\ \hline \end{array}$	**8.**	$\begin{array}{r} 89 \\ \times\ 7 \\ \hline \end{array}$
9.	$\begin{array}{r} 241 \\ \times\ 2 \\ \hline \end{array}$	**10.**	$\begin{array}{r} 416 \\ \times\ 4 \\ \hline \end{array}$	**11.**	$\begin{array}{r} 513 \\ \times\ 3 \\ \hline \end{array}$	**12.**	$\begin{array}{r} 505 \\ \times\ 5 \\ \hline \end{array}$
13.	$\begin{array}{r} 267 \\ \times\ 8 \\ \hline \end{array}$	**14.**	$\begin{array}{r} 216 \\ \times\ 6 \\ \hline \end{array}$	**15.**	$\begin{array}{r} 307 \\ \times\ 7 \\ \hline \end{array}$	**16.**	$\begin{array}{r} 199 \\ \times\ 9 \\ \hline \end{array}$

17. 7×345 **18.** 208×5 **19.** 6×3143 **20.** 6082×7

Work out

(a) $\begin{aligned} 42 \times 20 &\\ = 42 \times 2 \times 10 &\\ = 84 \times 10 &\\ = 840 & \end{aligned}$

(b) $\begin{aligned} 213 \times 300 &\\ = 213 \times 3 \times 100 &\\ = 639 \times 100 &\\ = 63\,900 & \end{aligned}$

(c) $\begin{aligned} 13 \times 5000 &\\ = 13 \times 5 \times 1000 &\\ = 65 \times 1000 &\\ = 65\,000 & \end{aligned}$

---

21. 43×20 **22.** 31×30 **23.** 24×50 **24.** 35×300

25. 52×400 **26.** 63×500 **27.** 600×211 **28.** 7000×21

29. 407×70 **30.** 312×600 **31.** 162×4000 **32.** $521 \times 30\,000$

33. Copy and complete this multiplication square.

×	3	5	4	
		40		16
			28	
4	12			8
				18

34. Copy and complete this multiplication square.

×		8		
7		56		
		16		10
	12			30
9			36	

Multiplication Keywords

The following words are all associated with multiplication.

"Multiplied by"   Two *multiplied by* three equals?
"Lots of"   Two *lots of* three equals?
"Times"   Two *times* three equals?
"Product"   What is the *product* of two and three?

All these statements are saying $2 \times 3 = 6$

Exercise 5

Write down the calculation and then work out the answer.

1. What is 7 multiplied by 12?

2. What are 11 lots of 5?

3. What is 7 times 6?

4. What is the product of 4 and 8?

5. Twenty-three boxes of eggs each contain six eggs. How many eggs are there altogether?

6. What is the product of three and nine?

7. In an orchard there are 15 apple trees and seven times as many pear trees. How many trees are there altogether?

8. What is ten times itself?

9. What are five lots of twelve?

10. What is the product of nine and seven?

11. A bus has 42 seats. How many passengers can be carried by a fleet of 6 buses?

12. A solid fuel stove uses 23 kilograms of coal per day. How much does it use in seven days?

13. Suppose you save 5 pence for every day you attend school (190 days). How much money will you have saved?

14. There are 52 playing cards in a 'deck'. How many playing cards are there altogether in six decks?

15. There are 80 tea bags per packet of tea. How many tea bags are there altogether in 7 packets?

16. Geoff grows peas with exactly nine peas per pod. Geoff picks 77 pods. How many peas will Geoff have to eat?

2.2 Turning

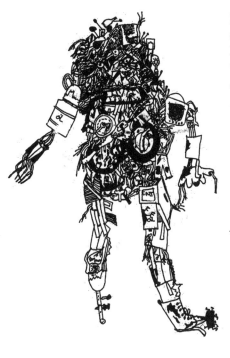

Professor M. Adman has designed a robot called 'The Rubbish Man' entirely from waste materials.

The robot is still in the early stages of development and is only able to move in four directions.

For example, as the 'Rubbish Man' approaches a crossroads, there are four directions he can take ...

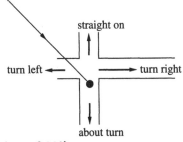

The 'Rubbish Man's' options are:-

1. Turn left (causing a change in direction of 90°).
2. Turn right (causing a change in direction of 90°).
3. Go straight on (meaning no change in direction).
4. About turn (causing a change in direction of 180°)

Three of the four options programmed into the 'Rubbish Man' cause a change in his direction. To change direction he needs to *turn* through an *angle*.

A *quarter turn* is a turn of **90°**, called *1 right angle*.
A *half turn* is a turn of **180°**, called *2 right angles*.
A *three-quarter* turn is a turn of **270°**, called *3 right angles*.
A *full turn* is a turn of **360°**, called *4 right angles*.

- A right angle is an angle of 90° and is always indicated by the following symbol.

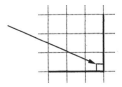

- When turning through right angles we have two options, we can turn clockwise (↷) or anti-clockwise (↶).
- Example:
  Draw the new direction of travel of 'Rubbish Man' after Professor Adman inputs the given instruction:

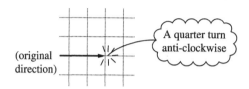

Solution:

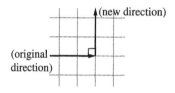

For each question you are given an arrow giving the original direction 'Rubbish man' is travelling. Copy each diagram and show his new direction of travel after each given instruction.

1.

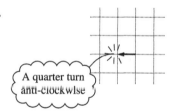

A quarter turn anti-clockwise

2.

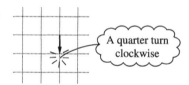

A quarter turn clockwise

3.

A half turn clockwise

4.

A half turn anti-clockwise

5.

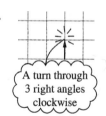

A turn through 3 right angles clockwise

6.

A turn through 3 right angles anti-clockwise

7.

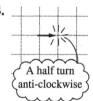

A quarter turn clockwise

8.

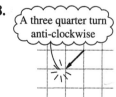

A three quarter turn anti-clockwise

9.

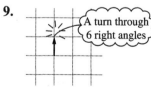

A turn through 6 right angles

10. These pictures have been hung incorrectly. Give instructions to turn them the right way round. Remember to give both the angle and the direction.

(a)

(b)

(c)

(d)

(e)

(f)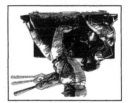

Exercise 2

In Questions **1** to **9** copy each diagram and then draw its new position after it has been turned. You can use tracing paper if you wish.

1.

A quarter turn
anti-clockwise

2.

A half turn

3.

A quarter turn
clockwise

4.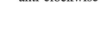

A three quarter
turn clockwise

5.

A right angle
turn anti-clockwise

6.

A turn through
2 right angles

7.

A 90° turn
anti-clockwise

8.

A 90° turn
clockwise

9.

One and a half
turns clockwise

In Questions **10** to **15** describe the turn.

10.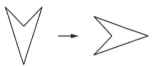

11.

12.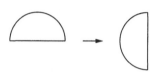

13.

14.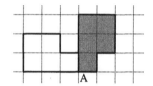

15.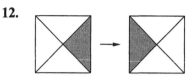

16. (a) This shape is going
     to be turned 90°
     clockwise around
     the point A

Here is
the result.

   (b) Turn this shape
       90° clockwise around
       the point B

Shade in the new
position of the shape

In Questions **17** to **19** copy the shape on squared paper and then
draw and shade its new position.

17.

Half turn around
the point C

18.

Quarter turn clockwise
around the point D

19.

Turn 90° anti-clockwise
around the point E

LOGO

LOGO is used to give commands to move a turtle on a computer.
Here is a list of the main commands.

FD 20   Go **F**orwar**D** 20 spaces
BK 30   Go **B**ac**K** 30 spaces

RT 90   **R**ight **T**urn 90 degrees
RT 45   **R**ight **T**urn 45 degrees
LT 90   **L**eft **T**urn 90 degrees

PU   **P**en **U**p   ⎫ These are used to move across the
PD   **P**en **D**own ⎬ screen without drawing a line.
                        ⎭

Here are two examples in which the turtle goes from A to B.

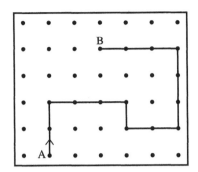

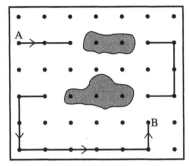

FD 20, RT 90, FD 30, RT 90, FD 10, LT 90, FD 20, LT 90, FD 30, LT 90, FD 30

In this one the turtle has to 'fly over' the obstacles shown.
FD 20, PU, FD 30, PD, FD 10, RT 90, FD 20, RT 90, FD 10, PU, FD 40, PD, FD 10, LT 90, FD 20, LT 90, FD 50, LT 90, FD 10

Exercise 2

1. Write down the commands that would move the turtle from A to B. The dots are 10 spaces apart

(a)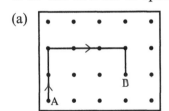

(b)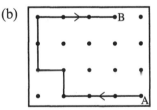

2. Write the commands that would move the turtle from A to B. In this question the turtle has to 'jump over' the obstacles shown by shaded areas.

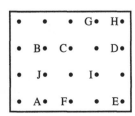

3. Write the commands that would move the turtle along the route given.
   (a) A → E → D → C → F → A
   (b) A → B → D → H → G → I → J → A
   (c) A → B → A → F → C

4. Leslie Smith wants to write her
   initials. Write down the LOGO
   commands.

5. Write down the LOGO commands for *your* own initials.

6. Draw the patterns given by the commands below.
   (a) FD 50, RT 90, FD 50, RT 90, FD 40, RT 90, FD 40, RT 90,
       FD 30, RT 90, FD 30, RT 90, FD 20, RT 90, FD 20, RT 90,
       FD 10, RT 90, FD 10.
   (b) FD 40, RT 90, FD 20, RT 90, FD 20, RT 90, FD 20, LT 90,
       FD 20, LT 90, PU, FD 30, PD, FD 20, LT 90, FD 20, LT 90,
       FD 20, BK 20, RT 90, FD 20, LT 90, FD 20.

Compass directions

Another way of describing a direction is provided by the *points* of the *compass*.

There are four major directions (called cardinal points) on a compass:

N represents north.
E represents east.
S represents south.
W represents west.

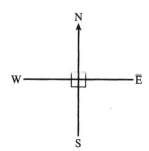

You can remember this easily by thinking in a clockwise order that
Naughty Elephants Squirt Water!

The directions between the four cardinal points are:

NE representing North-East.
SE representing South-East.
SW representing South-West.
NW representing North-West.

(a) You are facing north and then make a quarter turn anti-clockwise. In which direction are you now facing?

You must now be facing west.

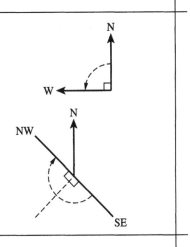

(b) You are facing south-east and then make a half-turn. In which direction are you now facing?

You must now be facing north-west.

Exercise 3

Copy and complete this table.

	You are facing	Movement (Angle and Direction)	Direction you are now facing
1.	N	180°	?
2.	E	360°	?
3.	S	90° clockwise	?
4.	W	90° clockwise	?
5.	NW	180°	?
6.	SE	90° anti-clockwise	?
7.	NE	270° clockwise	?
8.	SW	270° anti-clockwise	?
9.	S	90° anti-clockwise	?
10.	E	?	W
11.	NW	?	SW
12.	NE	?	E
13.	W	?	S
14.	?	90° clockwise	W
15.	?	90° anti-clockwise	S
16.	?	180°	NE
17.	?	90° clockwise	E
18.	SW	?	S
19.	N	?	SW
20.	S	?	NE

21. A ship is sailing around an
island. Copy and complete the
missing compass directions of
the ship's journey.

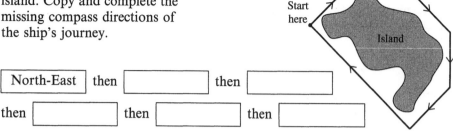

Start
here

Island

North-East	then		then	

then | | then | | then | |

22. The points A, B, C, D, E, F, G, H, I are places on a map.
Work out where I am in the following:

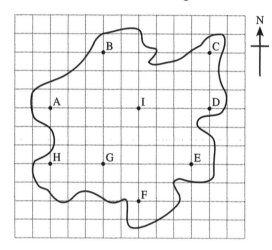

(a) I am North of G and West of C
(b) I am South of A and West of E
(c) I am West of D and North of F
(d) I am East of H and South of B
(e) I am South-East of G and South of I
(f) I am East of A and South of C
(g) I am South-West of C and East of H
(h) I am North-West of G and South-West of B.

Finding North

By Day: using the sun and your non-digital watch.

Step 1. Hold your arm in front of your stomach so that you
can read your watch.

Step 2. Turn your body so that the *hour* hand of your watch
points to the sun.

Step 3. Halve the angle between the hands on your watch. This
is the *north to south line*.

Step 4. In the morning as you look north the sun is on your
right (the east). As you look north in the afternoon the
sun is on your left.

Examples

(a)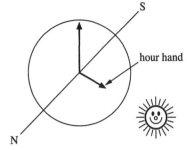

Time: 9.00 a.m.
Morning, so sun is on the right (eastward)

(b)

Time: 4.00 p.m.
Afternoon, so sun is on the left (westward)

2.3 Division

- Division is the reverse process of multiplication.

The numbers 2, 5 and 10 form a *number bond*

$2 \times 5 = 10$.   So $10 \div 2 = 5$ and $10 \div 5 = 2$

Exercise 1

Copy and complete the questions below. The number bonds are given
if you need them.

1.

$18 \div 3 = ?$

2.

$24 \div 6 = ?$

3.

$36 \div 4 = ?$

4.

$30 \div 6 = ?$

5.

$48 \div 8 = ?$

6.

$35 \div 5 = ?$

7.

$32 \div 8 = ?$

8.

$15 \div 3 = ?$

9.

$90 \div 10 = ?$

10.

$49 \div 7 = ?$

11.

$108 \div 9 = ?$

12.

$132 \div 11 = ?$

In questions **13** to **24** you are given three numbers, for example, 3, 6 and 18. There are four statements you can write connecting these numbers using the symbols ×, ÷ and =.

They are ... $3 \times 6 = 18$
$6 \times 3 = 18$
$18 \div 6 = 3$
$18 \div 3 = 6$

Write the four correct statements using ×, ÷ and = for the numbers given below.

13. 3, 4, 12   **14.** 5, 12, 60   **15.** 3, 8, 24
16. 5, 9, 45   **17.** 3, 7, 21   **18.** 7, 9, 63
19. 6, 9, 54   **20.** 3, 9, 27   **21.** 4, 9, 36
22. 4, 8, 32   **23.** 6, 7, 42   **24.** 5, 7, 35

Dividing larger numbers

- The order in which you divide numbers *is* important. For example $12 \div 3$ is *not* the same as $3 \div 12$.

- Here is a 'pencil and paper' method for dividing.

  (a) $625 \div 5$

  $$\begin{array}{r} 1\ 2\ 5 \\ 5\overline{)6^{\,1}2^{\,2}5} \end{array}$$

  (b) $936 \div 4$

  $$\begin{array}{r} 2\ 3\ 4 \\ 4\overline{)9^{\,1}3^{\,1}6} \end{array}$$

  (c) $3073 \div 7$

  $$\begin{array}{r} 0\ 4\ 3\ 9 \\ 7\overline{)3^{\,3}0^{\,2}7^{\,6}3} \end{array}$$

Exercise 2

Work out

1. $3\overline{)99}$ **2.** $2\overline{)42}$ **3.** $4\overline{)48}$ **4.** $7\overline{)84}$
5. $5\overline{)65}$ **6.** $6\overline{)72}$ **7.** $7\overline{)847}$ **8.** $9\overline{)558}$
9. $8\overline{)128}$ **10.** $9\overline{)729}$ **11.** $2\overline{)678}$ **12.** $6\overline{)3372}$
13. $3\overline{)729}$ **14.** $5\overline{)725}$ **15.** $4\overline{)1028}$ **16.** $8\overline{)1856}$
17. $6\overline{)1296}$ **18.** $7\overline{)343}$ **19.** $9\overline{)6561}$ **20.** $6\overline{)2796}$
21. $8\overline{)2056}$ **22.** $5\overline{)1025}$ **23.** $6\overline{)7776}$ **24.** $7\overline{)5082}$
25. $3050 \div 10$ **26.** $1387 \div 1$ **27.** $38\,199 \div 7$ **28.** $14\,032 \div 8$
29. $31\,386 \div 6$ **30.** $3490 \div 5$ **31.** $28\,926 \div 9$ **32.** $15\,638 \div 7$

Division keywords

The following words are all associated with division.

'Divided by'   Six *divided by* three equals?
'Shared between'   Six *shared between* three is equal to?
'Goes into'   Three *goes into* six, how many times?
'Lots of'   How many *lots of* three are there in six?

All these statements are saying . . . $6 \div 3 = 2$

Exercise 3

1. What is twenty-four divided by three?

2. What is fifty-six divided by seven?

3. How many nines go into sixty-three?

4. How many lots of six are there in seventy-two?

5. What is 120 divided by 10?

6. What is 108 shared between 9?

7. How many times does 4 go into 64?

8. How many lots of 3 are there in 78?

9. Woody has 240 matchsticks which he must divide into groups of 3. How many groups will he have?

10. Four dinosaurs each laid the same number of eggs. Altogether there are 104 eggs. How many eggs did each dinosaur lay?

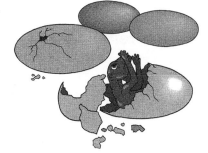

11. Davy, Dozy, Beaky, Mick and Tich are 5 dogs sharing a large tin of 'Muttmeat' which contains 215 delicious chunks. How many chunks does each dog get if it is shared out equally?

12. 'Guzzintas' fizzy drink, comes in six-can packets. Ellen has to pack them into a box which holds 216 cans. How many six-packs of 'Guzzintas' will the box hold?

13. Jake has to share his 'Megamunch' crisps with Max and Joe. He has 243 crisps in his packet. How many will Jake, Max and Joe get each if they are shared out equally?

14. (a) What is £132 divided between eleven?
    (b) What is £512 shared between 8 people?

Remainders

- Suppose you need to share 267 cakes between 5 people.

  Work out $267 \div 5$:

  $$5\overline{)2\,6\,^17} \quad \begin{array}{l} 5\,3 \;\; \textit{remainder 2} \end{array}$$

  Each person gets 53 cakes and there are 2 left over.

  Sometimes it is better to write the remainder as a fraction.
  In the calculation above the answer is $53\frac{2}{5}$.
  So each person could get $53\frac{2}{5}$ cakes.

- Work out $432 \div 7$:

  $$7\overline{)4\,3\,^12} \quad \begin{array}{l} 6\,1 \;\; \textit{remainder 5} \end{array}$$

  The answer is '61 remainder 5' or $61\frac{5}{7}$.

Exercise 4

Write the answer: (a) with a remainder,   (b) as a mixed fraction.

1. $5\overline{)432}$	**2.** $4\overline{)715}$	**3.** $6\overline{)895}$	**4.** $3\overline{)164}$
5. $8\overline{)514}$	**6.** $9\overline{)375}$	**7.** $5\overline{)2642}$	**8.** $2\overline{)7141}$
9. $4079 \div 7$	**10.** $2132 \div 5$	**11.** $4013 \div 8$	**12.** $235 \div 6$
13. $657 \div 10$	**14.** $8327 \div 10$	**15.** $85\,714 \div 6$	**16.** $4826 \div 9$
17. $2007 \div 7$	**18.** $9998 \div 9$	**19.** $6732 \div 11$	**20.** $84\,563 \div 7$

Think about the remainder

- How many teams of 5 can you make from 113 people?

  Work out $113 \div 5$.

  $$5\overline{)1\,1\,^13} \quad \begin{array}{l} 2\,2 \;\; \textit{remainder 3} \end{array}$$

  Here we round *down*. You can make 22 teams and there will be 3 people left over.

- An egg box holds 6 eggs. How many boxes do you need for 231 eggs?

  Work out $231 \div 6$.

  $$6\overline{)2\,3\,^51} \quad \begin{array}{l} 3\,8 \;\; \textit{remainder 3} \end{array}$$

  Here we round *up* because you must use complete boxes. You need 39 boxes altogether.

Exercise 5

In these questions you will get a remainder. Decide whether it is more sensible to round *up* or to round *down*.

1. Tins of spaghetti are packed 8 to a box. How many boxes are needed for 913 tins?

2. A prize consists of 10 000 one pound coins. The prize is shared between 7 people. How many pound coins will each person receive?

3. There are 23 children in a class. How many teams of 4 can be made?

4. Eggs are packed six in a box. How many boxes do I need for 33 eggs?

5. Tickets cost £6 each and I have £38. How many tickets can I buy?

6. I have 204 plants and one tray takes 8 plants. How many trays do I need?

7. There are 51 children in the dining room and a table seats 6. How many tables are needed to seat all the children?

8. I have 100 cans of drink. One box holds 8 cans. How many boxes can I fill?

9. A well organised flock of sheep queue up for their daily ration of 8 kg of grass. The farmer has only 2064 kg of grass.
   How many of his flock of 300 sheep will be disappointed?

10. Five people can travel in one car and there are altogether 93 people to transport. How many cars are needed?

11. There are 332 children in a school. One coach holds 50 children. How many coaches are needed for a whole school trip?

2.4 Mixed arithmetic

Checking that answers are reasonable

A. Check by doing the inverse.

To check:	$171 + 384 = 555$,	work out	$555 - 171$
	$67 - 38 = 29$,	work out	$29 + 38$
	$81 \times 4 = 324$,	work out	$324 \div 4$
	$228 \div 3 = 76$,	work out	76×3

B. Do addition or multiplication in a different order.

To check:	$281 + 631$,	work out	$631 + 281$
	15×7,	work out	7×15

C. Do an equivalent calculation.

To check:	$343 - 150$,	work out	$343 - 100 - 50$
	381×3,	work out	$(300 \times 3) + (80 \times 3) + (1 \times 3)$

D. Approximate by rounding.

$293 + 97$	is about	$300 + 100$
$5119 - 288$	is about	$5000 - 300$
307×19	is about	300×20
$2891 \div 11$	is about	$3000 \div 10$

Exercise 1

Work out the following and then check the answer by using the method stated.

Method A	**1.** $184 + 63$	**2.** $342 + 43$	**3.** $84 - 29$	**4.** $76 - 38$
	5. 91×4	**6.** 32×6	**7.** $396 \div 3$	**8.** $245 \div 5$

Method B	**1.** $84 + 92$	**2.** $7 + 17 + 83$	**3.** $207 + 184 + 17$	**4.** $658 + 2141$
	5. $8 \times 7 \times 2$	**6.** $7 \times 9 \times 3$	**7.** $18 + 88 + 111$	**8.** $309 + 21 + 123$

Method C	**1.** $687 - 150$	**2.** $872 - 250$	**3.** $690 - 110$	**4.** $242 + 150$
	5. 27×5	**6.** 81×6	**7.** 214×3	**8.** $815 - 750$

Method D	**1.** $298 + 105$	**2.** $896 - 307$	**3.** $5073 + 391$	**4.** $689 - 203$
	5. 98×11	**6.** 61×102	**7.** $8019 \div 11$	**8.** $708 - 589$

Mixed word problems

Exercise 2

1. A school has 1510 pupils, of which 718 are boys. How many are girls?

2. What number is twice as big as sixty-nine?

3. Find the difference between 93 and 47.

4. Seven people share a bingo prize of £2555. How much does each one receive?

5. By how much is three kilos more than 800 grams?

6. Mr Lo bought potatoes for 65p, carrots for 27p, onions for 43p and tomatoes for 57p. How much change did he receive from £5?

7. What number is three times as big as 55?

8. A bird remains airborn for five days. How many hours is that?

9. A large box of matches contained 297 matches on the evening of November 5th. If 49 matches were used during the evening, how many were left?

10. How many spots are there on an ordinary dice?

11. A school has nine forms with twenty-eight pupils in each form. How many pupils are there in the school?

12. What number is thirty-five more than eighty?

13. 456 people were invited to a banquet. How many tables were needed if eight people sat at each table?

14. In the last three days before Christmas the sales at "Toymart" were £12 501, £15 892 and £21 357: What were the total sales over the three day period?

15. A pile of 5p coins has a value of 80p. How many coins are there?

Exercise 3

1. Find the product of nine and eight.

2. A man has £1000. How much has he left after buying a television for £217 and a video recorder for £399?

3. A string of length 390 cm is cut in half. How long is each piece?

4. Find the sum of 85, 19 and 66.

5. £345 is to be divided evenly between three people. How much does each person receive?

6. How much more than £108 is £300?

7. A man died in 1993 aged 58. In what year was he born?

8. At a cricket match 2412 of the spectators were men and 172 were women. How many spectators were there altogether?

9. An egg box holds six eggs. How many boxes are needed for 100 eggs?

10. How many 5p coins are worth the same as a hundred 2p coins?

11. Multiply the sum of the numbers 415 and 707 by the difference between the numbers 33 and 26.

12. I bought a magazine for 79p and paid with £1 coin. My change consisted of five coins. What were they?

13. Five pounds of carrots cost 75p. How much do they cost per pound?

14. What is the total of 57 and 963?

15. 117 sweets are to be shared equally between 9 girls. How many sweets does each girl receive?

Number messages

Instructions:-

1. Start in the box marked X.
2. Work out the answer to the question at the bottom of the box.
3. Find the box which has the answer in the top right hand corner.
4. Write down the letter in this box. Now work out the answer to the question in that box.
5. Look for the answer as in (3.) Don't forget to record the letter!
6. Continue this process until you arrive back at box X.
7. Read the message.

1.

100	61	40	62	71
X	A	U	D	F
8 + 17	77 + 12	21 + 35	27 + 33	37 + 22
25	4	70	89	23
O	G	N	N	S
63 + 8	49 + 51	2 + 2	45 + 17	14 + 17
91	60	88	22	56
N	R	P	O	R
38 + 25	12 + 19	16 + 75	16 + 24	17 + 8
27	52	31	99	85
H	I	U	B	J
27 + 24	21 + 49	82 + 9	48 + 33	65 + 33
20	3	59	63	17
Y	W	F	N	A
13 + 9	12 + 80	28 + 33	37 + 15	27 + 11

2.

100	48	26	29	22
X	B	W	A	O
27 − 19	25 − 16	19 − 8	51 − 17	81 − 40
16	31	17	43	5
A	R	T	S	U
47 − 29	50 − 30	65 − 43	80 − 17	27 − 11
39	46	1	28	15
N	O	A	E	H
42 − 13	13 − 8	101 − 1	98 − 81	60 − 19
41	40	70	38	77
P	L	G	M	N
75 − 27	71 − 70	43 − 24	16 − 7	71 − 42
99	9	18	34	8
Q	A	R	N	Y
43 − 29	94 − 17	41 − 13	2 − 1	66 − 20

3.

100	41	24	42	27
X	B	O	A	C
3 × 5	3 × 2	2 × 9	7 × 8	7 × 7
81	32	51	83	21
C	A	S	T	K
6 × 7	2 × 8	7 × 4	6 × 8	7 × 9
20	14	56	7	45
E	R	L	E	O
3 × 10	3 × 8	3 × 9	2 × 7	1 × 1
15	49	18	16	1
L	U	O	T	R
6 × 4	10 × 5	3 × 7	5 × 9	10 × 10
64	72	90	50	63
O	P	H	L	N
9 × 9	10 × 9	9 × 8	4 × 8	8 × 8

4.

100	20	5	21	14
X	E	T	H	A
20 ÷ 5	9 ÷ 3	49 ÷ 7	8 ÷ 4	39 ÷ 3
12	16	3	18	11
A	M	H	C	B
99 ÷ 9	21 ÷ 3	15 ÷ 15	51 ÷ 17	20 ÷ 10
9	13	15	8	7
G	S	T	R	O
3 ÷ 1	60 ÷ 5	30 ÷ 6	12 ÷ 2	70 ÷ 7
10	4	19	20	21
N	B	P	E	D
100 ÷ 1	24 ÷ 3	81 ÷ 3	57 ÷ 3	30 ÷ 5
1	25	17	2	6
T	Y	S	U	I
28 ÷ 2	100 ÷ 50	99 ÷ 3	30 ÷ 2	90 ÷ 10

5.

100	19	96	6	81
X	I	E	P	S
12 × 7	9 × 9	18 ÷ 3	12 × 8	7 × 8
95	144	121	61	116
S	D	F	R	T
54 + 7	10 × 10	84 ÷ 7	7 × 5	43 − 17
84	91	29	0	22
O	R	Y	C	L
20 ÷ 4	71 − 49	0 × 7	32 − 7	12 × 12
12	35	26	9	8
T	A	O	O	H
38 + 47	2 ÷ 1	11 × 11	49 + 42	16 ÷ 4
56	37	5	10	85
W	U	U	I	H
72 ÷ 8	22 + 7	67 + 49	8 × 5	58 − 39

Inverse operations: Find the missing digits

The word inverse means 'opposite'.

- The inverse of adding is subtracting $7 + 11 = 18,\ 7 = 18 - 11$
- The inverse of subtracting is adding $20 - 5 = 15,\ 20 = 15 + 5$
- The inverse of multiplying is dividing $9 \times 5 = 45,\ 9 = 45 \div 5$
- The inverse of dividing is multiplying $12 \div 2 = 6,\ 12 = 6 \times 2$

Find the missing digits

(a) ☐ $85 \div 5 = 57$

Work out 57×5 because multiplying is the inverse of dividing.
Since $57 \times 5 = 285$, the missing digit is 2.

(b) $5\ ☐\ 2 \times 3 = 1626$

Work out $1626 \div 3$ because dividing is the inverse of multiplying.
Since $1626 \div 3 = 542$, the missing digit is 4.

(c)
```
   3 ☐ 5
 + 5 7 ☐
 ───────
   9 4 8
 ───────
```

Start from the right. $5 + 3 = 8$

Middle column. $7 + 7 = 14$

Check
```
   375
 + 573
 ─────
   948  ✓
 ─────
```

Find the missing digits.

1. (a)
```
   3 7 3
 + ☐ 1 4
 ───────
   5 ☐ ☐
```
(b)
```
   5 2 ☐
 + ☐ 4 3
 ───────
   7 ☐ 9
```
(c)
```
   ☐ 2 2
 + 1 7 ☐
 ───────
   5 ☐ 4
```

2. (a)
```
   1 4 7
 + 4 ☐ 5
 ───────
   5 8 ☐
```
(b)
```
   3 ☐ 3
 + 5 5 6
 ───────
   ☐ 3 9
```
(c)
```
   2 5 7
 + ☐ 3 ☐
 ───────
   9 ☐ 4
```

3. (a) ☐☐ $+ 63 = 118$ **(b)** ☐☐☐ $+ 134 = 589$

  (c) ☐☐☐ $- 41 = 99$ **(d)** ☐☐☐ $- 24 = 107$

4. (a)
$$
\begin{array}{r}
6\ \square \\
\times\qquad 7 \\
\hline
4\ \ 4\ \ 1
\end{array}
$$

(b)
$$
\begin{array}{r}
4\ \square \\
\times\qquad 8 \\
\hline
3\ \ 7\ \ 6
\end{array}
$$

(c)
$$
\begin{array}{r}
6\ \square \\
\times\qquad 7 \\
\hline
4\ \ 6\ \ 2
\end{array}
$$

5. (a) $\square\square\square \div 3 = 40$

(b) $\square\square \times 6 = 90$

(c) $7 \times \square = 56$

(d) $\square\square\square \div 5 = 23$

6. (a)
$$
\begin{array}{r}
3\ \square\ 4 \\
+\ 4\ \ 9\ \square \\
\hline
8\ \ 4\ \ 8
\end{array}
$$

(b)
$$
\begin{array}{r}
4\ \square\ 7 \\
+\ 3\ \ 5\ \square \\
\hline
\square\ 4\ 3
\end{array}
$$

(c)
$$
\begin{array}{r}
\square\ 7\ \square \\
+\ 5\ \square\ 4 \\
\hline
7\ \ 4\ \ 2
\end{array}
$$

7. (a) $\square\,\boxed{4} \times 8 = 592$

(b) $\square\square \times 10 = 530$

(c) $\boxed{5}\,\square \times 9 = 513$

(d) $\boxed{7}\,\square \times 7 = 5\square 8$

8. (a)
$$
\begin{array}{r}
\square\square\ 2 \\
4\,\overline{)\,7\ \ 2\ \square}
\end{array}
$$

(b)
$$
\begin{array}{r}
1\ \ 3 \\
6\,\overline{)\,\square\ \ 8}
\end{array}
$$

(c)
$$
\begin{array}{r}
2\ \ 9 \\
3\,\overline{)\,\square\ \ 7}
\end{array}
$$

9. (a) $\square\square\square \times 3 = 624$

(b) $\square\square\square \div 10 = 37$

(c) $495 + 20\square = 6\square 7$

(d) $674 - 34\square = 3\square 6$

10. There is more than one correct answer for each of these questions. Ask a friend to check your solution.

(a) $\boxed{3}\,\boxed{5} + \square\square - \square\square = 35$

(b) $\boxed{6}\,\boxed{3} - \square\square + \square\square = 64$

(c) $\boxed{8}\,\boxed{4} \times \square\square \div \square\square = 84$

(d) $\boxed{5}\,\boxed{0} \times \square\square \div \square = 100$

2.5 Angles 1

Estimating angles

When angles are measured accurately they are usually in *degrees*.
We write degrees as a number followed by the degree symbol °.

A full turn = 360°
A half turn = 180°
A quarter turn = 90°

An angle of 90° is called a *right angle*.

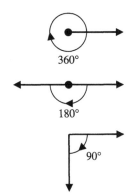

Decide which is the correct angle from the 2 answers given.
Do *not* measure the angles, *estimate*!

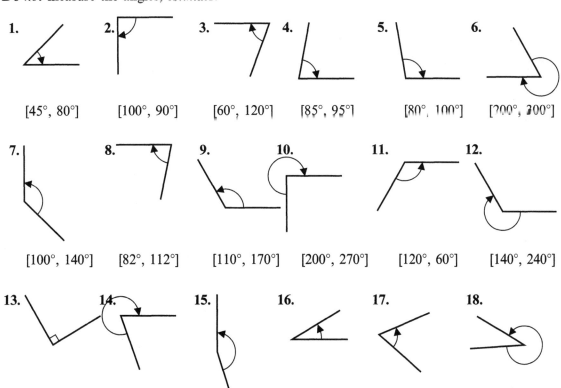

1. [45°, 80°]

2. [100°, 90°]

3. [60°, 120°]

4. [85°, 95°]

5. [80°, 100°]

6. [200°, 300°]

7. [100°, 140°]

8. [82°, 112°]

9. [110°, 170°]

10. [200°, 270°]

11. [120°, 60°]

12. [140°, 240°]

13. [90°, 110°]

14. [240°, 290°]

15. [120°, 160°]

16. [25°, 85°]

17. [70°, 110°]

18. [230°, 330°]

- Any angle between 0° and 90° is called an *acute* angle.
- Any angle between 90° and 180° is called an *obtuse* angle.
- Any angle bigger than 180° is called a *reflex* angle.

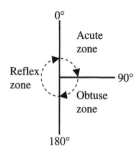

Exercise 2

State whether the following angles are acute, obtuse or reflex.

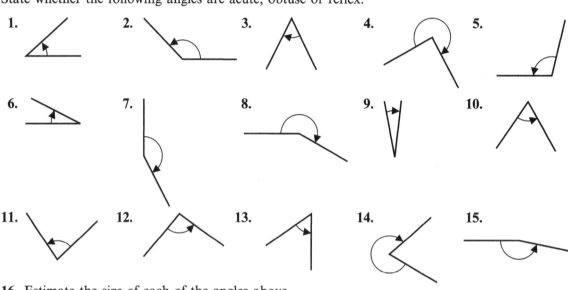

16. Estimate the size of each of the angles above.

Labelling angles

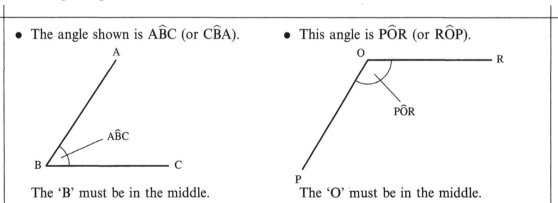

- The angle shown is AB̂C (or CB̂A).

The 'B' must be in the middle.

- This angle is PÔR (or RÔP).

The 'O' must be in the middle.

- Angles are labelled with capital letters and the middle letter wears a 'hat' to indicate an angle.

Copy each diagram and write down the size of each angle requested.

1.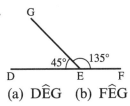
(a) DÊG   (b) FÊG

2.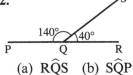
(a) RQ̂S   (b) SQ̂P

3.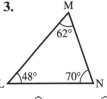
(a) MN̂L   (b) NL̂M

4.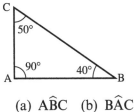
(a) AB̂C   (b) BÂC

5.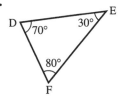
(a) DÊF   (b) FD̂E

6.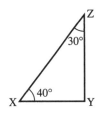
(a) YX̂Z   (b) XẐY

Using a protractor

A *protractor* is an instrument used to measure angles accurately. Most protractors are manufactured with two scales. One scale reads clockwise, the other anti-clockwise.

It is important to read the correct scale on any protractor in order to measure or draw an angle accurately.

Example:

Measure angle AÔB.

Step 1.   AÔB is acute (less than 90°).

Step 2.   Starting at 0° (along AO) you are moving clockwise. Read the clockwise scale. AÔB = 40°.

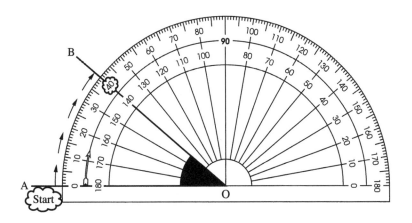

Exercise 4

Give the measurement of each angle listed below.
Remember to read the correct scale. Some questions are done for you, to remind you of this.

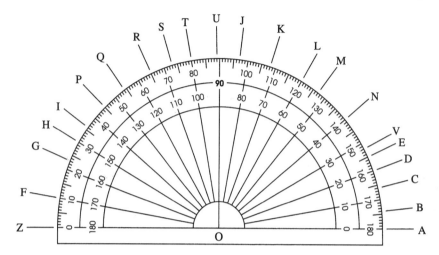

1. AÔD =	2. AÔN =	3. AÔL =	4. AÔK =
5. ZÔF =	6. ZÔP =	7. ZÔR =	8. ZÔT =
9. ZÔI =	10. ZÔG =	11. AÔC =	12. AÔV =
13. AÔQ =	14. AÔP =	15. AÔF =	16. AÔB =
17. ZÔH =	18. ZÔB =	19. ZÔC =	20. ZÔD =
21. AÔG =	22. AÔH =	23. AÔI =	24. AÔM =
25. AÔR =	26. ZÔE =	27. ZÔJ =	28. ZÔK =
29. ZÔL =	30. ZÔM =	31. AÔE =	32. AÔJ =
33. AÔU =	34. AÔS =	35. ZÔN =	36. ZÔQ =
37. ZÔS =	38. ZÔU =	39. ZÔV =	40. AÔT =

Exercise 5

Measure these angles.

1.

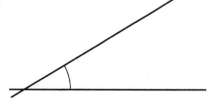

2.

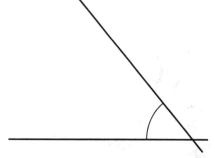

3.

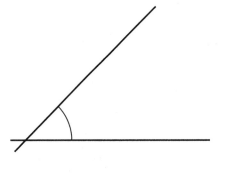

4.

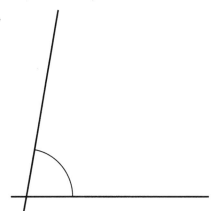

5.

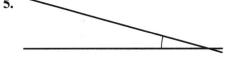

6.

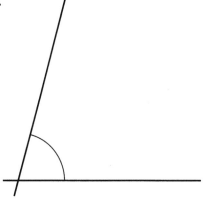

7.

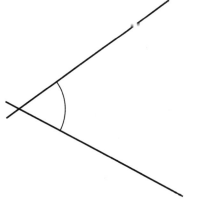

8.

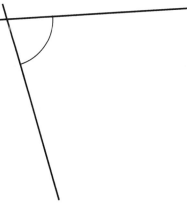

9.

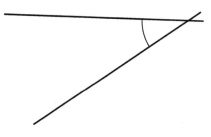

10.

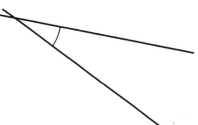

15.   **16.**

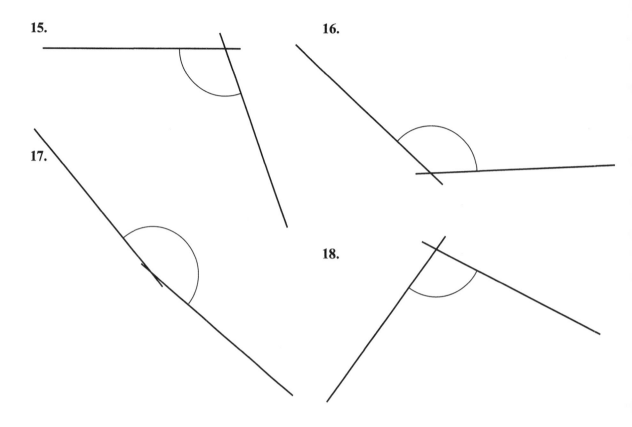

17.

18.

The 'Mystic Rose'

For this activity you need a circular protractor, a pencil and ruler.
(You *could* use a semi-circular protractor)

Step 1.   On a sheet of unlined paper, place a circular protractor with the zero pointing up the paper (↑).

Step 2.   With a sharp pencil draw around your protractor.

Step 3.   Mark where zero is, then mark 30°, 60°, 90°, 120° ... 330°.

Step 4.   Remove the protractor. Using a ruler and pencil join the 0° mark to all the marks made around the outside of the circle with straight lines. Next join the 30° mark to all other marks with straight lines. Repeat this for the 60°, 90° mark and so on up to the 330° mark so that each point is joined to every other point around the circle. This is the 'Mystic Rose'.

Step 5.   Colour in your Rose.

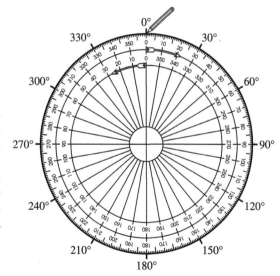

2.6 Decimals 1

- Decimals are used with money and with measurements of lengths, weights, times.

'The decimal

£13.55   2.65m

82.3 kg

5.2 seconds

separates the units from the tenths'

- The diagram below shows numbers we would see if we could 'zoom in' on an imaginary ruler.

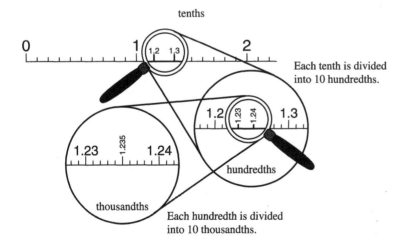

tenths

Each tenth is divided into 10 hundredths.

hundredths

thousandths

Each hundredth is divided into 10 thousandths.

The numbers between 1·2 and 1·3 go up by 0·01 at a time:
1·21, 1·22, 1·23, 1·24 ...

The numbers between 1·23 and 1·24 go up by 0·001 at a time:
1·231, 1·232, 1·233, 1·234, 1·235 ...

● Here are some decimal numbers.

Number	Hundreds H	Tens T	Units U	●	Tenths $\frac{1}{10}$	Hundredths $\frac{1}{100}$	Thousandths $\frac{1}{1000}$
538·1	5	3	8	●	1		
42·63		4	2	●	6	3	
0·04			0	●	0	4	
7·125			7	●	1	2	5

● £5·29 means £5 and $\frac{29}{100}$ths of a pound, or £5 and 29 pence.

9·6s means 9 seconds and $\frac{6}{10}$ths of a second.

18·29 metres means 18 metres and $\frac{29}{100}$ths of a metre or 18 m and 29 cm.

1·725 kilograms means 1 kilogram and $\frac{725}{1000}$ths of a kilogram or 1 kilogram and 725 grams.

Exercise 1

Copy and complete the table below putting each digit in its correct place.

Question number	Number	H	T	U	●	$\frac{1}{10}$	$\frac{1}{100}$	$\frac{1}{1000}$
1	56·7				●			
2	83·94				●			
3	137·071				●			
4	40·503				●			
5	179·03				●			
6	25·019				●			
7	3·142				●			
8	0·037				●			
9	2·004				●			
10	0·001				●			

In Questions **11** to **30** give the value of the underlined digit.

11. 4·5<u>3</u>   **12.** 3·8<u>2</u>   **13.** 7·<u>5</u>3   **14.** 9·<u>1</u>2   **15.** 15·0<u>2</u>

16. 5·0<u>4</u>   **17.** <u>6</u>·07   **18.** 3·<u>4</u>   **19.** <u>4</u>1·6   **20.** 5·3<u>6</u>2

21. 4·<u>8</u>57   **22.** 3·2<u>1</u>2   **23.** 2·52<u>2</u>   **24.** 7·1<u>6</u>4   **25.** 1·73<u>5</u>

26. 4·<u>8</u>07   **27.** 5·73<u>1</u>   **28.** 0·<u>1</u>01   **29.** <u>3</u>·142   **30.** 2·71<u>8</u>

Ordering decimals

Consider these three decimals ...

0·09, 0·101, 0·1.

Which is the correct order from lowest to highest?

- When ordering decimals it is always helpful to write them with the same number of figures after the decimal point.

0·09   ⟶ 0·090   Empty spaces can be
0·101 ⟶ 0·101   filled with zeros.
0·1   ⟶ 0·100

Now we can clearly see the correct order of these decimals from lowest to highest ... 0·090, 0·1, 0·101.

Exercise 2

In Questions **1** to **16** answer True (T) or False (F).

1. 0·7 is less than 0·71

2. 0·61 is more than 0·16.

3. 0·08 is more than 0·008

4. 0·5 is equal to 0·500

5. 0·613 is less than 0·631

6. 7·0 is equal to 0·7.

7. 6·2 is less than 6·02

8. 0·09 is more than 0·1.

9. 2·42 is equal to 2·420

10. 0·63 is less than 0·36

11. 0·01 is more than 0·001

12. 0·78 is less than 0·793

13. 8 is equal to 8·00

14. 0·4 is more than 0·35

15. 0·07 is less than 0·1

16. 0·1 is equal to $\frac{1}{10}$.

17. Here is a pattern of numbers based on 3. ⟶

Write a similar pattern based on 7 and extend it from 70 000 000 down to 0·0007. Write the numbers in figures and in words

three thousand	3000
three hundred	300
thirty	30
three	3
nought point three	0·3
nought point nought three	0·03

18. In mathematics, 5 > 2 means '5 *is greater than* 2'
and 6 < 20 means '6 *is less than* 20'

Write the correct symbol, either > or <, in place of the box

(a) 3.2 ☐ 3.02

(b) 0.01 ☐ 0.1

(c) 0.08 ☐ 0.1

(d) 0.8 ☐ 0.81

(e) 0.51 ☐ 0.15

(f) 0.03 ☐ 0.02

Exercise 3

In Questions **1** to **20** arrange the numbers in order of size, smallest first.

1. 0·21, 0·31, 0·12.   **2.** 0·04, 0·4, 0·35.

3. 0·67, 0·672, 0·7.   **4.** 0·05, 0·045, 0·07.

5. 0·1, 0·09, 0·089.   **6.** 0·75, 0·57, 0·705.

7. 0·41, 0·041, 0·14.   **8.** 0·809, 0·81, 0·8.

9. 0·006, 0·6, 0·059.   **10.** 0·15, 0·143, 0·2.

11. 0·04, 0·14, 0·2, 0·53.   **12.** 1·2, 0·12, 0·21, 1·12.

13. 2·3, 2·03, 0·75, 0·08.   **14.** 0·62, 0·26, 0·602, 0·3.

15. 0·5, 1·3, 1·03, 1·003.   **16.** 0·79, 0·792, 0·709, 0·97.

17. 1·23, 0·321, 0·312, 1·04.   **18.** 0·008, 0·09, 0·091, 0·075.

19. 2·05, 2·5, 2, 2·046.   **20.** 1·95, 9·51, 5·19, 5·1.

21. Here are numbers with letters
  (a) Put the numbers in order, smallest first. Write down just the letters.

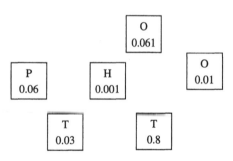

| O |
| 0.061 |

| P | | H | | O |
| 0.06 | | 0.001 | | 0.01 |

| T | | T |
| 0.03 | | 0.8 |

22. Increase the following numbers by $\frac{1}{10}$th:
  (a) 3·27   (b) 14·8   (c) 0·841

23. Increase the following numbers by $\frac{1}{100}$th:
  (a) 11·25   (b) 1·294   (c) 0·382

24. Increase the following numbers by $\frac{1}{1000}$th:
  (a) 3·142   (b) 2·718   (c) 1·414

25. Write the following amounts in pounds:
  (a) 11 pence.   (b) 2 pence.   (c) 5 pence.
  (d) 10 pence.   (e) 20 pence.   (f) 50 pence.

Adding and subtracting decimals

Remember: Line up the decimal points

(a) $2·4 + 3·23$

put a zero

$$
\begin{array}{r}
2·4\,0 \\
+\ 3·2\,3 \\
\hline
5·6\,3 \\
\end{array}
$$

(line up the points)

(b) $7 - 2·3$

$$
\begin{array}{r}
{}^{6}\not{7}·{}^{1}0 \\
-\ 2·3 \\
\hline
4·7 \\
\end{array}
$$

(write 7 as 7·0)

(c) $0·31 + 4 + 11·6$

$$
\begin{array}{r}
0·31 \\
4·00 \\
+\ 11·60 \\
\hline
15·91 \\
\end{array}
$$

(write 4 as 4·00)

Exercise 4

1. $1·2 + 3·4$ **2.** $2·7 + 5·1$ **3.** $9·4 + 0·2$

4. $5·6 + 2·7$ **5.** $4·9 + 0·8$ **6.** $6·3 + 2·9$

7. $7·4 + 9·6$ **8.** $14·3 + 9·8$ **9.** $46·7 + 8·0$

10. $5 + 0·26$ **11.** $2·9 + 4·37$ **12.** $8·62 + 7·99$

13. $0·078 + 2·05$ **14.** $10·04 + 3·005$ **15.** $13·47 + 27·084$

16. $1·97 + 19·7$ **17.** $4·56 + 7·890$ **18.** $456·7 + 8·901$

19. $16·374 + 0·947 + 27$ **20.** $3·142 + 2·71 + 8$

Now do these.

21. $3·8 - 2·4$ **22.** $8·7 - 6·5$ **23.** $4·8 - 6·5$

24. $4·8 - 0·7$ **25.** $7·1 - 4·6$ **26.** $5 - 3·8$

27. $13·8 - 6·5$ **28.** $11·2 - 7·4$ **29.** $19·9 - 8·1$

30. $29·6 - 14$ **31.** $59·2 - 34·8$ **32.** $81·8 - 29·9$

33. $8 - 2·7$ **34.** $6·7 - 4·29$ **35.** $47·2 - 27·42$

36. $94·63 - 5·9$ **37.** $2·97 - 1·414$ **38.** $25·52 - 1·436$

39. $3·142 - 1·414$ **40.** $2·718 - 1·732$

Exercise 5

Work out

1. $£1·45 + 75\,p$ **2.** $£1·00 + £0·75 + 19\,p$

3. $£2·60 + £4·05 + £0·59$ **4.** $35\,p + 85\,p + £1·65$

5. $£5·00 - £1·50$ **6.** $£3 - 25\,p$

7. $£10 - 75\,p$ **8.** $£20 - £3·99$

9. Geri bought her local team's cycling kit, shirt costing £10·75, shorts costing £3·99 and socks for £2·59. How much did she spend?

10. Winona spent £5·15 in the supermarket and £10·99 in the music shop. How much change did she get from £20?

11. What must be added to £5·63 to make £18?

12. Which five different coins make a total of £1·37?

13. David has £3·20 and wants to buy articles costing £1·10, 66 p, £1·99 and 45 p. How much more money does he need?

14. Which six different coins make £1·78?

15. Jane went to a shop and bought a book for £2·95 and a compact disc for £10·95. She paid with a £50 note. What change did she receive?

Top Banana!   The Banana man of Tesco's.

The following article is a true story. Read the article (which deliberately contains blanks) and then answer the questions below.

He is called the Banana man of Tesco. In a special offer Phil Calcott bought almost half a ton of bananas. He then gave it all away and still made a profit on the deal. In a way Mr Calcott made his local store pay him to take away its own fruit.

The offer said that if you bought a 3 lb bunch of bananas at £1.17, you would gain 25 Tesco 'Club Card' points. These points could be used to buy goods worth £1.25.

Mr Calcott asked the store to load up his Peugeot 205 with bananas.

'I took a car load at a time because even with the back seat down and the boot full I could only fit in 460 lbs of bananas,' he said.

He returned for another load the next day and altogether spent £____ buying 942 lbs of the fruit. This earned him almost ____,000 Tesco 'Club Card' points.

1. How much would it cost to buy ten 3 lb bunches of bananas?

2. How many Tesco Club Card points would you get?

3. How much would the points be worth?

4. How much profit would you make on this deal?

5. Do you like bananas?

6. Write down the paragraph, which starts 'He returned ...' and fill in the missing numbers.

Part 3

3.1 Accurate drawing

When an architect designs a house he
has to draw accurate plans for a
builder to follow. In this section you
will use a protractor and a pair of
compasses to construct accurate
diagrams involving triangles and
quadrilaterals. Later you will also
construct nets from which three
dimensional shapes can be made.

Drawing angles

Example: To draw an angle of 70°.

Step 1. Draw a horizontal line.

Step 2. Put your protractor on one
end of the line. (In this case
we shall use the right hand
end of the line.)

Step 3. Starting from zero, move
around the scale clockwise
and mark 70°.

Step 4. Remove the protractor and
join the right hand end of
the line to your 70° mark.

right hand end of line.

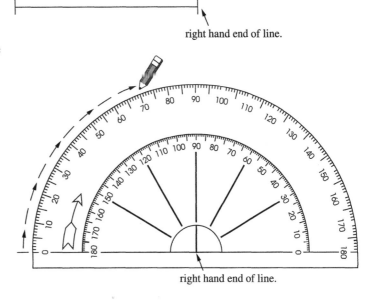

right hand end of line.

Exercise 1

Use your protractor to draw the following angles.

1. 60°	**2.** 20°	**3.** 45°	**4.** 79°	**5.** 9°
6. 115°	**7.** 90°	**8.** 51°	**9.** 18°	**10.** 130°
11. 47°	**12.** 170°	**13.** 94°	**14.** 135°	**15.** 87°

Constructing triangles

A triangle is an extremely rigid structure. It is used extensively in the real world to support many objects. These objects can range from large structures, such as the roof on your house, to smaller structures, such as the brackets holding up your bookshelf.

Draw the triangle ABC full size and measure the length x.
(a) Draw a base line *longer than* 8·5 cm
(b) Put the centre of the protractor on A and measure an angle 64°. Draw line AP.
(c) Similarly draw line BQ at an angle 40° to AB.
(d) The triangle is formed.
     Measure $x = 5·6$ cm.

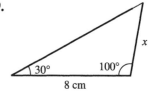

Exercise 2

Construct the triangles and measure the lengths of the sides marked x.

1.

2.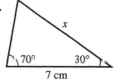

3.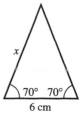

4.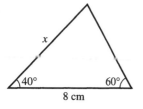

5.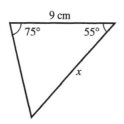

6.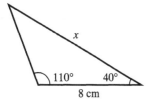

7.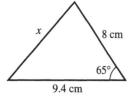

8.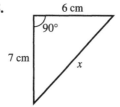

9.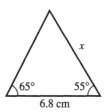

Constructing a triangle given three sides

Draw triangle XYZ and measure XẐY.

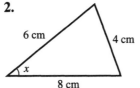

(a) Draw a base line longer than 7 cm and mark X and Y exactly 7 cm apart.
(b) Put the point of a pair of compasses on X and draw an arc of radius 8 cm.
(c) Put the point of the pair of compasses on Y and draw an arc of radius 5 cm.
(d) The arcs cross at the point Z so the triangle is formed.

Measure XẐY = 60°

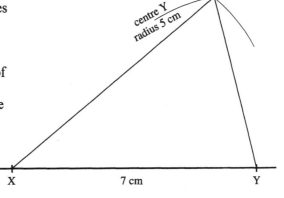

Exercise 3

In Questions 1 to 6 use a pair of compasses and measure the angle x.

1.
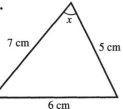
7 cm   5 cm   6 cm

2.
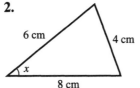
6 cm   4 cm   8 cm

3. 7 cm
6 cm   5 cm

4.
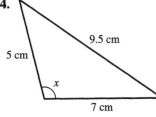
5 cm   9.5 cm   7 cm

5.
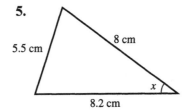
5.5 cm   8 cm   8.2 cm

6.
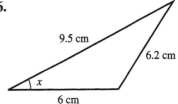
9.5 cm   6.2 cm   6 cm

3.2 Number patterns

Prime numbers

A *prime* number is divisible by only two different numbers: by itself and by one. The first six prime numbers are 2, 3, 5, 7, 11, 13. Note that one is *not* a prime number.

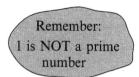

Remember:
1 is NOT a prime
number

Exercise 1

1. Use a number square like the one shown.

   (a) Cross out in pencil the number 1.

   (b) Cross out in pencil all the even numbers, but leave the number 2.

   (c) Draw a red circle around all the numbers divisible by 3, but leave the number 3.

   (d) Cross out in pencil all the numbers divisible by 5, but leave the number 5.

   (e) Draw a green circle around all the numbers divisible by 7, but leave the number 7.

   (f) Cross out in red all the numbers divisible by 11, but leave the number 11.

1	2	3	4	5	6	7	8	9	10
11	12	13	14	15	16	17	18	19	20
21	22	23	24	25	26	27	28	29	30
31	32	33	34	35	36	37	38	39	40
41	42	43	44	45	46	47	48	49	50
51	52	53	54	55	56	57	58	59	60
61	62	63	64	65	66	67	68	69	70
71	72	73	74	75	76	77	78	79	80
81	82	83	84	85	86	87	88	89	90
91	92	93	94	95	96	97	98	99	100

You should be able to see several patterns in the table.

(g) The numbers divisible by 3 form diagonals across the table.

(h) The numbers divisible by 11 form one diagonal across the table.

(i) The numbers divisible by 7 form a pattern which is not so obvious. Can you describe it?

The numbers which have been left blank are all the prime numbers between 1 and 100. You have drawn a square for finding prime numbers known as the 'sieve of Eratosthenes'. Eratosthenes was a famous Greek mathematician working over 2000 years ago.

2. How many prime numbers are there between 1 and 100?

3. Write down two prime numbers which add up to another prime number.

4. How many of the prime numbers are even?

5. How many of the prime numbers are odd?

6. Find three prime numbers which add up to another prime number.

7. (Harder) Use a calculator to find which of the following are prime numbers. Divide each number by the prime numbers 2, 3, 5, 7, 11 and so on.

(a) 103   (b) 145   (c) 151   (d) 188
(e) 143   (f) 108   (g) 221   (h) 293
(i) 493   (j) 323   (k) 1999   (l) 2639

8. What is the smallest 4-digit prime number?

Factors

- The number 12 can be written as two numbers multiplied together in three different ways

$$\boxed{1 \times 12} \qquad \boxed{2 \times 6} \qquad \boxed{3 \times 4}$$

The numbers 1, 12, 2, 6, 3, 4 are all the *factors* of 12.

- $\boxed{1 \times 8} = 8 \qquad \boxed{2 \times 4} = 8$

The factors of 8 are 1, 2, 4, 8.

- $\boxed{1 \times 6} = 6 \qquad \boxed{2 \times 3} = 6$

The factors of 6 are 1, 2, 3, 6.
The *prime numbers* of 6 are 2 and 3

Exercise 2

Write down all the factors of the following numbers

1. 6	**2.** 4	**3.** 10	**4.** 7	**5.** 15
6. 18	**7.** 24	**8.** 21	**9.** 36	**10.** 40
11. 32	**12.** 31	**13.** 60	**14.** 63	**15.** 85

16. Factors of a number which are also prime numbers are called prime factors. We can find these prime factors using a 'factor tree'

(a) Here is a factor tree for 60   (b) Here is a factor tree for 24

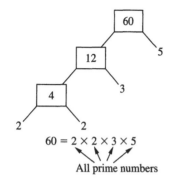

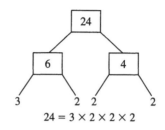

$24 = 3 \times 2 \times 2 \times 2$

$60 = 2 \times 2 \times 3 \times 5$

All prime numbers

(c) You can turn the diagram upside down and then draw a trunk around the number and branches to give a real 'tree shape'. Some people like to draw the prime factors inside apples, pears, bananas and so on.

(d) Draw a factor tree for 36.

In Questions **17** to **28** draw a factor tree for each number.

17. 28   **18.** 32   **19.** 34   **20.** 81

21. 84   **22.** 216   **23.** 294   **24.** 200

25. 1500   **26.** 2464   **27.** 4620   **28.** 98 175

29.* Which number less than 100 has the most prime factors?

30.* Which number less than 1000 has the most *different* prime factors? (You cannot repeat a factor.)

Multiples

The *multiples* of 5 divide by 5 with no remainder.
The first four multiples of 5 are 5, 10, 15, 20.
The first four multiples of 6 are 6, 12, 18, 24.

Exercise 3

Write down the first four multiples of:

  1. 3   **2.** 4   **3.** 2   **4.** 7   **5.** 10

Write down the first six multiples of:

  6. 5   **7.** 8   **8.** 9   **9.** 11   **10.** 20

11. Find which numbers the following sets are multiples of
   (a) 8, 12, 20, 28
   (b) 25, 30, 55, 60
   (c) 14, 21, 35, 70

In Questions **12** to **16** find the 'odd one out'. (The number which is
not a multiple of the number given.)

12. Multiples of 6:   18, 24, 32, 48, 54.

13. Multiples of 11:   33, 77, 101, 132.

14. Multiples of 10:   5, 10, 20, 30, 60.

15. Multiples of 9:   18, 27, 45, 56, 72.

16. Multiples of 7:   49, 77, 91, 105, 18.

17. Find three numbers that are multiples of 3 and 4.

18. Find three numbers that are multiples of 2 and 5.

19. Find three numbers that are multiples of 2, 3 and 5.

20. Find two numbers that are multiples of 2, 4 and 6.

Square numbers and cube numbers

Exercise 4

1.

  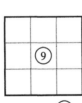 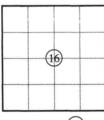

$1 \times 1 = ①$ $2 \times 2 = ④$ $3 \times 3 = ⑨$ $4 \times 4 = ⑯$

   (a) The first four *square* numbers are 1, 4, 9, 16.
   (b) Draw diagrams with labels to show the next three square
       numbers.

2. A square number is obtained by multiplying a number by itself.
   3×3 is written 3^2 (We say '3 squared...')
   4×4 is written 4^2

   Work out
   (a) 5^2 (b) 8^2 (c) 10^2 (d) 1^2

3. Work out
   (a) $3^2 + 4^2$ (b) $1^2 + 2^2 + 3^2$ (c) $9^2 + 10^2$

4. (a) Write down this sentence and fill in the missing numbers

$$1 \qquad\qquad = 1 \qquad = 1^2$$

$$1+3 \qquad\quad = 4 \qquad = 2^2$$

$$1+3+5 \qquad = \boxed{} \qquad = \boxed{}^2$$

$$1+3+5+7 \quad = \boxed{} \qquad = \boxed{}^2$$

(b) Write down the next five lines of the sequence.

5. The *square root* of a number is the number which is multiplied by itself to give that number. The symbol for square root is $\sqrt{}$. So $\sqrt{9} = 3$, $\qquad \sqrt{16} = 4$, $\qquad \sqrt{100} = 10$

Work out

(a) $\sqrt{25}$ (b) $\sqrt{81}$ (c) $\sqrt{49}$ (d) $\sqrt{1}$

6. *Lagrange's theorem.* A famous mathematician called Lagrange proved that every whole number could be written as the sum of four or fewer square numbers.

For example: $21 = 16 + 4 + 1$

$$19 = 16 + 1 + 1 + 1$$

$$35 = 25 + 9 + 1$$

Check that the theorem applies to the following numbers.

(a)   10   (b)   24   (c)   47

(d)   66   (e)   98   (f)   63

(g)   120   (h)   141   (i)   423

If you can find a number which needs more than four squares you will have disproved Lagrange's theorem and a new theorem will be named after you.

7. The numbers 1, 8, 27 are the first three *cube* numbers.

$$1 \times 1 \times 1 = 1^3 = 1 \qquad \text{(we say '1 cubed')}$$

$$2 \times 2 \times 2 = 2^3 = 8 \qquad \text{(we say '2 cubed')}$$

$$3 \times 3 \times 3 = 3^3 = 27 \qquad \text{(we say '3 cubed')}$$

The odd numbers can be added in groups to give an interesting sequence:

$$1 \qquad\qquad = 1 \qquad\quad = 1^3$$

$$3+5 \qquad\quad = 8 \qquad\quad = 2^3$$

$$7+9+11 \quad = 27 \qquad = 3^3$$

Write down the next three rows of the sequence to see if the sum of each row always gives a cube number.

Happy numbers

- (a) Take any number, say 23.
  (b) Square the digits and add: $2^2 + 3^2 = 4 + 9 = 13$
  (c) Repeat (b) for the answer: $1^2 + 3^2 = 1 + 9 = 10$
  (d) Repeat (b) for the answer: $1^2 + 0^2 = 1$

  23 is a so-called 'happy' number because it ends in one.

- Take another number, say 7.

  Write 7 as 07 to maintain the pattern of squaring and adding the digits.
  Here is the sequence:

$$
\begin{array}{c}
07 \\
\swarrow \quad \searrow \\
0 + 49 = \quad 49 \\
\swarrow \quad \searrow \\
16 + 81 = \quad 97 \\
\swarrow \quad \searrow \\
81 + 49 = \quad 130 \\
\swarrow \ \downarrow \ \searrow \\
1 + 9 + 0 = \quad 10 \\
\swarrow \quad \searrow \\
1 + 0 = 1
\end{array}
$$

So 7 is a happy number also.

With practice you may be able to do the arithmetic in your head and write: $07 \to 49 \to 97 \to 130 \to 10 \to 1$.

You may find it helpful to make a list of the square numbers 1^2, 2^2, $3^2, \ldots 9^2$.

- Your task is to find all the happy numbers from 1 to 100 and to circle them on a grid like the one shown.
  This may appear to be a very time-consuming and rather tedious task!
  But remember: Good mathematicians always look for short cuts and for ways of reducing the working.

  So think about what you are doing and good luck!
  As a final check you should find that there are 20 happy numbers from 1 to 100.

1	2	3	4	5	6	7	8	9	10
11	12	13	14	15	16	17	18	19	20
21	22	23	24	25	26	27	28	29	30
31	32	33	34	35	36	37	38	39	40
41	42	43	44	45	46	47	48	49	50
51	52	53	54	55	56	57	58	59	60
61	62	63	64	65	66	67	68	69	70
71	72	73	74	75	76	77	78	79	80
81	82	83	84	85	86	87	88	89	90
91	92	93	94	95	96	97	98	99	100

3.3 Three dimensional objects

Three dimensional objects have three dimensions ... length, width and depth.
Three dimensional is abbreviated to '3D'.
3D objects are often referred to as 'solids' or 'solid objects'.
Below are some familiar 3D objects.

Special Names are given to certain 3D solid objects ...

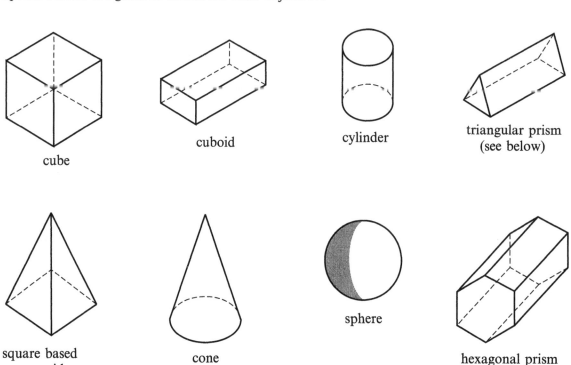

cube

cuboid

cylinder

triangular prism
(see below)

square based
pyramid

cone

sphere

hexagonal prism
(see below)

- A *prism* has the same cross section throughout its length. Here is a triangular prism.

  If you cut through the prism parallel to its end, (the face marked A in the diagram) you produce a congruent shape (marked A′).

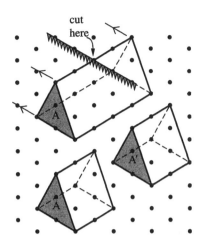

Exercise 1

Copy the following diagrams and complete the accompanying sentence using words from the page opposite.

1.

A dice is a _____

2.

A filing cabinet is a

3.

A tin of soup is a _____

4.

White light is changed by directing it through a _____

5.

The tepee is in the shape of a _____

6.

A snooker ball is a _____

7.

The ice hockey puck is a _____

8.

The roof of this bell tower is a _____

9.

A pencil is a _____ with a _____ at one end

Exercise 2

Below are drawn ten 3D objects labelled A to J.

1. Write down the letters of all objects that are prisms and write next to the letter the name of the object.

2. Write down the letters of all the objects that are non-prisms and write next to the letter the name of the object.

3. For the 10 objects given, sort the objects into two groups (other than prisms and non-prisms). Write down your two groups and how you chose your groups.

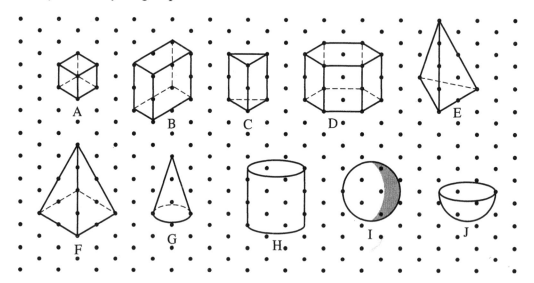

Faces, edges and vertices

Many three-dimensional shapes have *faces*, *edges* and *vertices* (plural of *vertex*). The diagram opposite shows a cuboid.

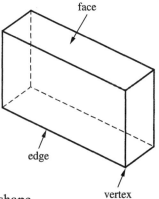

The *faces* of the cuboid are the flat surfaces on the shape.
There are 6 faces on a cuboid.
The *edges* of the cuboid are the lines that make up the shape.
There are 12 edges on a cuboid.
The vertices of the cuboid are where the edges meet at a point.
There are 8 vertices on a cuboid.

Exercise 3

In Questions **1** to **8** you are given the diagrams of different three-dimensional objects. Copy and complete the table below the diagrams. The details for the cuboid above have been done for you.

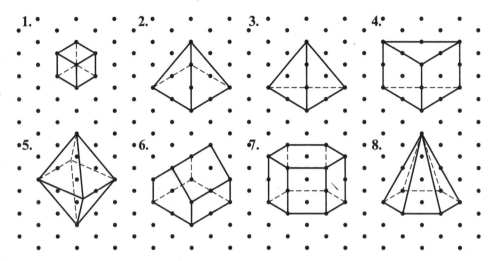

No	Shape	Faces	Edges	Vertices
Example	cuboid	6	12	8
1.	cube			
2.	square based pyramid			
3.	tetrahedron			
4.	triangular based prism			
5.	octahedron			
6.	pentagonal based prism			
7.	hexagonal based prism			
8.	hexagonal based pyramid			

9. Examine carefully the results of your table.

    (a) Try to find a connection between the number of faces, edges and vertices of the three-dimensional objects given.

    (b) A certain shape has 9 faces and 6 vertices. How many edges does it have?

Nets for making shapes

- If the cube shown was made of cardboard, and you cut along some of the edges and laid it out flat, you would have a *net* of the cube.

  There is more than one net of a cube as you will see in the exercise below.

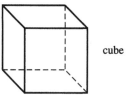

cube

- To make a cube from card you need to produce the net shown below complete with the added 'tabs' for glueing purposes.

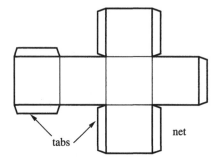

tabs   net

- In this section you will make several interesting 3D objects. You will need a pencil, ruler, scissors and either glue (Pritt Stick) or Sellotape.
  Score all lines before cutting out the net. This makes assembly of the object easier. Don't forget the tabs!

Exercise 4

1. Here are several nets which may or may not make cubes. Draw the nets on squared paper, cut them out and fold them to see which ones do make cubes.

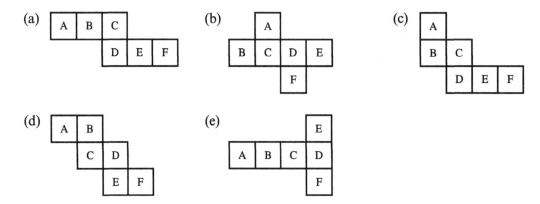

(a) (b) (c)

(d) (e)

2. For the nets which *did* make cubes in Question **1**, state which of the faces **B, C, D, E** or **F** was opposite face **A** on the cube.

In Questions **3** and **4** draw the net and cut it out to make the object shown.

3.

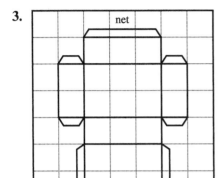

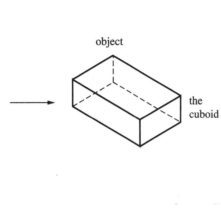

the cuboid

4.

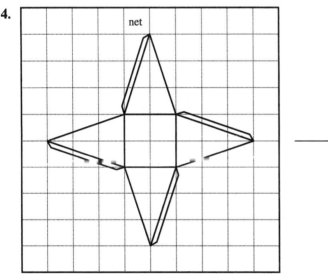

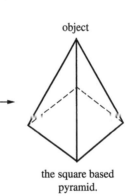

the square based pyramid.

5. Draw a net which could be used to make the closed box shown. Use squared paper.

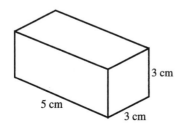

3 cm

5 cm

3 cm

6. Each diagram below shows *part* of the net of a cube. Each net needs one more square to complete the net.

(a)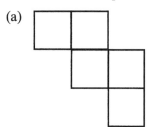

(b)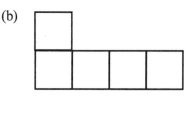

Cut out each of the shapes given and then draw the four possible nets which would make a cube with each one.

7. Some interesting objects can be made using triangle dotty paper. The basic shape for the nets is an equilateral triangle. With the paper as shown the triangles are easy to draw.

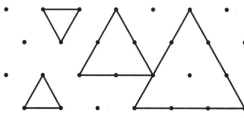

Make the sides of the triangles 3 cm or 4 cm long so that the objects are easy to make.
Here is the net of a tetrahedron.
Draw it and then cut it out.

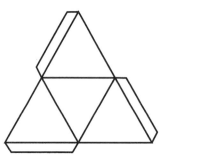

8. Here are two more.
  (a) Octahedron (octa: eight; hedron: faces)

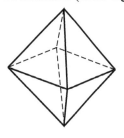

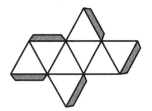

  (b) Icosahedron (an object with 20 faces)

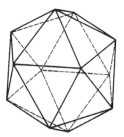

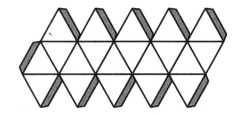

3.4 Time

Analogue – 12 hour watch

Digital – 24 hour watch

The 24 hour clock

The times which most people use in their everyday lives are times measured from midnight or from mid-day (noon). In the morning 9 o'clock is 9 hours after midnight and is written 9.00 a.m. In the afternoon 4 o'clock is 4 hours after mid-day (noon) and is written 4.00 p.m.

Using the 24 hour clock all times are measured from midnight. This means 9.00 a.m. is written 09.00 and 4.00 p.m. is written 16.00.

Here are three times converted from the 12 hour clock to the 24 hour clock

(a) 8.00 a.m. = 08.00
(b) 9.30 p.m. = 21.30
(c) 3.15 p.m. = 15.15

Remember   a.m. is an abbreviation of ante meridiem and means before mid-day,
p.m. is an abbreviation of post meridiem and means after mid-day

Exercise 1

Write the following in the 24-hour system.

1. 8.00 a.m.   2. 9.30 p.m.   3. 6.00 p.m.
4. 5.30 a.m.   5. 7.40 p.m.   6. 10.00 p.m.
7. 7.15 p.m.   8. 10.45 p.m.   9. 8.30 a.m.
10. 4.15 a.m.   11. 2.25 a.m.   12. 1.30 p.m.
13. 7.20 p.m.   14. 6.50 a.m.   15. 7.10 a.m.

16. Two minutes before midnight.   17. Two and a half hours before midnight.
18. Five minutes before noon.   19. Three and a half hours after noon.
20. One hour after midnight.   21. One and a half hours before noon.
22. Twenty minutes after midnight.   23. Five hours before midnight.
24. Six minutes after noon.   25. Fifty minutes after midnight.

Write the following in the 12-hour system.

26. 07.00	**27.** 19.30	**28.** 11.20	**29.** 04.45
30. 20.30	**31.** 21.15	**32.** 09.10	**33.** 11.45
34. 23.10	**35.** 20.00	**36.** 12.00	**37.** 01.40
38. 04.00	**39.** 07.07	**40.** 13.13	**41.** 12.15
42. 12.30	**43.** 15.45	**44.** 16.20	**45.** 05.16

Time intervals

- Find the time interval between 15.40 and 18.05.

From 15.40 to 16.00 : 20 minutes   (count on to the next hour)
From 16.00 to 18.05 : 2 hours 5 minutes   (count on from 16.00)
Altogether there is 2 hours 25 minutes

Exercise 2

Find the number of hours and minutes between the following.

1. 20.10 and 21.20	**2.** 21.40 and 23.50
3. 22.15 and 23.10	**4.** 19.30 and 20.05
5. 20.16 and 23.36	**6.** 11.25 and 13.10
7. 09.40 and 12.00	**8.** 21.17 and 23.10
9. 23.04 and 23.57	**10.** 17.45 and 23.10
11. 05.15 and 07.05	**12.** 11.26 and 14.40
13. 9.50 a.m. and 11.05 a.m.	**14.** 9.30 a.m. and 2.05 p.m.

3.5 Mental arithmetic

Mental calculation strategies

A. 'Easy-to-add' numbers

When numbers are added the order of the numbers does not matter:

$$23 + 17 \qquad = 17 + 23$$
$$41 + 9 + 110 = 110 + 9 + 41$$

Many pairs of numbers are easy to add together mentally

e.g. $17 + 23 = 40$, $18 + 32 = 50$, $33 + 7 = 40$

Practice questions

Look for 'easy-to-add' pairs of numbers in the following. If necessary change the order of the numbers in your head and then write down the answer without working.

1. $5 + 17 + 15$	**2.** $8 + 27 + 12$	**3.** $17 + 13 + 16$
4. $22 + 48 + 11$	**5.** $9 + 87 + 11$	**6.** $19 + 41 + 37$
7. $17 + 15 + 25$	**8.** $18 + 2 + 57$	**9.** $16 + 3 + 24$
10. $90 + 110 + 58$	**11.** $75 + 37 + 25$	**12.** $215 + 49 + 51$

B. Splitting the numbers

- $23 + 48$: $20 + 40 = 60$ and $3 + 8 = 11$
    So $23 + 48 = 60 + 11 = 71$

- $255 + 38$: $250 + 30 = 280$ and $5 + 8 = 13$
    So $225 + 38 = 280 + 13 = 293$

- Other way
    $23 + 48 = 23 + 40 + 8 = 63 + 8 = 71$
    $255 + 38 = 255 + 30 + 8 = 285 + 8 = 293$

    $576 - 43 = 576 - 40 - 3 = 536 - 3 = 533$
    $95 - 48 = 95 - 40 - 8 = 55 - 8 = 47$

Practice questions

1. $34 + 47$ **2.** $65 + 28$ **3.** $78 + 23$ **4.** $57 + 24$

5. $88 - 31$ **6.** $97 - 42$ **7.** $84 + 17$ **8.** $82 - 35$

9. $66 + 37$ **10.** $58 + 34$ **11.** $62 - 44$ **12.** $206 + 105$

C. Add/subtract

$9, 19, 29 \ldots 11, 21, 31, \ldots$, adjusting by one.

- $54 + 19 = 54 + 20 - 1 = 73$
- $77 + 41 = 77 + 40 + 1 = 118$
- $63 + 59 = 63 + 60 - 1 = 122$
- $54 - 31 = 54 - 30 - 1 = 23$
- $77 - 39 = 77 - 40 + 1 = 38$
- $95 - 29 = 95 - 30 + 1 = 66$

Practice questions

1. $67 + 21$ **2.** $37 + 51$ **3.** $36 + 41$ **4.** $76 + 29$

5. $45 + 29$ **6.** $70 + 21$ **7.** $80 + 41$ **8.** $44 + 39$

9. $33 + 59$ **10.** $80 - 41$ **11.** $53 + 41$ **12.** $90 - 51$

13. $70 - 19$ **14.** $50 - 29$ **15.** $95 - 19$ **16.** $81 - 19$

D. Doubling large numbers: work from the left

- double $63 =$ double $60 +$ double $3 = 120 + 6 = 126$
- double $79 =$ double $70 +$ double $9 = 140 + 18 = 158$
- double $127 =$ double $100 +$ double $20 +$ double $7 = 200 + 40 + 14 = 126$

Practice questions

1. double 54	**2.** double 34	**3.** double 27	**4.** double 73
5. double 28	**6.** double 74	**7.** double 115	**8.** double 57
9. double 65	**10.** double 66	**11.** double 87	**12.** double 49
13. double 123	**14.** double 208	**15.** double 236	**16.** double 342

E. Doubling and halving

(a) Multiplying by doubling and then by halving:

- 23×5 $23 \times 10 = 230$ $230 \div 2 = 115$
- 7×45 $7 \times 90 = 630$ $630 \div 2 = 315$
- 11×15 $11 \times 30 = 330$ $330 \div 2 = 165$

(b) To multiply by 50, multiply by 100, then halve the result.

- 23×50 $23 \times 100 = 2300$ $2300 \div 2 = 1150$
- 38×50 $38 \times 100 = 3800$ $3800 \div 2 = 1900$

(c) To multiply by 25, multiply by 100, then divide by 4

- 44×25 $44 \times 100 = 4400$ $4400 \div 4 = 1100$
- 56×25 $56 \times 100 = 5600$ $5600 \div 4 = 1600$

9×35
$9 \times 70 = 630$
$630 \div 2 = 315$

Practice questions

1. 22×50	**2.** 32×50	**3.** 24×25	**4.** 16×25
5. 36×50	**6.** 8×15	**7.** 7×45	**8.** 44×50
9. 14×50	**10.** 13×20	**11.** 18×50	**12.** 12×25

Mental arithmetic tests

There are several sets of mental arithmetic questions in this section. It is intended that a teacher will read out each question twice, with all pupils' books closed. The answers are written down without any written working. Alternatively the questions can be done with the pupils' books open.

Mental Arithmetic Test 1

1. Write the number six thousand and thirty-one in figures.

2. What number should you subtract from fifty-one to get the answer twenty-four?

3. What is twenty multiplied by ten?

4. What is thirty-five divided by seven?

5. Add together nine, three and eighteen.

6. Write nought point five as a fraction.

7. How many centimetres are there in ninety millimetres?

8. What is two point three multiplied by ten?

9. How many quarters make up two whole ones?

10. The side of a square is four metres. What is the area of the square?

11. If sixty per cent of teachers in a school are female what percentage of teachers are male?

12. A bus journey starts at seven twenty. It lasts fifty-five minutes. At what time does it end?

13. In the morning the temperature is minus three degrees celsius. What will be the temperature after it rises eleven degrees?

14. Write a factor of twenty-four which is greater than one.

15. What is three squared?

16. Write down any multiple of nine.

17. How much change from ten pounds would you get after spending eight pounds and fifty pence?

18. Write down the number that is halfway between fourteen and twenty?

19. Fifty per cent of a number is thirty-two. What is the number?

20. What is the reflex angle between clock hands showing three o'clock?

Mental Arithmetic Test 2

1. Add together seven, three and twelve.

2. Write the number that is thirteen less than one hundred.

3. What is nine multiplied by seven?

4. Write the number two thousand and thirty-seven in figures.

5. Write nought point two five as a fraction.

6. What is two hundred and ten divided by one hundred?

7. Change thirteen centimetres into millimetres.

8. What is double seventeen?

9. How many ten pence coins make three pounds and seventy pence?

10. What is four hundred and fifty-eight to the nearest ten?

11. What number is half way between six and thirteen?

12. A television programme starts at five minutes to seven and lasts thirty-five minutes. At what time does the programme finish?

13. One third of a number is six. What is the number?

14. How many twenty pence coins would you get for ten pounds?

15. What number is eight squared?

16. What is three quarters of one hundred?

17. If seventy-seven per cent of pupils in a school are right-handed, what percentage are left-handed?

18. Write seven tenths as a decimal number.

19. The temperature in Weston-super-Mare was minus two degrees, the temperature in Benidorm was eleven degrees warmer. What was the temperature in Benidorm?

20. David ate one hundred and twenty degrees of a circular wedding cake. Jacqui ate sixty degrees. How many degrees of cake were left?

Mental Arithmetic Test 3

1. Write the number two thousand one hundred and four in figures

2. What number is eight more than thirty-seven?

3. If oranges cost twelve pence each, how many can I buy for one pound?

4. With three darts I score seven, double five and treble eleven. What is my total score?

5. A film lasting one and half hours starts at seven twenty-five p.m. What time does the film finish?

6. If I buy a pen for twenty-eight pence and a note pad for forty-two pence, how much change do I get from one pound?

7. What number is nine less than forty-six?

8. What is half of half of sixty?

9. How many twenty pence coins make five pounds?

10. What is the perimeter of a rectangular lawn fifteen metres by six metres?

11. I am facing South-West and the wind is hitting me on my back. What direction is the wind coming from?

12. If eight per cent of pupils of a school are absent, what percentage of pupils are present?

13. Write nought point nine as a fraction.

14. What is twenty-fifteen in twelve hour clock time?

15. How many degrees are there in three right angles?

16. A quarter of my wages is taken in tax. What percentage have I got left?

17. How many grams are there in half a kilogram?

18. What four coins make seventy-six pence?

19. One angle in an isosceles triangle is one hundred and ten degrees. How large is each of the other two angles?

20. What number is one hundred times bigger than nought point two?

Mental Arithmetic Test 4

1. What are eight twenties?

2. What number is nineteen more than eighty-seven?

3. Write in figures the number six-thousand and eleven.

4. What is one quarter of twenty-eight?

5. What is the sum of sixty-three and twenty-nine?

6. How many sevens are there in eighty-four?

7. A pair of shorts costs £8·99, how much change do you get from a £10 note?

8. Subtract forty-five centimetres from two metres giving your answer in metres as a decimal number.

9. If you have three thousand and eleven pennies, how much do you have in pounds and pence?

10. The perimeter of a square is sixteen centimetres. What is the length of the side of the square?

11. How many metres are there in 1·5 kilometres?

12. What is fifty per cent of fifty pounds?

13. How many sides has a heptagon?

14. I think of a number, double it and the answer is five. What was the number I thought of?

15. What is three thousand four hundred and sixty-nine to the nearest hundred?

16. What is nought point two squared?

17. Two angles of a triangle add up to one hundred and fifty-five degrees. What size is the third angle?

18. Write noon in twenty-four hour clock time.

19. You are facing south and turn through three right angles anti-clockwise, what direction are you now facing?

20. A thermometer in a freezer compartment shows minus five degrees. The temperature outside the freezer is thirteen degrees celsius. What is the difference in temperature between inside and outside?

Mental Arithmetic Test 5

1. What is nought point one as a percentage?

2. How many edges has a triangular based pyramid?

3. What is three quarters of sixty pounds?

4. Change nineteen forty-five into twelve hour clock time.

5. I am facing north-west and turn through one and a half right-angles in a clockwise turn. In which direction am I now facing?

6. What is the product of ten and twenty-five?

7. What is the sum of the numbers 1, 2, 3, 4, 5?

8. How much change from a ten pound note will I receive if I spend three pounds and ninety-nine pence?

9. How many 2 p coins are worth the same as twenty 5 p coins?

10. How many centimetres are there in one hundred and five millimetres?

11. Two angles in a triangle are forty-five and sixty-five degrees. What is the third angle?

12. A 'pools' prize of six million pounds is shared equally between one hundred people. How much does each person receive?

13. What is the probability I roll an even number on a fair dice?

14. What is the next prime number after thirteen?

15. How many seconds are there in one hour?

16. I bought a magazine for 79 p and paid with a £1 coin. My change consisted of five coins. What were they?

17. What is the perimeter of a square whose area is nine centimetres squared?

18. What is the name given to a triangle which has two sides the same length and a pair of equal triangles?

19. Write down the number that is halfway between twenty-seven and eighty-three.

20. Answer true or false: 1 km is longer than 1 mile.

Mental Arithmetic Test 6

1. Write ten million pence in pounds.

2. Write down a sensible estimate for eleven multiplied by ninety-nine.

3. Write the number two thousand one hundred and seven in figures.

4. What is nine hundred and fifty-eight to the nearest hundred?

5. In a survey three quarters of people like football. What percentage of people like football?

6. What decimal number is twenty-three divided by one hundred?

7. How many twenty pence coins make three pounds?

8. How many twelve pence pencils can you buy for one pound?

9. One third of a number is eight. What is the number?

10. Write nine tenths as a decimal number.

11. What is the name of the quadrilateral which has only one pair of parallel sides?

12. What number is 10 less than ninety thousand?

13. A sphere is a prism. True or false?

14. What is the probability of scoring less than six on a fair dice?

15. I think of a number, divide it by three and the answer is seven. What number did I think of?

16. What is the area of a rectangle nine metres by seven metres.

17. How many quarters are there in one and a half?

18. How many millimetres are there in one metre?

19. How many hours of recording time are there on a two hundred and forty minute video tape?

20. What number is squared to produce eighty-one?

3.6 Mid book review

This section contains six review exercises
Review exercises 1 and 2 cover material in part 1
Review exercise 3 covers material in part 2
Review exercise 4 covers material in part 3.

Review exercise 1

Work out

1. $\begin{array}{r} 81 \\ -45 \\ \hline \end{array}$
2. $\begin{array}{r} 682 \\ +\ 74 \\ \hline \end{array}$
3. $\begin{array}{r} 599 \\ -315 \\ \hline \end{array}$
4. $\begin{array}{r} 235 \\ +409 \\ \hline \end{array}$

5. $566 + 278$ 6. $657 - 340$ 7. $171 + 681$ 8. $963 - 148$

9. $534 - 208$ 10. $589 - 99$.

11. There were 122 peaches in a box. 63 were sold. How many peaches were left?

12. There are 763 books in a library. A further 128 books are put on the shelves. How many books does the library now have altogether?

13. There are exactly 135 worms in a garden. A
hungry Robin ate 49 of them for breakfast.
How many worms are left?

14.

This is a number triangle. The numbers
along each edge add up to 9.

Copy and complete the triangle.

The six numbers are 1, 2, 3, 4, 5, 6.

15. A box has a mass of 230 g when empty.
When it is full of sugar the total mass is 650 g.
What is its mass when it is half full?

[Hint: First work out the mass of all the sugar.]

Review exercise 2

1. In a school 316 of the pupils have lunch at the school and 97 go
home to lunch. How many pupils have lunch altogether?

2. Two shops usually sell compact discs at the same price. Today there
is a sale at both shops. Each shop has a different offer on compact
discs.

**Dharal's
discs
$\frac{1}{4}$ off
all C.D.s**

**Stefan's
sounds
30% off
all C.D.s**

Which shop is more expensive for compact discs?

3. Write down the co-ordinates of the points which
make up the 'S'. You must give the points in the
correct order starting at the bottom left.

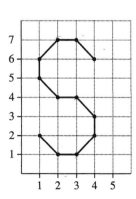

4. Draw a grid with values from 0 to 10. Plot the points below and join them up in order. You should obtain two letters of the alphabet

(a) (1, 5)   (3, 1)   (4, 3)   (5, 1)   (7, 5)
(b) (8, 5)   (8, 1)   (8, 3)   (10, 3)   (10, 5)   (10, 1)

5. Here are three number cards.
One number that can be made with the three cards is 617.

(a) Use the three cards to make a number which is *more* than 617.
(b) Use the three cards to make a number which is *less* than 617.
(c) Use the three cards to make an even number.

6. Here are four number cards.

Use *all four* cards for the following
(a) An add. The answer must be less than 100.

(b) A take away
The answer must be less than 20.

7. Make a copy of the cross number pattern and complete the puzzle using the clues given.

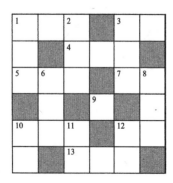

Clues across

1. $63 + 79$
3. $71 - 37$
4. $965 - 668$
5. $839 + 126$
7. $100 - 49$
9. $17 - 9$
10. $329 + 267$
12. $604 - 528$
13. $1036 - 643$

Clues down

1. $527 - 418$
2. $136 + 89$
3. $241 + 134$
6. $840 - 211$
8. $1001 - 815$
10. $924 - 867$
11. $25 + 38$
12. $100 - 27$

Review exercise 3

In Questions **1** to **6** arrange the numbers in order of size, smallest first.

1. 0·79, 0·791, 0·709, 0·97

2. 0·3, 0·33, 0·303, 0·033

3. 1, 0·99, 0·989, 0·09

4. 1·2, 0·12, 0·21, 1·12

5. 0·08, 0·096, 1, 0·4

6. 0·008, 0·09, 0·091, 0·0075

7. Which list is arranged in ascending order?

    A   0·14, 0·05, 0·062, 0·09

    B   0·14, 0·09, 0·062, 0·05

    C   0·050, 0·062, 0·09, 0·14

    D   0·050, 0·090, 0·14, 0·062

8. Lucy puts 4 pegs in a board. She turns the board through one right angle.
Draw a picture to show how the board looks now.

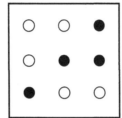

9. There are 5 tyres to each new car. How many tyres are there on 27 new cars?

10. If Jenny has 40 flowers and she puts 8 flowers in each bunch, How many bunches will she have?

11. If your school holiday is for 42 days and there are 7 days to a week, how many weeks holiday is this?

12. A teacher marked 2000 questions. There were 25 pupils in the class. If each pupil did the same number of questions, how many questions did each pupil do?

13. Work out the missing digits in each division.

    (a)   ☐☐2   (b)   2 9
         4)7 2☐   3)☐ 7

14. How many hundreds make a million?

Review exercise 4

1. Without a calculator, work out $7.2 + 11 + 0.32 + 0.09$.

2. Find the number of hours and minutes between:

(a) 15.30 and 18.00
(b) 05.35 and 09.10
(c) 9.30 a.m. and 1.40 p.m.

3. Choose the correct answer: The number of seconds in a day is *about*:

A 9000   **B** 90 000   **C** 30 000   **D** 300 000

4. This is a rough sketch of a triangle.
Draw the triangle accurately and full size.
Measure the side marked h.

5. I left the cinema at 22.25. The film lasted 2 hours and 35 minutes. At what time did it begin?

6. A man's heart beats at 70 beats/min. How many times will his heart beat between 03.30 and 23.30 on the same day?

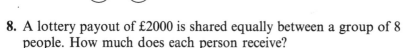

7. Write the following with the correct signs inside the circles.

(a) $4 \times 3 \times 2 \bigcirc 1 = 25$

(b) $5 \times 2 \times 4 \bigcirc 3 = 37$

(c) $6 + 5 \bigcirc 4 \bigcirc 1 = 8$

8. A lottery payout of £2000 is shared equally between a group of 8 people. How much does each person receive?

9. Ron and Pete were playing a video game. Pete scored 1089 and Ron scored 995. What was the difference in their scores?

10. In one million seconds which of these would you be able to do?

(a) Take a term off school.
(b) Go without sleep for two whole days.
(c) Spend ten days on the beach in France.
(d) Go to Africa for a year.

Explain your working.

Part 4

4.1 Sequences

- Sequences are lists of numbers (and sometimes letters) which have a pattern to them. An important part of any mathematician's job is to search for and explain hidden patterns or structures.

- 2, 9, 4, 7, 6, 41, ... is a list. There is no underlying pattern to the numbers – and so we have no real way of predicting what comes next.

- These are sequences. Their underlying patterns are shown.

Sequence	Structure
3, 5, 7, 9, ...	3 5 7 9 $(+2)$ $(+2)$ $(+2)$ $(+2)$
20, 17, 14, 11, ...	20 17 14 11 (-3) (-3) (-3) (-3)
5, 8, 12, 17, ...	5 8 12 17 $(+3)$ $(+4)$ $(+5)$ $(+6)$
2, 2, 4, 12, 48, ...	2 2 4 12 48 $(\times 1)$ $(\times 2)$ $(\times 3)$ $(\times 4)$ $(\times 5)$
1, 1, 2, 3, 5, 8, ...	1 1 2 3 5 $(1+1)$ $(1+2)$ $(2+3)$

This is a *Fibonacci* sequence

Exercise 1

1. The numbers in boxes form a sequence. Find the next number.

   (a) 10 12 14 16 ☐

   (b) 3 8 13 18 ☐

   (c) 11 9 7 5 ☐

Winter

In Questions **2** to **17** write down the sequence and find the next number

2. 4, 8, 12, 16,   **3.** 2, 5, 8, 11,
4. 21, 17, 13, 9,   **5.** 2, 4, 8, 16,
6. 1, 2, 4, 7, 11,   **7.** 3, 5, 9, 17,
8. 2, 4, 6, 8,   **9.** 1, 4, 8, 13,
10. 80, 40, 20, 10,   **11.** 5, 8, 12, 17,
12. $\frac{1}{2}$, 1, $1\frac{1}{2}$, 2,   **13.** 2, 20, 200, 2000,
14. 45, 36, 28, 21,   **15.** 1, 3, 9, 27,
16. 56, 28, 14, 7,   **17.** 1, 1, 2, 3, 5, 8, [Hint see page 93]

18. Write down the sequence and find the missing number.

(a) [2] [6] [ ] [14] [18]

(b) [3] [ ] [12] [24] [48]

(c) [$\frac{1}{2}$] [2] [$3\frac{1}{2}$] [5] [ ]

(d) [ ] [8] [4] [0] [−4]

19. Copy each sequence and write down the next number
(a) 3·2, 3·4, 3·6, 3·8, …
(b) 1·76, 1·77, 1·78, 1·79, …
(c) 0·402, 0·403, 0·404, 0·405, …
(d) 4·192, 4·194, 4·196, 4·198, …

20. The rule for the sequences below is '*double and take away 1*'. Find the missing numbers

(a) 3 → 5 → 9 → 17 → [ ]

(b) [ ] → 7 → 13 → 25 → 49

(c) [ ] → 19 → [ ] → 73

21. The rule for the sequences here is '*multiply by 3 and add 1*'. Find the missing numbers

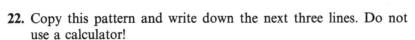

(a) 1 → 4 → 13 → [ ]

(b) [ ] → 7 → 22 → 67

(c) [ ] → 2 → [ ] → 22

22. Copy this pattern and write down the next three lines. Do not use a calculator!

$$1 \times 99 = 99$$
$$2 \times 99 = 198$$
$$3 \times 99 = 297$$
$$4 \times 99 = 396$$

23. (a) Copy this pattern and write down the next two lines

$$4 \times 8 = 32$$
$$44 \times 8 = 352$$
$$444 \times 8 = 3552$$
$$4444 \times 8 = 35\,552$$

(b) Copy and complete $444\,444\,444 \times 8 =$

Exercise 2

Use your knowledge of sequences to help you answer these questions.

1.

	6			10			14			18
5		7	9		11	13		15	17	
4			8			12			16	

M1   M2   M3   M4

The numbers M1, M2, M3, M4 form a sequence
(a) Find M5, M6, M7.
(b) Think of a rule and use it to find M15 and M30.

2.

D1   D2   D3

	7			13			19	
6		8	12		14	18		20	
5		9	11		15	17		21	
4			10			16			22

C1   C2   C3   C4

(a) Find C5, D5.
(b) Use a rule to find C10 and D10.

3.

	B1				B2				B3				
5	6	7		15	16	17		25	26	27			
4		8		14		18		24		28			
3		9		13		19		23		29		33	
2		10	11	12		20	21	22		30	31	32	
			A1				A2				A3		

(a) Find A5 and B5

(b) Use a rule to find A10 and B20.

4. Here is a sequence of touching triangles.

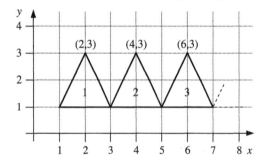

Find the coordinates of:

(a) the top of triangle 5

(b) the top of triangle 50

(c) the bottom right corner of triangle 50

(d) the bottom right corner of triangle 100.

5. Write down the coordinates of the centres of squares 1, 2 and 3.

Find the coordinates of:

(a) the centre of square 4

(b) the centre of square 40

(c) the top right corner of square 4

(d) the top right corner of square 40.

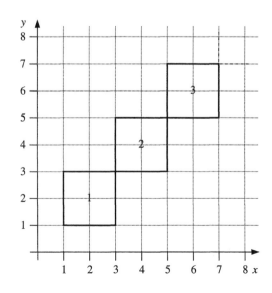

6.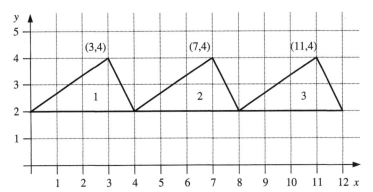

Find the coordinates of the top vertex of:
(a) triangle 4
(b) triangle 20
(c) triangle 2000.

7.* Write down the coordinates of the centres of squares 1, 2 and 3.
Find the coordinates of:
(a) the centre of square 4
(b) the centre of square 10
(c) the centre of square 70.

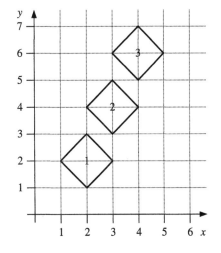

8.* Write down the coordinates of the centres of the first six squares.
Find the coordinates of:
(a) the centre of square 60
(b) the centre of square 73
(c) the top left corner of square 60
(d) the top left corner of square 73.

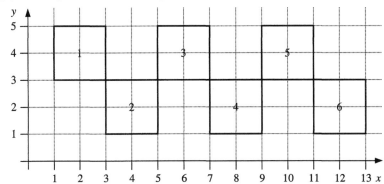

9. Now design some patterns of your own.

Count the crossovers: an investigation

Two straight lines have a maximum of one crossover

Three straight lines have a maximum of three crossovers.

Notice that you can have less than three crossovers if the lines all go through one point. Or the lines could be parallel.
In this work we are interested only in the *maximum* number of crossovers.

Four lines have a maximum of six crossovers.

▨ Draw five lines and find the maximum number of crossovers.

▨ Does there appear to be any sort of sequence in your results?
If you can find a sequence, use it to *predict* the maximum number of crossovers with six lines.

▨ Now draw six lines and count the crossovers to see if your prediction was correct.
(Remember not to draw three lines through one point.)

▨ Predict the number of crossovers for seven lines and then check if your prediction is correct by drawing a diagram.

▨ Write your results in a table:

Number of lines	Number of crossovers
2	1
3	3
4	6
5	
6	

(a) Predict the number of crossovers for 20 lines.

(b) (Harder) Predict the number of crossovers for 2000 lines.

4.2 Decimals 2

Multiplying decimals by whole numbers

Method 1

- $7 \cdot 93 \times 4 \approx 8 \times 4 = 32$
  (Estimate first)

  $$\begin{array}{r} 7 \cdot 93 \times 4 \quad 7 \cdot 00 \times 4 = 28 \cdot 00 \\ 0 \cdot 90 \times 4 = \quad 3 \cdot 60 \\ 0 \cdot 03 \times 4 = \quad \underline{0 \cdot 12} \; + \\ \hline 31 \cdot 72 \end{array}$$

- $3 \cdot 16 \times 6 \approx 3 \times 6 = 18$
  (Estimate first)

  $$\begin{array}{r} 3 \cdot 16 \times 6 \quad 3 \cdot 00 \times 6 = 18 \cdot 00 \\ 0 \cdot 10 \times 6 = \quad 0 \cdot 60 \\ 0 \cdot 06 \times 6 = \quad \underline{0 \cdot 36} \; + \\ \hline 18 \cdot 96 \end{array}$$

Method 2

- $7 \cdot 24 \times 4 \approx 7 \times 4 = 28$
  (Estimate first)

  $$\begin{array}{r} 7 \cdot 24 \\ \times \quad 4 \\ \hline 28 \cdot 96 \\ \hline {\scriptstyle 1} \end{array}$$

- $0 \cdot 096 \times 9 \approx 0 \cdot 1 \times 9 = 0 \cdot 9$
  (Estimate first)

  $$\begin{array}{r} 0 \cdot 096 \\ \times \quad 9 \\ \hline 0 \cdot 864 \\ \hline {\scriptstyle 8\,5} \end{array}$$

> The answer has the same number of figures after the point as there are in the numbers being multiplied.

Exercise 1

Work out

1. $\begin{array}{r} 5 \cdot 1 \\ \times \quad 2 \end{array}$
2. $\begin{array}{r} 2 \cdot 3 \\ \times \quad 3 \end{array}$
3. $\begin{array}{r} 3 \cdot 7 \\ \times \quad 4 \end{array}$
4. $\begin{array}{r} 5 \cdot 6 \\ \times \quad 5 \end{array}$

5. $\begin{array}{r} 6 \cdot 13 \\ \times \quad 6 \end{array}$
6. $\begin{array}{r} 10 \cdot 22 \\ \times \quad 7 \end{array}$
7. $\begin{array}{r} 5 \cdot 34 \\ \times \quad 8 \end{array}$
8. $\begin{array}{r} 1 \cdot 29 \\ \times \quad 9 \end{array}$

9. $0 \cdot 63 \times 7$ 10. $1 \cdot 452 \times 6$ 11. $0 \cdot 074 \times 9$ 12. $11 \cdot 3 \times 5$

13. $13 \cdot 6 \times 5$ 14. $0 \cdot 074 \times 5$ 15. $6 \times 2 \cdot 22$ 16. $8 \cdot 04 \times 3$

17. Copy and complete with the missing numbers.

(a) $0 \cdot 3 \times 4 = \boxed{}$

(b) $0 \cdot 6 \times \boxed{} = 4 \cdot 2$

(c) $\boxed{} \times 5 = 2 \cdot 0$

(d) $2 \cdot 4 = 6 \times \boxed{}$

(e) $\boxed{} \times 7 = 3 \cdot 5$

(f) $8 \times \boxed{} = 1 \cdot 6$

18. Find the cost of 4 calculators at £6.95 each.

19. What is the cost of 2 CDs at £10.95 each?

20. If one brick weighs $1 \cdot 35 \, \text{kg}$, how much do 5 weigh?

1. What is the total cost of 6 books at £2·13 each?

2. A basket ball costs £29·99.
   What is the total cost of 4 basket balls?

3. Find the total cost of 8 batteries at £1·19 each.

4. If 1 kg of cheese costs £4·59, find the cost of 3 kg.

5. Ink cartridges cost £1·25 a packet. What is the cost of 10 packets?

6. A sack of coal costs £6·90. Find the total cost of 9 sacks.

7. If 1 litre equals 1·76 pints, how many pints is 8 litres?

8. Find the total cost of 3 lb of leeks at 18p per lb and 2 packets of
   sugar at £2.30 each.

Copy and complete the bills:

9. 2 jars at £1·75 each   = ☐

   4 boxes at £0·40 each = ☐

   1 bottle at £1·25   = ☐

                  Total = ☐

10. 3 tins at £0·51 each   = ☐

    5 packets at £1·10 each   = ☐

    2 pints of milk at 22p per pint. = ☐

                              Total = ☐

Multiplying by 10, 100, 1000

- Using a calculator, $3·24 \times 10 = 32·4$
  $16·17 \times 10 = 161·7$
  $0·53 \times 10 = 5·3$
  $1·414 \times 10 = 14·14$

> When you multiply by 10 you move
> the point one place to the right.

- What do you notice in these calculations?
  $4·235 \times 100 = 423·5$
  $1·138 \times 100 = 113·8$
  $0·258 \times 100 = 25·8$

- Without a calculator, write down the answer to the following:
  $1·174 \times 100$
  $32·56 \times 10$
  $1·2359 \times 1000$

Do the following calculations

1. $4·23 \times 10$	**2.** $5·63 \times 10$	**3.** $0·427 \times 10$	**4.** $4·63 \times 10$
5. $0·075 \times 100$	**6.** $0·0063 \times 100$	**7.** $1·147 \times 100$	**8.** $10·7 \times 100$
9. $6·33 \times 1000$	**10.** $0·00714 \times 1000$	**11.** $6·36 \times 1000$	**12.** $8·142 \times 1000$
13. $0·71 \times 1000$	**14.** $8·9 \times 1000$	**15.** 12×100	**16.** 13×10
17. 7×1000	**18.** $9·2 \times 100$	**19.** $0·7 \times 100$	**20.** $0·5 \times 1000$

21. 0.01×10 **22.** 5.2×100 **23.** 14×1000
24. 0.1×10 **25.** 0.2×1000 **26.** 8.31×1000
27. 9.2×1 million   **28.** 8.34×1 million   **29.** 0.71×1 million
30. 8.6×100 **31.** 27×1000 **32.** 53×100

Division of decimals by whole numbers

(a) $9.6 \div 3$

$$3 \overline{) 9.6} = 3.2$$

(b) $22.48 \div 4$

$$4 \overline{) 22.^2 48} = 5.62$$

(c) $6.7 \div 5$

$$5 \overline{) 6.^1 7 \, ^2 0} = 1.34$$

notice the zeros

(d) $6.1 \div 4$

$$4 \overline{) 6.^2 1 \, ^1 0 \, ^2 0} = 1.525$$

Exercise 4

1. $8.42 \div 2$ **2.** $205.2 \div 6$ **3.** $18.52 \div 4$
4. $4.984 \div 7$ **5.** $236.0 \div 5$ **6.** $18.93 \div 3$
7. $49.92 \div 8$ **8.** $487.26 \div 9$ **9.** $3.12 \div 4$

In Questions **10** to **18** you may need extra zeros.

10. $6.8 \div 5$ **11.** $7.2 \div 5$ **12.** $3.1 \div 2$
13. $11.1 \div 2$ **14.** $8.7 \div 4$ **15.** $87.2 \div 4$
16. $0.67 \div 5$ **17.** $9.0 \div 4$ **18.** $17.1 \div 5$

Exercise 5

1. The total bill for a meal for nine people is £76.23. How much does each person pay if they each paid the same?

2. A pie weighing $2.43\,$kg is divided into 9 equal pieces. How much does each piece weigh?

3. A father shares £4.56 between his three children. How much does each receive?

4. If 5 bricks weigh 4·64 kg, find the weight of one brick.

5. Five people share the fuel cost of a car journey which amounts to £18·65. How much does each person pay?

6. Six cows produce 33·84 litres of milk each day. What is the average milk production of each cow?

7. How many times will a 9 litre bucket have to be filled and emptied to completely empty a water drum containing 139·5 litres?

8. A telephone call costs £0·10. How many calls can I make if I have £3.50?

9. A steel rod of length 2·38 m is divided into 7 equal pieces. How long is each piece?

10. Ten ball bearings weigh 2·5 kg. What is the weight of one?

Dividing by 10, 100, 1000 etc

The rules for dividing decimals are very similar to the rules for multiplying decimals.

- To divide by 10 move the point one place to the left.

- To divide by 100 move the point two places to the left.

- To divide by 1000 move the point three places to the left.

   (a) $56 \div 10 = 5\cdot6$ (b) $6\cdot24 \div 100 = 0\cdot0624$

   (c) $3\cdot14 \div 10 = 0\cdot314$ (d) $57 \div 1000 = 0\cdot057$

Exercise 6

Do the following calculations. WARNING: They are not all dividing!

1. $57\cdot2 \div 10$	**2.** $89\cdot2 \div 10$	**3.** $5\cdot3 \div 10$	**4.** $47\cdot1 \div 100$
5. $141\cdot2 \div 100$	**6.** $19\cdot3 \div 10$	**7.** $1518 \div 100$	**8.** $4\cdot7 \div 100$
9. $25\cdot2 \div 1000$	**10.** $0\cdot63 \div 10$	**11.** $47\cdot2 \div 100$	**12.** $27\cdot9 \div 1000$
13. $6\cdot2 \div 1000$	**14.** $198\cdot7 \div 100$	**15.** $47 \div 10$	**16.** $416 \div 1000$
17. $2400 \div 100$	**18.** $89 \div 100$	**19.** $63 \div 100$	**20.** $7 \div 1000$
21. $0\cdot86 \div 10$	**22.** $516 \div 1000$	**23.** $0\cdot077 \div 100$	**24.** $21\cdot9 \div 1000$
25. $5\cdot6 \times 10$	**26.** $5\cdot6 \div 10$	**27.** $8\cdot1 \times 10$	**28.** $8\cdot1 \div 10$
29. $0\cdot3 \times 100$	**30.** $0\cdot3 \div 100$	**31.** $0\cdot4 \times 10$	**32.** $0\cdot4 \div 10$
33. $0\cdot414 \times 100$	**34.** $0\cdot0631 \times 1000$	**35.** $0\cdot005 \times 100$	**36.** $0\cdot0063 \times 1000$
37. $47\cdot4 \div 10$	**38.** $8\cdot97 \div 100$	**39.** $54\cdot2 \div 1000$	**40.** 63×100
41. 47×10	**42.** $0\cdot84 \times 1000$	**43.** $0\cdot7 \div 100$	**44.** $6\cdot2 \div 10$
45. $4\cdot73 \times 10$	**46.** $0\cdot001 \times 1000$	**47.** $47 \div 100$	**48.** 47×100

49. Here is a table giving some lengths.

distance from train station	10 000 m
distance from home to school	1000 m
length of football pitch	100 m
width of road bridge	10 m
width of door	1 m
length of Pritt Stick	0·1 m
size of a dice	0·01 m
thickness of a 5 p coin	0·001 m

(a) What is ten times the size of a dice?
(b) What is 1000 times the size of a dice?
(c) What is one hundredth of the length of a football pitch?
(d) What is one thousandth of the width of a door?
(e) What is one million times the thickness of a 5 p coin?
(f) How many Pritt Sticks end to end would be the distance from home to school?

50. Make up your own table like the one above and think of distances and objects for lengths from 100 000 m down to 0·001 m.

51. On a calculator $\frac{1}{9} = 0·111\,111\,1$

Without using a calculator, write down $\frac{1}{900}$ as a decimal.

4.3 Metric and Imperial units

Originally measurements were made by using appropriately sized bits of human being. The inch was measured using the thumb, (hence we still sometimes say 'rule of thumb' when we mean rough measurement), the foot by using the foot.

Other measurements were based on actions. The Mile was taken from the Latin *Milia passuus*, meaning a thousand passing-paces (the distance covered from one foot touching the ground to the same foot touching the ground again).

Even today many people, when asked their height or weight, will give the answer as '5 feet 3' or '9$\frac{1}{2}$ stone' rather than '1 metre 59' or 60 kg.

After the French Revolution in 1789 the standard unit of length became the metre and the unit of mass became the kilogram. All the smaller and larger units are obtained by dividing or multiplying by ten, a hundred, a thousand and so on.

I'm 5 feet 6... or is it 56 kg?

Here is a table with details of the most commonly used units for length, mass and volume.

Metric units		Imperial units
Length	10 mm = 1 cm	12 inches = 1 foot
	100 cm = 1 m	3 feet = 1 yard
	1000 m = 1 km	1760 yards = 1 mile
Mass	1000 mg = 1 g	16 ounces = 1 pound
	1000 g = 1 kg	14 pounds = 1 stone
	1000 kg = 1 tonne	2240 pounds = 1 ton
Volume	1000 ml = 1 litre	8 pints = 1 gallon
	1 ml = 1 cm^3	

Exercise 1

What unit would you use to measure the following:
Give two answers: metric and Imperial.

1. The mass of this book.
2. The length of a pencil.
3. The distance from London to Paris.
4. The length of an ant.
5. The mass of a heavy goods vehicle.
6. The amount of water in a swimming pool.
7. Your height.
8. Your mass.
9. The capacity of a car's petrol tank.
10. The amount of liquid in a cup of tea.

Copy and complete the following:

11. $1{\cdot}25\,m =$ _____ cm   12. $0{\cdot}35\,m =$ _____ cm   13. $3\,m =$ _____ cm

14. $17\,cm =$ _____ m   15. $250\,cm =$ _____ m   16. $5\,cm =$ _____ m

17. $40\,mm =$ _____ cm   18. $300\,mm =$ _____ cm   19. $5\,mm =$ _____ cm

20. $1500\,m =$ _____ km   21. $750\,m =$ _____ km   22. $10\,000\,m =$ _____ km

23. $2\,kg =$ _____ g   24. $8{\cdot}52\,kg =$ _____ g   25. $0{\cdot}625\,kg =$ _____ g

26. $325\,g =$ _____ kg   27. $1627\,g =$ _____ kg   28. $2\ tonnes =$ _____ kg

29. $440\,ml =$ _____ l 30. $1976\,ml =$ _____ l 31. $2500\,ml =$ _____ l

32. $2{\cdot}5\,l =$ _____ ml   33. $75\,l =$ _____ ml   34. $1{\cdot}76\,l =$ _____ ml

Exercise 2

Copy and complete

1. 57 cm =   m   **2.** 1·3 km =   m   **3.** 0·24 kg =   g   **4.** 600 g =   kg

5. 17 mm =   cm   **6.** 3000 kg =   t   **7.** 0·6 m =   cm   **8.** 14 mm =   cm

9. 2000 ml =   ℓ   **10.** 305 g =   kg   **11.** 80 cm =   m   **12.** 200 mm =   m

13. 2·5 t =   kg   **14.** 2·4 m =   mm   **15.** 20 g =   kg   **16.** 4·5 ℓ =   ml

17. 2 ℓ =   cm^3 **18.** 5·5 m =   cm   **19.** 56 mm =   m   **20.** 7 g =   kg

Questions **21** to **30** involve imperial units

21. 3 feet =   inches   **22.** 5 yards =   feet

23. 2 pounds =   ounces   **24.** 9 stones =   pounds

25. 24 inches =   feet   **26.** $\frac{1}{2}$ pound =   ounces

27. 2 feet 6 inches =   inches   **28.** 1 ton =   pounds

29. 8 stones 4 pounds =   pounds   **30.** 5 feet 2 inches =   inches

Questions **31** to **45** involve a mixture of metric and imperial units.

31. 0·032 kg =   g   **32.** 6 feet =   yards   **33.** 8 ounces =   pound

34. 1 mile =   feet   **35.** 235 mm =   cm   **36.** 0·42 t =   kg

37. 11·1 cm =   m   **38.** $\frac{1}{4}$ pound =   ounces   **39.** 7 litres =   ml

40. 4 yards =   feet   **41.** 7 mm =   cm   **42.** 2 gallons =   pints

43. 400 m =   km   **44.** 5 gallons =   pints   **45.** 10 miles =   yards

Converting between metric and imperial units

- It is sometimes necessary to convert imperial units into metric units and vice versa. Try to remember the following *approximate equivalents*:

1 inch ≈ 2·5 cm	1 kg ≈ 2 pounds
1 foot ≈ 30 cm	30 g ≈ 1 ounce
1 km ≈ $\frac{5}{8}$ mile	1 gallon ≈ 5 litres

[The '≈' sign means 'is approximately equal to'.]

- Here are some familiar objects to help you remember.

A one pound coin has a mass of about 10 grams.

A standard bag of sugar has a mass of 1 kg.

A 'tall' adult man is about 6 feet tall. [180 cm]

Exercise 3

Copy each sentence and choose the number which is the best estimate.

1. The Prime Minister is about [1 m, 6 feet, 8 feet] tall.

2. An egg weighs about [$\frac{1}{2}$ oz, 60 g, 1 kg].

3. The distance from London to Dover is about [60 miles, 300 km, 10 miles].

4. A bag of crisps weighs about [25 g, 100 g, 1 lb].

5. The thickness of a pound coin is about [1 mm, 3 mm, 6 mm].

6. The perimeter of the classroom is about [30 m, 10 m, $\frac{1}{10}$ mile].

7. A can of coke contains about [500 ml, 2 litres, 20 ml].

8. The width of one of my fingers is about [1 mm, 5 mm, 10 mm].

9. Suppose you have just won a prize which is one million grams of gold! Which of the following would you need to take away your prize?
   (a) A large suitcase
   (b) A van
   (c) Two large delivery lorries

10. Which is heavier:
    (a) 100 ounces of butter or 100 grams of butter?
    (b) 6 lb of apples or 6 kg of apples?

11. Write down one thing you would measure in:
    (a) kilometres
    (b) kilograms
    (c) litres
    (d) gallons

12. Choose a *metric* unit to measure:
    (a) the distance from Paris to Berlin
    (b) the thickness of a 5p coin
    (c) the weight of a calculator
    (d) the amount of petrol in a car's tank

13. Choose a suitable *imperial* unit to measure:
    (a) the weight of your mother
    (b) the height of the classroom door
    (c) the amount of butter in a cake recipe
    (d) the distance from New York to Manchester

4.4 Rounding off

Here are cuttings from two newspapers:

A. '39748 people paid £511,615 to watch
   Arsenal play ...'

B. '40000 people paid over £500,000 to
   watch Arsenal play ...'

In B the figures have been *rounded off* because the reporter thinks that his readers will not be interested in the exact numbers in the report.

Rules for rounding

- Rounding to the nearest whole number.

  If the first digit after the decimal point is *5 or more* round *up*.
  Otherwise round down.

  $$57 \cdot 3 \rightarrow 57$$
  $$89 \cdot 8 \rightarrow 90$$
  $$5 \cdot 5 \rightarrow 6$$

- Rounding to the nearest 100.

  If the digit in the tens column is 5 or more round up.
  Otherwise round down.

  $$593 \rightarrow 600$$
  $$247 \rightarrow 200$$
  $$2643 \rightarrow 2600$$

- Rounding to the nearest 10.

  If the digit in the units column is 5 or more round up.
  Otherwise round down.

  $$27 \rightarrow 30$$
  $$42 \rightarrow 40$$
  $$265 \rightarrow 270$$

- Rounding to the nearest 1000.

  If the digit in the hundreds column is 5 or more round up.
  Otherwise round down.

  $$1394 \rightarrow 1000$$
  $$502 \rightarrow 1000$$
  $$11\,764 \rightarrow 12\,000$$

- From the above you will see that when a number is 'right in the middle' we round *up*. This is an internationally accepted rule.

Exercise 1

1. Round off these numbers to the nearest 10.
   (a) 73   (b) 58   (c) 24   (d) 99
   (e) 56   (f) 127   (g) 242   (h) 18
   (i) 29   (j) 589   (k) 37   (l) 51

2. Round off these numbers to the nearest 100.
   (a) 584   (b) 293   (c) 607   (d) 914
   (e) 285   (f) 655   (g) 222   (h) 1486

3. Round off these numbers to the nearest 1000.
   (a) 4555   (b) 757   (c) 850   (d) 2251
   (e) 614   (f) 2874   (g) 25712   (h) 13568

4. Work out these answers on a calculator and then round off the answer to the *nearest whole number*.

(a) $235 \div 17$	(b) $4714 \div 58$	(c) $2375 \div 11$	(d) $999 \div 17$
(e) $5 \cdot 62 \times 7 \cdot 04$	(f) $19 \cdot 3 \times 1 \cdot 19$	(g) $53 \cdot 2 \times 2 \cdot 3$	(h) $12 \cdot 6 \times 0 \cdot 93$
(i) $119 \cdot 6 \div 5 \cdot 1$	(j) $109 \div 0 \cdot 7$	(k) $63 \cdot 4 \div 11$	(l) $1 \cdot 92 \div 0 \cdot 09$

5. Round off these numbers to the nearest $\frac{1}{10}$.

(a) $8 \cdot 59$	(b) $6 \cdot 18$	(c) $2 \cdot 49$	(d) $0 \cdot 78$
(e) $5 \cdot 21$	(f) $8 \cdot 72$	(g) $16 \cdot 27$	(h) $1 \cdot 23$

6. Work out these answers on a calculator and then round off the answer to the nearest $\frac{1}{10}$.

(a) $6 \cdot 7 \div 7 \cdot 2$	(b) $8 \cdot 13 \times 2 \cdot 1$	(c) $4 \cdot 3 \div 6$	(d) $12 \cdot 3 \times 0 \cdot 41$
(e) $11 \cdot 1 \div 9$	(f) $109 \div 7$	(g) $0 \cdot 89 \times 5 \cdot 1$	(h) $12 \cdot 6 \div 13 \cdot 7$

Exercise 2

In Questions **1** to **8** rewrite the sentences by rounding off the numbers involved and using the word 'about'. (E.g. Jim swam *about* 300 m.)

1. Mr Sadler drove 3478 miles on his holiday (nearest 100).

2. David saw 5173 cars go past his window (nearest 100).

3. The Sainsbury supermarket took in £49 713·21 last Saturday (nearest 1000).

4. There are 19 763 Junior schools in England and Wales (nearest 1000).

5. The winner of the National Lottery won £6 913 214. (nearest million).

6. There are 15 214 714 cars in the UK (nearest million).

7. Applecroft School raised £2611·26 for charity last year (nearest 100).

8. The population of the USA is 223 516 718 (nearest million).

9. Decide whether you would round these numbers to the nearest 10, 100, 1000, 10 000, 100 000 or 1 000 000.

(a) The number of children in your school.
(b) The number of people in Britain.
(c) The number of people on a full Eurostar.
(d) The daily circulation of 'The Sun' newspaper.
(e) The number of miles from London to Birmingham.

Estimating lengths

Exercise 3

1. Estimate the lengths shown. Use the ruler as a guide.

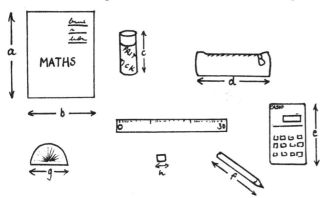

2. Look at the picture. The person is about 2 metres tall.

Estimate the height of:

(a) The top of the roof of the house
(b) The ladder
(c) The tree
(d) The telegraph pole
(e) The nest box on the tree.

3. Estimate the reading on each thermometer.

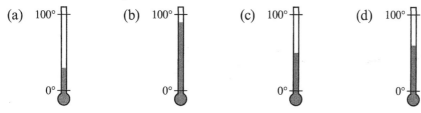

4.5 Negative numbers

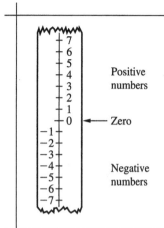

- All numbers above zero are positive numbers.
- Zero is not positive or negative.
- All numbers below zero are negative numbers.
- If a minus symbol appears before a number then it is a negative number.

- The most common application of negative numbers is in illustrating temperature.

This is a weather map showing temperatures across the United Kingdom and Ireland on a day in Winter.

The temperatures are given in degrees Celsius (°C).

Water freezes at 0°C.

The weather map shows lower temperatures in the north than in the south.

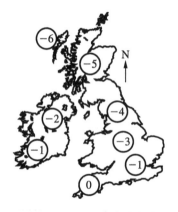

Exercise 1

1. What temperature is shown at each arrow?

(a) (b) (c) (d)

2.

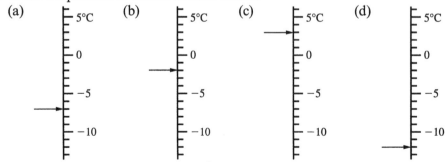

(a) Which of these temperatures is the coldest?
(b) Which of these temperatures is the hottest?
(c) Which temperatures are below freezing?

3. The graph shows the temperatures for one day in Greenland.

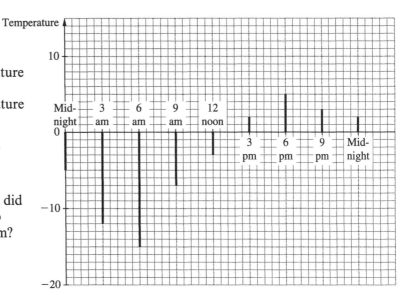

(a) What was the temperature at 6 pm?

(b) What was the temperature at 9 am?

(c) What was the lowest temperature recorded?

(d) At what time was it −12°C?

(e) By how many degrees did the temperature go up between 6 am and 6 pm?

4. Find the new temperature in the following problems.

(a) The temperature is 5°C and falls by 9°C.

(b) The temperature is −7°C and falls by 4°C.

(c) The temperature is −6°C and rises by 13°C.

(d) The temperature is −9°C and rises by 11°C.

5. State in the following questions whether the temperature has risen or fallen and by how many degrees.

(a) It was −3°C and it is now −7°C.

(b) It was 6°C and is now −2°C.

(c) It was 11°C and is now −3°C.

(d) It was −9°C and is now 1°C.

6. Copy and complete the following table:

	Temperature	Change	New temperature
(a)	6°C	+5°C	
(b)	15°C	+8°C	
(c)	18°C	−11°C	
(d)	0°C	−3°C	
(e)	−2°C	−12°C	
(f)		+7°C	12°C
(g)		−8°C	−3°C
(h)	−4°C		−6°C

Exercise 2

1. The *range* is the difference between the highest and the lowest. The scale shows the highest and lowest temperatures one day in Paris.
The range of the temperatures is 10°C.

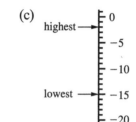

Find the range in these temperatures

(a)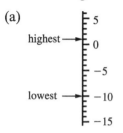

(b)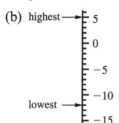

(c)

2. This table shows the highest and lowest temperatures in five places.

	Highest	Lowest
Glasgow	3°C	−11°C
London	12°C	−4°C
Moscow	2°C	−23°C
North Pole	−40°C	−53°C
Rome	15°C	1°C

Find the temperature range for
(a) Glasgow.
(b) Moscow.
(c) Which place had the greatest range in temperature?

3. Here is a number line from −10 to +10

−10 −9 −8 −7 −6 −5 −4 −3 −2 −1 0 1 2 3 4 5 6 7 8 9 10

Find the difference between
(a) −7 and 2   (b) −6 and −1   (c) 8 and −3
(d) −5 and 0   (e) −8 and 8   (f) −3 and −10.

4. Write down each sequence and fill in the missing number.

(a)   6   4   2   0   −2   ☐

(b)   10   6   2   −2   ☐

(c)   10   7   4   1   −2   ☐

(d)   9   5   1   ☐   −7

4.6 Fractions 1

- Express the shaded part of the diagram as a fraction of the whole.

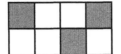

  3 out of 8 sections are shaded.
  The fraction shaded $= \frac{3}{8}$.

- It is not possible to express the shaded part in this diagram as a fraction of the whole. This is because the shape has not been divided equally.

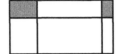

Exercise 1

In each of the following diagrams, express the shaded part of the diagram as a fraction of the whole where possible.

1.

2.

3.

4.

5.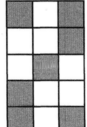

6.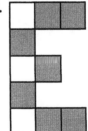

7.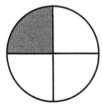

8.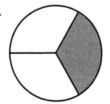

9.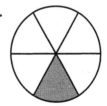

10.

11.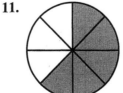

12.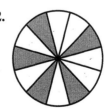

Writing fractions in their simplest form

A fraction is composed of two numbers:

The top number is called the $\longrightarrow$ Numerator

The bottom number is called the $\longrightarrow$ Denominator.

The method of changing a fraction into a simpler form is known as '*cancelling down*'.

The fraction $\frac{15}{20}$ *cancels down* to $\frac{3}{4}$.

To do this, Find the **highest** possible number that divides exactly into **both** the numerator and denominator

$$\frac{15 \div 5}{20 \div 5} = \frac{3}{4}$$ The highest possible number that divides exactly into 15 and 20 is 5.

Here are two more examples of cancelling down fractions …

Fraction	Method of cancelling down	Simplest form of fraction
$\frac{8}{12}$	4 goes into 8, 2 times 4 goes into 12, 3 times	$\frac{2}{3}$
$\frac{12}{15}$	3 goes into 12, 4 times 3 goes into 15, 5 times	$\frac{4}{5}$

Exercise 2

Use the fraction charts to find the missing numbers

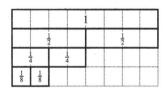
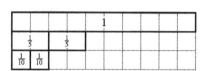

1. $\dfrac{6}{8} = \dfrac{\square}{4}$

2. $\dfrac{2}{6} = \dfrac{\square}{3}$

3. $\dfrac{6}{10} = \dfrac{\square}{5}$

4. $\dfrac{2}{8} = \dfrac{\square}{4}$

5. $\dfrac{4}{10} = \dfrac{\square}{5}$

6. $\dfrac{4}{8} = \dfrac{1}{\square}$

7. $\dfrac{4}{6} = \dfrac{2}{\square}$

8. $\dfrac{8}{10} = \dfrac{\square}{5}$

Copy and complete the table below to cancel down each fraction into its simplest form:

No.	Fraction	Method of cancelling down	Simplest form of fraction
9.	$\frac{9}{12}$	3 goes into 9: ___ times 3 goes into 12: ___ times	———
10.	$\frac{6}{24}$	6 goes into 6: ___ time 6 goes into 24: ___ times	———
11.	$\frac{8}{10}$	2 goes into 8: ___ times 2 goes into 10: ___ times	———

Express each fraction in its simplest form:

12. $\frac{8}{20}$ **13.** $\frac{9}{36}$ **14.** $\frac{8}{12}$ **15.** $\frac{9}{15}$ **16.** $\frac{6}{18}$

17. $\frac{7}{21}$ **18.** $\frac{32}{36}$ **19.** $\frac{24}{30}$ **20.** $\frac{4}{12}$ **21.** $\frac{4}{18}$

22. $\frac{20}{30}$ **23.** $\frac{12}{18}$ **24.** $\frac{14}{42}$ **25.** $\frac{20}{24}$ **26.** $\frac{6}{15}$

Equivalent fraction anagrams

Example: Jn the table given below, pick out all the letters above the fractions which are equivalent to one half ($\frac{1}{2}$).

C	Q	E	A	Y	P	R	N	H	F	letters
$\frac{5}{10}$	$\frac{3}{4}$	$\frac{2}{4}$	$\frac{21}{42}$	$\frac{1}{3}$	$\frac{3}{5}$	$\frac{6}{12}$	$\frac{3}{6}$	$\frac{4}{7}$	$\frac{5}{10}$	fractions

The letters are C, E, A, R, N, F
because ... $\frac{5}{10}, \frac{2}{4}, \frac{21}{42}, \frac{6}{12}, \frac{3}{6}, \frac{5}{10}$ are all the same as $\frac{1}{2}$.

Now rearrange the letters to make the name of a country.

C, E, A, R, N, F $\longrightarrow$ FRANCE

Exercise 3

As in the example above, find the fractions in the table which are equivalent to the given fraction. Rearrange the letters to make a word using the clue.

1. ($\frac{1}{3}$, city)

L	P	A	U	R	I	D	N	S	B
$\frac{3}{9}$	$\frac{2}{8}$	$\frac{5}{7}$	$\frac{4}{12}$	$\frac{7}{20}$	$\frac{6}{18}$	$\frac{8}{24}$	$\frac{10}{30}$	$\frac{3}{5}$	$\frac{5}{15}$

2. ($\frac{1}{4}$, fruit)

B	O	P	A	E	I	H	C	R	T
$\frac{2}{7}$	$\frac{4}{16}$	$\frac{11}{44}$	$\frac{2}{8}$	$\frac{3}{9}$	$\frac{10}{40}$	$\frac{6}{25}$	$\frac{5}{20}$	$\frac{12}{48}$	$\frac{3}{12}$

3. ($\frac{3}{4}$, sport)

R	O	F	G	A	U	B	D	Y	J
$\frac{8}{10}$	$\frac{6}{8}$	$\frac{15}{25}$	$\frac{5}{7}$	$\frac{21}{32}$	$\frac{9}{12}$	$\frac{30}{45}$	$\frac{15}{20}$	$\frac{66}{99}$	$\frac{75}{100}$

4. ($\frac{1}{10}$, drink)

R	E	F	E	F	T	O	W	C	A
$\frac{2}{20}$	$\frac{5}{60}$	$\frac{9}{108}$	$\frac{5}{50}$	$\frac{12}{96}$	$\frac{3}{30}$	$\frac{4}{20}$	$\frac{10}{100}$	$\frac{6}{50}$	$\frac{7}{70}$

5. ($\frac{2}{3}$, country)

A	N	E	R	S	B	I	Z	Q	L
$\frac{4}{6}$	$\frac{9}{12}$	$\frac{14}{22}$	$\frac{60}{90}$	$\frac{16}{25}$	$\frac{8}{12}$	$\frac{22}{33}$	$\frac{20}{30}$	$\frac{32}{49}$	$\frac{12}{18}$

6. ($\frac{1}{2}$, animal)

N	C	U	E	A	N	T	Y	R	B
$\frac{5}{10}$	$\frac{3}{18}$	$\frac{7}{14}$	$\frac{6}{9}$	$\frac{1}{3}$	$\frac{17}{34}$	$\frac{5}{12}$	$\frac{25}{50}$	$\frac{5}{15}$	$\frac{9}{18}$

7. Now make up your own question and test it on a friend.

Equivalent fraction pairs: an activity

This is an activity for 2, 3 or 4 players using the equivalent fraction cards.

How to play:

- Shuffle the cards, place them face down in a pattern of 6 rows by 4 columns.

- Decide who will go first.

- Each turn requires a player to turn over a pair of cards.

- If the pair of cards are equivalent such as $\frac{1}{5}$ and $\frac{2}{10}$ the player keeps the pair. If the cards are not equivalent turn the cards face down again.

- Try to remember which cards are where!

- If you find a pair you get another go, the player with the most pairs when no cards are left is the winner.

- Teacher's note. The fraction cards can be photocopied from the answer book. Alternatively many teachers prefer to have the cards made by pupils.

Proper and improper fractions

- A *proper* fraction is one in which the *numerator* (top number) is less than the *denominator* (bottom number).

  The fractions $\frac{1}{2}$, $\frac{2}{3}$, $\frac{3}{4}$ and $\frac{99}{100}$ are all examples of *proper* fractions.

- An *improper* fraction is one in which the *numerator* is larger than the *denominator*. They are sometimes called 'top-heavy' fractions.

  The fractions $\frac{3}{2}$, $\frac{4}{3}$, $\frac{8}{5}$ and $\frac{100}{33}$ are all examples of *improper* fractions.

- A *mixed number* is one which contains both a whole number and a fraction. *Improper* fractions can be changed into *mixed numbers* and vice versa.

(a) $\frac{3}{2} = 1\frac{1}{2}$ Step 1. 2 into 3 goes once, giving the whole number 1.
Step 2. The remainder is 1 which is written as $\frac{1}{2}$.

(b) $\frac{16}{3} = 5\frac{1}{3}$ Step 1. 3 into 16 goes five times, giving the whole number 5.
Step 2. The remainder is 1, which is written $\frac{1}{3}$.

(c) $2\frac{1}{2} = \frac{5}{2}$ Step 1. 2 times 2, gives 4 (4 halves).
Step 2. Add 1 from the numerator to 4 giving 5.
Step 3. Express 5 as a fraction of 2 which is $\frac{5}{2}$.

(d) $3\frac{5}{6} = \frac{23}{6}$ Step 1. 3 times 6 is 18 (18 sixths).
Step 2. There are 5 sixths to add from the numerator giving 23.
Step 3. Express 23 as a fraction of 6 which is $\frac{23}{6}$.

Exercise 4

Change the following improper fractions to mixed numbers or whole numbers where applicable.

1. $\frac{7}{2}$ 2. $\frac{5}{3}$ 3. $\frac{7}{3}$ 4. $\frac{5}{4}$ 5. $\frac{8}{3}$

6. $\frac{8}{6}$ 7. $\frac{9}{3}$ 8. $\frac{9}{2}$ 9. $\frac{9}{4}$ 10. $\frac{10}{2}$

11. $\frac{10}{6}$ 12. $\frac{10}{7}$ 13. $\frac{13}{8}$ 14. $\frac{35}{15}$ 15. $\frac{42}{21}$

16. $\frac{120}{10}$ 17. $\frac{22}{7}$ 18. $\frac{15}{9}$ 19. $\frac{12}{5}$ 20. $\frac{150}{100}$

In Questions **21** to **35** change the mixed numbers to improper fractions.

21. $1\frac{1}{4}$ 22. $1\frac{1}{3}$ 23. $2\frac{1}{4}$ 24. $2\frac{2}{3}$ 25. $1\frac{7}{8}$

26. $1\frac{1}{3}$ 27. $3\frac{1}{7}$ 28. $2\frac{1}{6}$ 29. $4\frac{3}{4}$ 30. $7\frac{1}{2}$

31. $3\frac{5}{8}$ 32. $4\frac{2}{5}$ 33. $3\frac{2}{5}$ 34. $8\frac{1}{4}$ 35. $1\frac{3}{10}$

Mixed questions

Exercise 5

1. How many halves are in: (a) $1\frac{1}{2}$,   (b) $2\frac{1}{2}$,   (c) $10\frac{1}{2}$?

2. How many thirds are in: (a) $1\frac{2}{3}$,   (b) $3\frac{1}{3}$,   (c) $5\frac{2}{6}$?

3. How many quarters are in: (a) $2\frac{1}{4}$,   (b) $3\frac{1}{2}$,   (c) $4\frac{3}{4}$?

4. Copy each sequence and write down the next four numbers

   (a) $\frac{1}{2} = \frac{2}{4} = \frac{3}{6} = \frac{4}{8} = \frac{5}{10} = \ldots\ldots$

   (b) $\frac{1}{3} = \frac{2}{6} = \frac{3}{9} = \frac{4}{12} = \frac{5}{15} = \ldots\ldots$

5. Write down the first five numbers in the sequence which starts
$\frac{1}{5} = \frac{2}{10} = \ldots\ldots$

6. Draw these fraction charts, using squared paper.

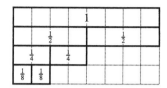

7. Use your fraction charts to answer the following:

(a) $\frac{3}{4} = \frac{?}{8}$ (b) $\frac{3}{5} = \frac{?}{10}$ (c) $\frac{1}{2} + \frac{1}{4} = \frac{?}{4}$

(d) $\frac{1}{5} + \frac{1}{10} = \frac{?}{10}$ (e) $\frac{2}{3} + \frac{1}{6} = \frac{?}{6}$ (f) $\frac{1}{4} + \frac{2}{8} = ?$

8. What fraction of the months of the year begin with the letters J, A or M?

9. What fraction of one hour is one minute?

10. What fraction of one complete turn is two right-angles?

11. What fraction of one minute is ten seconds?

12. What fraction of £1 is 60 p?

13. In a class of 30 pupils writing an essay, 23 are right-handed. What fraction are left-handed?

14. What fraction of the numbers from zero to ninety-nine contain the number 7?

15. Here are four numbers   2   4   7   11
You can use two of the numbers to make a fraction less than one (e.g. $\frac{4}{7}, \frac{2}{7} \ldots$)
(a) What is the smallest fraction you can make?
(b) What is the largest fraction you can make?

16. What number is half way between $3\frac{1}{4}$ and $3\frac{1}{2}$?

17. What fraction of the square is shaded?

18. Find six ways of adding two fractions to make one.

4.7 Angles 2

Angles on a straight line

- The angles on a straight line add up to 180°.

- Angles that add up to 180° are called supplementary.

- Angles that add up to 90° are called complementary.

Find the angles marked with letters.

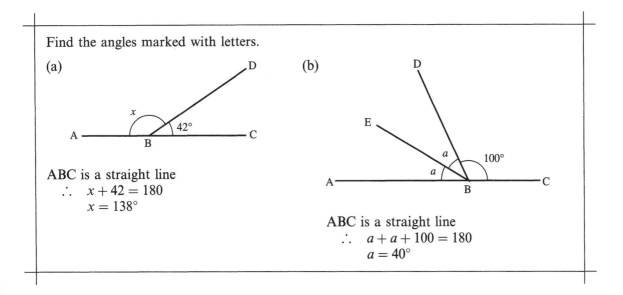

(a)

ABC is a straight line
$$\therefore \quad x + 42 = 180$$
$$x = 138°$$

(b)

ABC is a straight line
$$\therefore \quad a + a + 100 = 180$$
$$a = 40°$$

Find the angles marked with letters. In some questions you may
need to work out a division.

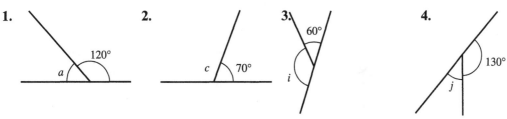

1. 2. 3. 4.

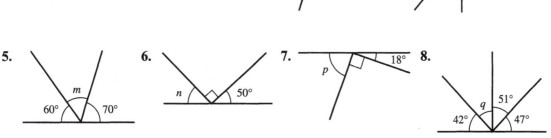

5. 6. 7. 8.

9.

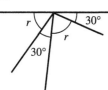

10.

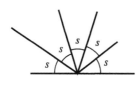

11.

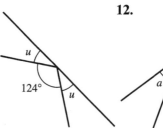

12.

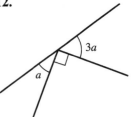

13.

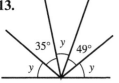

14.

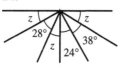

15.

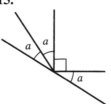

16.

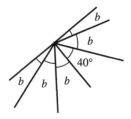

Angles at a point

The angles at a point add up to 360°

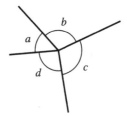

$$a + b + c + d = 360°$$

Exercise 2

Find the angles marked with letters.

1.

2.

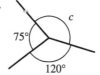

3.

4.

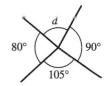

5.

6.

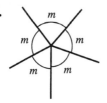

7.

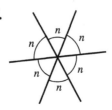

8.

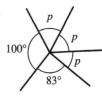

9.

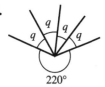

10.

11.

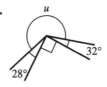

12.

Angles in a triangle

Draw a triangle of any shape on a piece of card and cut it out accurately. Now tear off the three corners as shown.

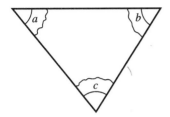

When the angles a, b and c are placed together they form a straight line.

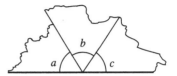

We see that:

> The angles in a triangle add up to 180°

Isosceles and equilateral triangles

An *isosceles* triangle has two equal sides and two equal angles.

The sides AB and AC are equal (marked with a dash) so angles $\widehat{B}$ and $\widehat{C}$ are also equal.

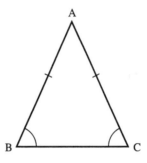

An *equilateral* triangle has three equal sides and three equal angles (all 60°).

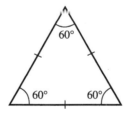

Intersecting lines

When two lines intersect, the opposite angles are equal.
In the diagram, $a = 36°$ and $b = 144°$.

The angles are called *vertically opposite* angles.

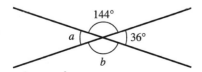

Find the angles marked with letters

(a)
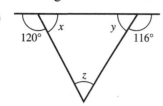

(b)
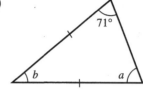

$x = 60°$ (angles on a straight line)
$y = 64°$ (angles on a straight line)
$z + 60 + 64 = 180$
$z = 56°$

$a = 71°$ (isosceles triangle)
$b + 71 + 71 = 180°$
$b = 38°$

Exercise 3

Find the angles marked with letters.

1.

2.

3.

4.

5.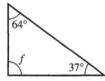

6.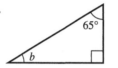

7.

8.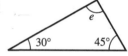

9.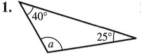

10.

11.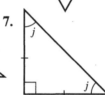

12.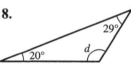

13.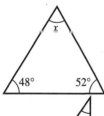

14.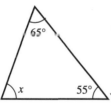

15.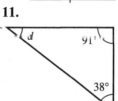

16.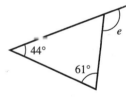

17.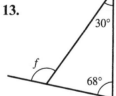

18.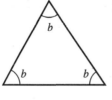

19.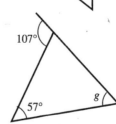

20.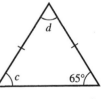

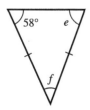
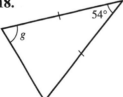
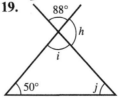
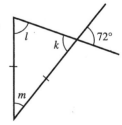

Part 5

5.1 Area and perimeter

We use area to describe how much *surface* a shape has.

1	2		9	10
3	4	7	8	
5	6			

B

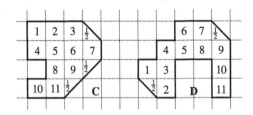

C   **D**

B contains 10 squares.
B has an area of 10 squares.

C has an area of $12\frac{1}{2}$ squares.
D has an area of 12 squares.

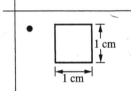

A square one centimetre by one centimetre
has an area of one square centimetre.
This is written $1\,cm^2$.

In the diagrams below each square represents $1\,cm^2$. Copy each
shape and find its area by counting squares.

1.   **2.** 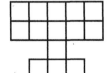   **3.**   **4.**

5.   **6.**   **7.** 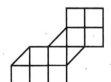   **8.**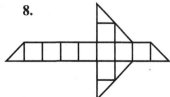

9. 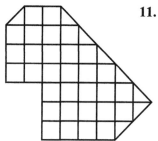 **10.** 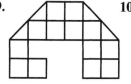 **11.** 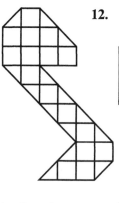 **12.**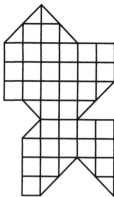

Areas of rectangles

1	2	3	4	5	6
7	8	9	10	11	12
13	14	15	16	17	18
19	20	21	22	23	24
25	26	27	28	29	30

5 cm

|←——— 6 cm ———→|

The area of a rectangle can be found by counting squares. This rectangle has an area of 30 squares.
If each square is $1\,cm^2$, this rectangle has an area of $30\,cm^2$.

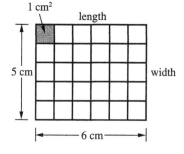

It is easier to multiply the length by the width of the rectangle than to count squares.

$$\text{Area of rectangle} = \text{length} \times \text{width}$$
$$= (6 \times 5)\,cm^2$$
$$= 30\,cm^2$$

Area of a rectangle = length × width   Remember!

A square is a special rectangle in which the length and width are equal.

Area of a square = length × length

Exercise 2

Calculate the areas of the following rectangles. All lengths are given in centimetres.

1.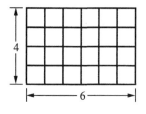

4

|←——— 6 ———→|

2.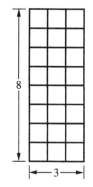

8

|←— 3 —→|

3.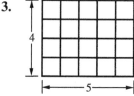

4

|←——— 5 ———→|

4.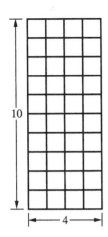

10

4

5.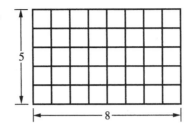

5

8

6.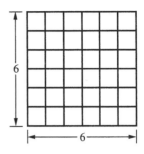

6

6

7. Measure the length and width of these rectangles and then work out the area of each one.

length

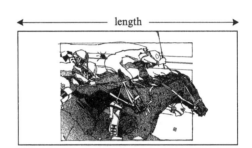

8. Find a magazine or newspaper and cut out pictures with the following areas:

(a) $12\,\text{cm}^2$ (b) $16\,\text{cm}^2$ (c) $24\,\text{cm}^2$

Stick the pictures in your book and write down the area of each one.

In Questions **9** to **12** the area is written inside the shape. Calculate the length of the side marked x.

9.
$45\,\text{cm}^2$ 5 cm

x

10.
x $150\,\text{m}^2$

10 m

11.
$72\,\text{m}^2$ 9 m

x

12.
$64\,\text{m}^2$ x

x

Areas of irregular shapes

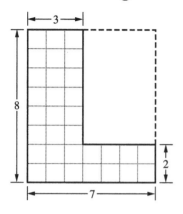

This is an irregular shape. It is possible to find its area by counting squares. A better method is to surround the irregular shape with a rectangle.

Step 1 Area of surrounding rectangle.
$$\begin{aligned} \text{Area} &= \text{length} \times \text{width} \\ &= (8 \times 7)\,\text{cm}^2 \\ &= 56\,\text{cm}^2 \end{aligned}$$

Step 2 Find the unwanted area.
$$\begin{aligned} \text{Area} &= \text{length} \times \text{width} \\ &= (8 - 2) \times (7 - 3)\,\text{cm}^2 \\ &= (6 \times 4)\,\text{cm}^2 \\ &= 24\,\text{cm}^2 \end{aligned}$$

Step 3 Required area $= (56 - 24)\,\text{cm}^2$
$$= 32\,\text{cm}^2$$

Exercise 3

Find the areas of the following irregular shapes. Each square represents $1\,\text{cm}^2$.

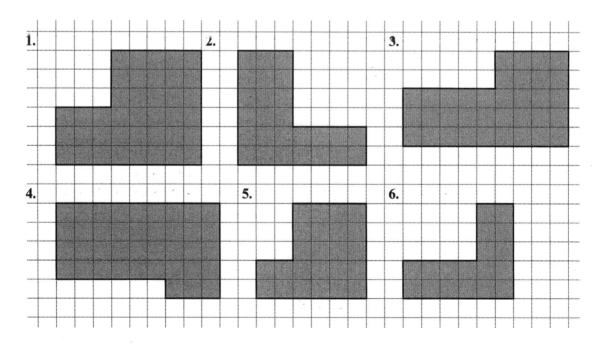

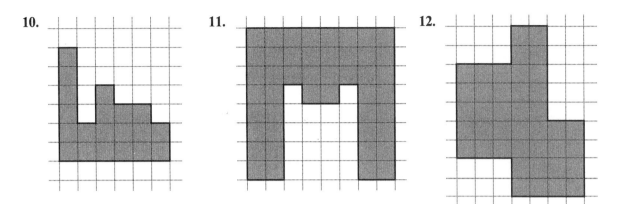

10. **11.** **12.**

Exercise 4

Draw each shape on squared paper and then find the area. All measurements are in centimetres.

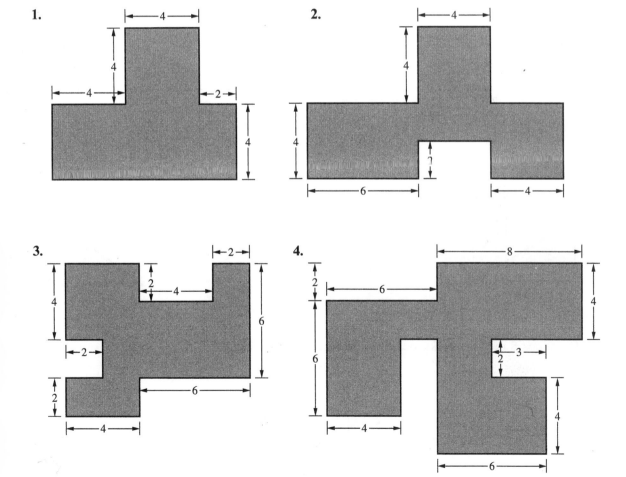

1. **2.**

3. **4.**

Triangles

This triangle has base 6 cm, height 4 cm and a right angle at A.

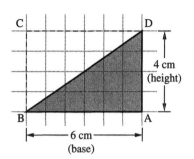

Area of rectangle ABCD $= (6 \times 4)\,\text{cm}^2$
$$= 24\,\text{cm}^2.$$

Area of triangle ABD = area of triangle CDB.

$\therefore$ Area of triangle ABD $= 24 \div 2$
$$= 12\,\text{cm}^2$$

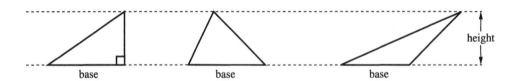

For any triangle, area $= \left(\dfrac{\text{base} \times \text{height}}{2} \right)$

Exercise 5

Find the area of each shape.

1.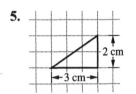

2.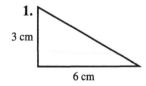

3.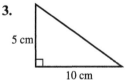

4.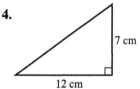

In Questions **5** to **8** the background squares are 1 cm by 1 cm.

5.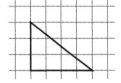

6.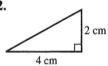

7.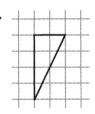

8.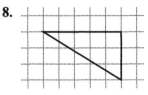

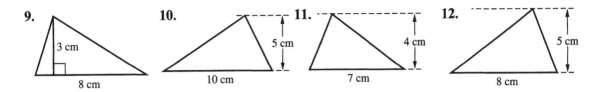

9. 10. 11. 12.

In Questions **13** to **18** the lengths are in cm.

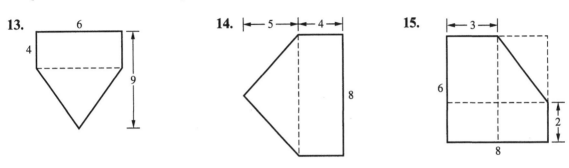

13. 14. 15.

16. Find the shaded area.

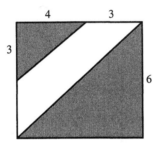

17. Find the shaded area

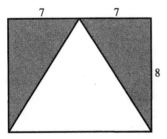

18.* The triangle shown has base 10 cm and area 40 cm². Find the height of the triangle.

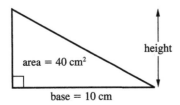

Perimeter

The perimeter of a shape is the distance around its outline.

(a) The perimeter of this rectangle
is $4 + 10 + 4 + 10 = 28$ cm

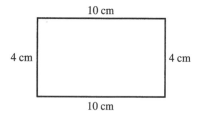

10 cm

4 cm   4 cm

10 cm

(b) The perimeter of this triangle
is $7 + 5 + 9 = 21$ cm.

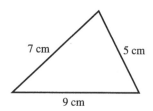

7 cm   5 cm

9 cm

1. Measure the sides of these shapes and work out the perimeter of
each one.

(a)

(b)

(c)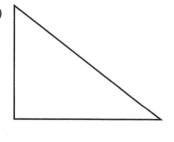

2. Find the perimeter of these pictures.

(a)

(b)

(c)

3. Find the perimeters of these shapes

    (a) rectangle 7 cm by 4 cm   (b) square of side 6 cm

    (c) equilateral triangle of side 7 cm   (d) rectangle 3·5 cm by 2·5 cm

    (e) square of side 20 m   (f) regular hexagon of side 5 cm

The shapes in Questions **4** to **11** consist of rectangles joined together. Find the missing lengths and then work out the perimeter of each shape. The lengths are in cm.

4.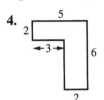

5.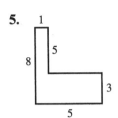

6.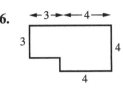

7.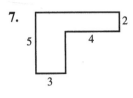

8.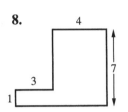

9.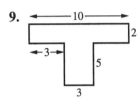

10.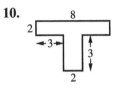

11.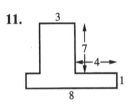

<img: Exercise 7 heading bar>

Exercise 7 [Perimeter *and* area]

1. Here are four shapes made with centimetre squares.

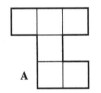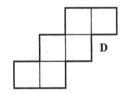

(a) Which shape has an area of $5\,\text{cm}^2$?
(b) Which two shapes have the same perimeter?

2. Each of the shapes here has an area of $2\,\text{cm}^2$.
(a) On square dotty paper draw three more shapes with area $2\,\text{cm}^2$
(b) Draw three shapes with area $3\,\text{cm}^2$.
(c) Draw one shape with area $4\,\text{cm}^2$ *and* perimeter $10\,\text{cm}$.

3. A picture frame has its length twice its height.
The total length of wood used in the frame is $132\,\text{cm}$.
Work out the length of the frame.

height

length

15. Here are five shapes made from equilateral triangles of side 1 cm.

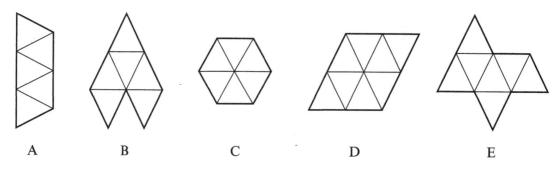

    A   B   C   D   E

(a) Which shape has the longest perimeter?
(b) Which shape has the smallest area?
(c) Which shape has the same perimeter as D?

5. The perimeter of a rectangular lawn is 40 m. The shortest side is 7 m. How long is the longest side?

6.* The diagram shows the areas of 3 faces of a rectangular box. What are the measurements of the box?

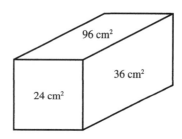

Area and perimotor: an investigation

A • Draw *four* different rectangles which all have a *perimeter* of 24 cm.

B • Draw *three* different rectangles which all have an *area* of 24 cm².

C • Draw at least four rectangles which have a perimeter of 20 cm.
    • Work out the area of each rectangle.
    • Which of your rectangles has the largest area?

D • The perimeter of a new rectangle is 32 cm.
    • Try to *predict* what the sides will be for the rectangle with the largest possible area.
    • Now check to see if your prediction was correct.

E • Try to find the rectangle with perimeter 32 cm which has the *smallest* possible area.

5.2 Volume

- Volume is a measure of how much physical space an object takes up. The volume of a container, like a bottle or a tin, is the quantity of liquid it could contain.

- We measure volume in cubic centimetres. This is a natural choice because we measure length in centimetres, and area in square centimetres.

A cube measuring 1 cm by 1 cm by 1 cm has a → volume of 1 cm³.

This shape takes up the same amount of space → as 4 unit cubes. It has a volume of 4 cm³

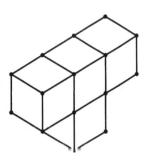

Exercise 1

For Questions **1** to **6** copy the object onto paper and write down the volume of the object. All the objects are made from centimetre cubes.

1.

2.

3.

4.

5.

6.

Find the volume of each object

7.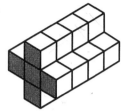

8.

9.

Calculating volumes

Blocks A and B are each made from eight cubes, measuring $1\,cm \times 1\,cm \times 1\,cm$. They each have a volume of 8 cubic cm, which is written $8\,cm^3$.

Rectangular blocks like these are called *cuboids*.

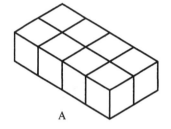

A

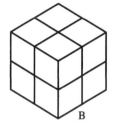

B

A cube like block B, in which all dimensions are equal, is a special kind of cuboid.
The volume of a cuboid is given by the formula,

$$\text{Volume} = (\text{length}) \times (\text{width}) \times (\text{height})$$

(a) Find the volume of the cuboid

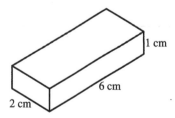

1 cm

6 cm

2 cm

Volume $= 2 \times 6 \times 1$
$= 12\,cm^2$

(b) Find the volume of the cuboid

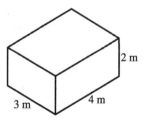

2 m

3 m   4 m

Volume $= 3 \times 4 \times 2$
$= 24\,m^3$

(Notice that the units of volume are m^3 because the lengths are in metres.)

Exercise 2

In Questions **1** to **8** work out the volume of each cuboid. Give your
answer in the correct units

1.

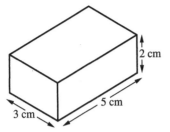

2.

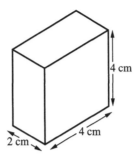

3.

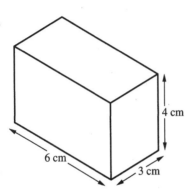

4.

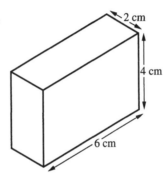

5.

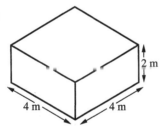

6.

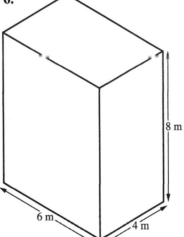

7.

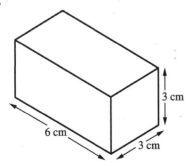

8.

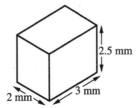

Exercise 3

1. How many times can the small box be filled from the large container which is full of grass seed?

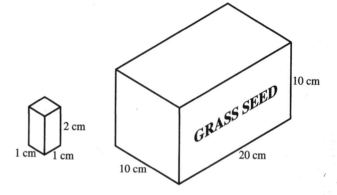

2. A cubical dice is 2 cm by 2 cm by 2 cm. Calculate the total volume of 1000 dice.

3. The diagram shows an empty swimming pool. Water is pumped into the pool at a rate of $2\,m^3$ per minute. How long will it take to fill the pool?

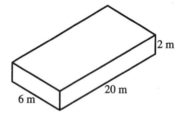

4.

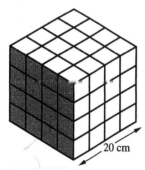

The large cube is cut into lots of identical small cubes as shown. Calculate the volume of each small cube.

5. The shapes below are nets for closed boxes. Work out the volume of the box in each case, giving your answer in cubic cm.

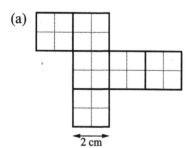

(a)

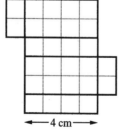

(b)

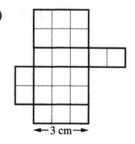

(c)

5.3 Mixed problems

Exercise 1

Each empty square contains either a number or a mathematical symbol (+, −, ×, ÷,). Copy each square and fill in the missing details.

1.

	×	4	→	
×		÷		
8	÷	2	→	
↓		↓		
16	÷		→	8

2.

9	×	8	→	
÷		÷		
		2	→	1
↓		↓		
3	×		→	

3.

15	÷	3	→	
+		×		
6	×		→	
↓		↓		
	−	18	→	

4.

	×	9	→	27
+		−		
	×	4	→	
↓		↓		
8	×		→	

5.

	×	5	→	
−				
7	×	6	→	
↓		↓		
3			→	90

6.

	×	10	→	100
−		÷		
3	×	5	→	
↓		↓		
	−		→	

7.

	+	69	→	
×		+		
7		15	→	105
↓		↓		
	−		→	133

8.

50	×	12	→	
+		÷		
60	÷		→	15
↓		↓		
	×		→	

9.

80	×	50	→	
÷		÷		
8	×	25	→	
↓		↓		
	÷		→	

10.

300		2	→	298
÷		×		
	+		→	25
↓		↓		
		38	→	12

11.

48	−	7.5	→	
3		2	→	1.5
↓		↓		
16	−		→	1

12.

	×	0.3	→	1.8
÷		+		
	−		→	
↓		↓		
0.6	+	1	→	

Exercise 2

1. Work out
   (a) 4×8 (b) $70 - 25$ (c) 8×0
   (d) $48 \div 6$ (e) $279 + 182$ (f) $314 - 276$

2. Write the number 'three thousand and fourteen' in figures.

3. (a) Copy and shade one quarter
        of this shape:
    (b) What fraction of the shape
        is left unshaded?

4. Steve has read 97 of the 448 pages in his book. How many more
pages must be read to reach the middle?

5. There are 15 piles of magazines. Eight piles have 20 magazines
each, of the other piles each have 25 magazines. How many
magazines are there altogether?

6. There are 27 youngsters playing football.
How many teams of five can be formed?
How many will be left over?

7. It cost 6 children a total of £12.90 to
watch a film. What did it cost each child?

8. Copy and complete this multiplication square

×	2	5		
		40		72
			18	
7	14			
			24	36

9. Write 25555p in pounds and pence.

10. Write the number 4307 in words.

Exercise 3

1. On average the amount of potato lost through peeling is 12%. What percentage of potato is left after peeling?

2. 36715 people saw Arsenal's match against Spurs. This is 2368 more than for their match against Everton. How many people saw the game against Everton?

3. Two thirds of the 246 children in a school have pets. 52 children have a rabbit and 37 have a snake. How many children have other kinds of pets?

4.

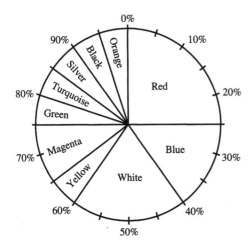

The diagram shows the distribution of colours of cars produced by the 'Cheetah' motor company.

(a) What percentage of cars produced are red, white or blue?

(b) What percentage of cars produced are green or yellow?

(c) List the four most popular colours produced and give each percentage from highest to lowest.

5. How much does *one* cost in each case?

(a) 5 for £2.65

(b) 10 for £4.50

(c) 100 for £81

6. (a) What is the length of this line in millimetres?
   (b) What is this length in centimetres?

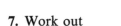

7. Work out
   (a) £5 − £1·35   (b) 0·14 × 1000   (c) 4·2 ÷ 5

8. Write down what fraction of each shape is shaded.

(a) 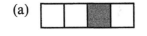   (b)    (c)

9. James is 1·31 m tall and Samita is 6 cm taller. How tall is Samita in metres?

10. A carton of 'Bisto' weighs 0·8 kg. How much would 100 cartons weigh?

Exercise 4

1. How many grams of sugar must be added to 1·3 kg to make 3 kg altogether?

2. Serena bought a packet of 100 raspberries.
She ate a quarter of them on Monday.
She ate a fifth of the remaining
raspberries on Tuesday.
How many raspberries
did she have left?

3. For sports day a school has 40 litres of drink. One cup of drink is 200 ml. How many cups of drink can be provided?

4. Change this cake recipe for 4 people to a recipe for 6 people.

320 g	mixed fruit
90 g	butter
200 ml	milk
4	eggs

5. Stainless steel contains Iron, Chromium and Nickel. 74% of stainless steel is Iron, 8% is Nickel. What percentage is Chromium?

6. Write the number 'two and a half million' in figures.

7. How many minutes are there from 08·20 to 09·15?

8. Measure the sides of the rectangle
and work out
(a) the area
(b) the perimeter

9. Work out the missing numbers

(a) $310 + 560 = \boxed{}$ (b) $530 + \boxed{} = 700$ (c) $734 + \boxed{} = 780$

(d) $\boxed{} + 210 = 500$ (e) $338 + \boxed{} = 558$ (f) $\boxed{} - 420 = 535$

10. Work out the missing numbers

(a) $5·6 + \boxed{} = 6$ (b) $3·7 - \boxed{} = 2$ (c) $0·54 + \boxed{} = 0·74$

(d) $0·4 - \boxed{} = 0·15$ (e) $\boxed{} - 0·7 = 1·4$ (f) $0·86 - \boxed{} = 0·5$

Exercise 5

1. There are 35 rows of chairs and there are 20 chairs in each row.
   (a) How many chairs are there altogether?
   (b) How many rows of chairs are needed for 300 people?

2. One whole number divided by eleven gives 0·63636363. Use a calculator to find the number.

3. At the end of year 6 Mark said 'I have now lived for over one million hours'. Work out if Mark was right.

4. I think of a number, add 2·3 and then multiply by 4. The answer is 23·4. What is the number I am thinking of?

5. How many roses, costing 42p each, can be bought for £20? How much change will there be?

6. The words for the numbers from one to ten are written in a list in alphabetical order. What number will be third in the list?

7. Find two consecutive whole numbers with a product of 210.

8. Use each of the digits 1 to 6. Put one digit in each box to make the statement true.

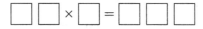

9. A restaurant has 5000 litres of milk. It sells 350 litres per day on average. How many days will the milk last?

10. Julie runs across the playground, which is 90 m wide, in 15 seconds. What was her average speed in metres per second?

Exercise 6

1. Mark is paid a basic weekly wage of £65 and then a further 30p for each item completed. How many items must be completed in a week when he earns a total of £171·50?

2. What number, when divided by 7 and then multiplied by 12, gives an answer of 144?

3. A 10p coin is 2 mm thick. Alex has a pile of 10p coins which is 16·6 cm tall. What is the value of the money in Alex's pile of coins?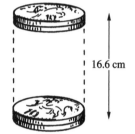

2 mm

16.6 cm

4. An Air France Concorde leaves Paris at 07 00 and arrives in New York at 10 20.
A PanAm 747 leaves Paris at 07 10 and flies at half the speed of the Concorde. When should it arrive in New York?

5. The numbers 1 to 12 are arranged on the star so that the sum of the numbers along each line is the same.

Copy and complete the star.

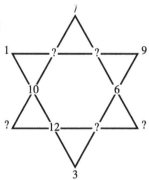

6. Find two numbers which multiply together to give 60 and which add up to 19.

 × = 60, + = 19

7. A shopkeeper buys coffee beans at £4·20 per kg and sells them at 95p per 100 g. How much profit does he make per kg?

8. A Jaguar XJ6 uses 10 litres of petrol for every 50 km travelled. Petrol costs 60p per litre. Calculate the cost in £'s of travelling 500 km.

9. A school play was attended by 226 adults, each paying £1·50, and 188 children, each paying 80p. How much in £'s was paid altogether by the people attending the play?

10. Arrange the following numbers in order, smallest first:
8711, 8171, 8117, 817, 8710

Exercise 6

1. Find the total cost of 4 litres of oil at 97p per litre and 3lb of meat at £2.12 per lb.

2. As an incentive to tidy her bedroom,
a girl is given 1p on the first day,
2p on the second day, 4p on the
third day and so on,
doubling the amount each day.

How much has she been given
after 10 days?

3. A shopkeeper has a till containing a large number of the following coins:
£1; 50p; 20p; 10p; 5p; 2p; 1p.
He needs to give a customer 57p in change. List all the different ways in which he can do this using no more than six coins.

4. Place the following numbers in order of size, smallest first:
0·34; 0·334; 0·032; 0·04; 0·4.

5. A book has 150 pages and the thickness of the book is 15 mm. How thick is each page?

6. In an election 7144 votes were cast for the two candidates. Mr Dewey got 3216 votes. How many people voted for the other candidate?

7. The tenth number in the sequence 1, 4, 16, 64 ...... is 262 144. What is (a) the ninth number,
     (b) the eleventh number?

8. Two fifths of the children in a swimming pool are boys. There are 72 girls in the pool. How many boys are there?

9. How many minutes are there between:

(a) 09.20 and 11.10,
(b) 07.15 and 10.00,
(c) 14.45 and 17.15,
(d) 02.10 and 06.10?

10. A large lump of 'Playdoh' weighing 3·6 kg is cut up into 800 identical pieces. Find the weight of each piece in grams.

Exercise 8

1. Lisa is 12 years old and her father is 37 years older than her. Lisa's mother is 3 years younger than her father. How old is Lisa's mother?

2. 36 small cubes are stuck together to make the block shown and the block is then painted on the outside. How many of the small cubes are painted on:

(a) 1 face   (b) 2 faces
(c) 3 faces   (d) 0 faces?

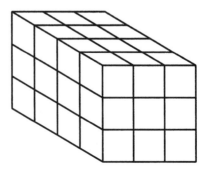

3. Find the letters in these additions.

(a)
```
    8  7  A
    3  B  5
 +  C  4  2
 ----------
 D  8  4  1
```

(b)
```
 A  2  4  5
 5  B  8  4
+1  4  C  6
------------
E 0  5  2  D
```

4. (a) Which four coins make a total of 77p?
(b) Which five coins make a total of 86p?
(c) Which five coins make a total of £1·67?

5. Which of the shapes below can be drawn without taking the pen from the paper and without going over any line twice?

(a)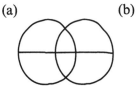

(b)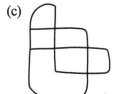

(c)

6. Petrol costs 52p per litre. How many litres can be bought for £13? Give your answer to the nearest litre.

Questions **7** to **12** involve speed. [speed = distance ÷ time]

7. A flight on Concorde takes 2 h 10 min. How long would the same flight take on a plane travelling at half the speed of Concorde?

8. An arctic tern flies a distance of 245 km in 9 hours. How fast does it fly?

9. A steamroller takes 180 seconds to travel 60 m. What is its speed, in m/s?

10. How long does it take a train to travel 270 km at a constant speed of 90 km/h?

11. A tram travels a distance of 200 m at a speed of 25 m/s. How long does it take?

12. A man runs at a speed of 8 m/s. How far will he run in 4 seconds?

In a code the 25 letters from A to Y are obtained from the square using a 2 digit grid reference similar to coordinates.

So letter 'U' is 42 and 'L' is 54.

The missing letter 'Z' has code 10.

5	G	A	P	C	Q
4	O	F	R	H	L
3	N	K	B	M	Y
2	D	S	I	U	E
1	J	T	V	W	X
[Second digit]	1	2	3	4	5

[First digit]

Decode the following messages:

1. 41, 52
   13, 52, 52, 12
   43, 14, 34, 52
   22, 42, 43, 22

2. 44, 25, 31, 52
   25
   13, 32, 45, 52
   12, 25, 53

3. 22, 35, 42, 34, 22
   25, 34, 52
   34, 42, 33, 33, 32, 22, 44

In Question **4** each pair of brackets gives one letter

4. $\left(\frac{1}{4} \text{ of } 140\right)$, $(7^2 + 5)$, $(7 \times 8 - 4)$, $(4^2 + 3^2)$, $\left(\frac{1}{5} \text{ of } 110\right)$, $\left(26 \div \frac{1}{2}\right)$

   $(3 \times 7 + 1)$, $(83 - 31)$, $(2 \times 2 \times 2 \times 2 + 5)$

   $(100 - 57)$, $(4^2 - 2)$, (17×2), $(151 - 99)$

   $(2 \times 2 \times 2 \times 5 + 1)$, $\left(\frac{1}{4} \text{ of } 56\right)$, $(2 \times 3 \times 2 \times 3 - 2)$, $(5^2 - 2)$.

5. Write your own message in code and ask a friend to decode it.

5.4 Number machines

- A number machine performs an *operation* on numbers.
- A simple *operation* could be

	add	(+)
	subtract	(−)
	multiply	(×)
or	divide	(÷)

- The *input* number goes into the machine.   input
- The *output* number comes out of the machine.   output

Examples

input	machine	output	output solution	reason
1.	5 → + 7 → ?		? = 12	(5 + 7 = 12)
2.	8 → − 3 → ◆		◆ = 5	(8 − 3 = 5)
3.	3 → × 6 → ■		■ = 18	(3 × 6 = 18)

Exercise 1

Find the outputs from these number machines.

1. 4 → + 5 → ☺   2. 7 → + 11 → ◢

3. 10 → − 3 → ▮   4. 14 → − 9 → ▬

5. 6 → × 7 → 〰   6. 8 → × 2 → ⊃◁

7. 25 → ÷ 5 → ?   8. 24 → ÷ 4 → ☺

9. 39 → + 13 → ▮   10. 7 → × 9 → ◤

11. 64 → − 46 → ⊡   12. 66 → ÷ 6 → 👢

13. 8 → × 9 → ⊃◁   14. 73 → + 37 → ✠

15. 45 → ÷ 5 → ◆   16. 51 → − 15 → ▮

17. 33 → × 3 → ◤   18. 8 → × 8 → 🌲

19. 120 → ÷ 20 → π   20. 52 → ÷ 4 → ∅

Exercise 2

Find the output.

1. $6 \rightarrow \boxed{+5} \rightarrow \boxed{+2} \rightarrow$?

2. $3 \rightarrow \boxed{+6} \rightarrow \boxed{+8} \rightarrow$ ●

3. $13 \rightarrow \boxed{-9} \rightarrow \boxed{-3} \rightarrow$ ▲

4. $17 \rightarrow \boxed{-8} \rightarrow \boxed{-5} \rightarrow$ ◆

5. $4 \rightarrow \boxed{\times 2} \rightarrow \boxed{\times 5} \rightarrow$ π

6. $3 \rightarrow \boxed{\times 3} \rightarrow \boxed{\times 3} \rightarrow$ ∅

7. $20 \rightarrow \boxed{\div 5} \rightarrow \boxed{\div 2} \rightarrow$ ◢

8. $48 \rightarrow \boxed{\div 4} \rightarrow \boxed{\div 6} \rightarrow$ ◤

9. $17 \rightarrow \boxed{+71} \rightarrow \boxed{-8} \rightarrow$ ♟

10. $34 \rightarrow \boxed{+43} \rightarrow \boxed{-70} \rightarrow$ 👢

11. $5 \rightarrow \boxed{+4} \rightarrow \boxed{\times 3} \rightarrow$ 🐟

12. $7 \rightarrow \boxed{+9} \rightarrow \boxed{\times 0} \rightarrow$ ☺

13. $12 \rightarrow \boxed{+6} \rightarrow \boxed{\div 6} \rightarrow$ ◆

14. $39 \rightarrow \boxed{+13} \rightarrow \boxed{\div 4} \rightarrow$ 〰

15. $89 \rightarrow \boxed{-15} \rightarrow \boxed{+4} \rightarrow$ 〰

16. $73 \rightarrow \boxed{-5} \rightarrow \boxed{+9} \rightarrow$ ▬

17. $42 \rightarrow \boxed{-38} \rightarrow \boxed{\times 7} \rightarrow$ 👢

18. $100 \rightarrow \boxed{-81} \rightarrow \boxed{\times 3} \rightarrow$ ♟

19. $85 \rightarrow \boxed{-58} \rightarrow \boxed{\div 9} \rightarrow$ 🌲

20. $76 \rightarrow \boxed{-67} \rightarrow \boxed{\div 9} \rightarrow$ ⚃

In Questions **21** to **25** there are several operations.

21. $5 \rightarrow \boxed{\times 3} \rightarrow \boxed{-10} \rightarrow \boxed{\times 2} \rightarrow \boxed{\div 10} \rightarrow$ ☂

22. $7 \rightarrow \boxed{\times 9} \rightarrow \boxed{\times 2} \rightarrow \boxed{-66} \rightarrow \boxed{\div 12} \rightarrow$ ⌢

23. $50 \rightarrow \boxed{\times 10} \rightarrow \boxed{-123} \rightarrow \boxed{+13} \rightarrow \boxed{\div 10} \rightarrow \boxed{\div 13} \rightarrow$ ↑

24. $17 \rightarrow \boxed{\times 5} \rightarrow \boxed{+25} \rightarrow \boxed{\div 11} \rightarrow \boxed{\times 13} \rightarrow \boxed{\div 2} \rightarrow \boxed{+7} \rightarrow$ ⚑

25. $13 \rightarrow \boxed{+84} \rightarrow \boxed{\times 0} \rightarrow \boxed{+14} \rightarrow \boxed{\times 5} \rightarrow \boxed{-15} \rightarrow \boxed{\div 11} \rightarrow$ **!**

Inverse operations

- Using the *inverse* (or reverse) we can find the input for any machine, by using the output.

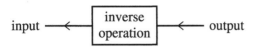

input ⟵ | inverse operation | ⟵ output

Operation	Inverse operation
+7	−7
−8	+8
×4	÷4
÷6	×6

- Example: Find the input.

$$? \rightarrow \boxed{+9} \rightarrow 20$$

Solution: Change arrows direction and use the inverse operation

$$? \leftarrow \boxed{-9} \leftarrow 20$$

$$? = 11 \text{ since } 20 - 9 = 11$$

Exercise 3

Find the input to these systems

1. ● → $\boxed{+6}$ → 11

2. ▲ → $\boxed{+4}$ → 13

3. ⚅ → $\boxed{-7}$ → 2

4. ◢ → $\boxed{-12}$ → 24

5. ■ → $\boxed{\times 3}$ → 18

6. ☺ → $\boxed{\times 5}$ → 45

7. $ → $\boxed{\div 8}$ → 4

8. 👢 → $\boxed{\div 7}$ → 8

9. ⊂× → $\boxed{+14}$ → 72

10. ▨ → $\boxed{+11}$ → 29

11. ◢ → $\boxed{-13}$ → 31

12. ◆ → $\boxed{-72}$ → 27

13. Ø → $\boxed{\times 5}$ → 60

14. π → $\boxed{\times 9}$ → 72

15. ? → $\boxed{\div 4}$ → 8

16. ▶ → $\boxed{\div 6}$ → 7

17. ▬ → $\boxed{\times 9}$ → 54

18. ? → $\boxed{\times 8}$ → 56

19. ☺ → $\boxed{\div 7}$ → 7

20. ◢ → $\boxed{\div 3}$ → 27

Exercise 4

Find the input to these machines

1. ∅ →| + 8 |→| + 6 |→ 18   2. ● →| + 2 |→| + 5 |→ 14

3. ▶ →| − 5 |→| − 8 |→ 7   4. ◆ →| − 9 |→| − 3 |→ 6

5. ∀ →| × 3 |→| × 3 |→ 36   6. ∅ →| × 5 |→| × 2 |→ 70

7. ☺ →| ÷ 6 |→| ÷ 4 |→ 4   8. ◢ →| ÷ 2 |→| ÷ 5 |→ 13

9. ▬ →| + 7 |→| − 11 |→ 11   10. π →| + 1 |→| − 17 |→ 1

11. ◢ →| + 3 |→| × 2 |→ 16   12. ▲ →| + 3 |→| × 4 |→ 52

13. 🎄 →| + 4 |→| ÷ 5 |→ 3   14. 🐟 →| + 7 |→| ÷ 9 |→ 2

15. 🥾 →| − 2 |→| + 17 |→ 34   16. ● →| − 16 |→| + 61 |→ 84

17. ▨ →| − 11 |→| × 8 |→ 40   18. $ →| − 8 |→| × 7 |→ 21

19. ✦ →| − 1 |→| ÷ 11 |→ 4   20. ⚅ →| − 6 |→| ÷ 8 |→ 32

Mystery machines

The following inputs go into a mystery machine ...

      3,   6,   27   and   0.

The diagram shows the outputs produced ...

input	machine	output
3 →	?	→ 6
6 →	?	→ 9
27 →	?	→ 30
0 →	?	→ 3

The 'mystery' machine has added three to produce the outputs because it links *all* the inputs to the outputs in the same way.

The mystery machine was ...   input →| +3 |→ output

Exercise 5

What operation is taking place in each of these machines?

1.

input	output
1 →⊢? ⊢→ 5	
2 →⊢? ⊢→ 10	
3 →⊢? ⊢→ 15	

2.

input	output
63 →⊢? ⊢→ 7	
54 →⊢? ⊢→ 6	
27 →⊢? ⊢→ 3	

3.

input	output
10 →⊢? ⊢→ 8	
9 →⊢? ⊢→ 7	
8 →⊢? ⊢→ 6	

4.

input	output
3 →⊢? ⊢→ 6	
8 →⊢? ⊢→ 11	
7 →⊢? ⊢→ 10	

5.

input	output
12 →⊢? ⊢→ 6	
2 →⊢? ⊢→ 1	
50 →⊢? ⊢→ 25	

6.

input	output
19 →⊢? ⊢→ 57	
9 →⊢? ⊢→ 27	
7 →⊢? ⊢→ 21	

7.

input	output
2 →⊢? ⊢→ 20	
5 →⊢? ⊢→ 50	
8 →⊢? ⊢→ 80	

8.

input	output
9 →⊢? ⊢→ 63	
4 →⊢? ⊢→ 28	
8 →⊢? ⊢→ 56	

9.

input	output
8 →⊢? ⊢→ 64	
1 →⊢? ⊢→ 8	
3 →⊢? ⊢→ 24	

For Questions **10** to **15** copy and complete the number machines after working out the operation for each.

10.

input	output
1 →⊢ ⊢→ 7	
7 →⊢ ⊢→ 13	
13 →⊢ ⊢→ ?	
? →⊢ ⊢→ 26	

11.

input	output
2 →⊢ ⊢→ 8	
3 →⊢ ⊢→ 12	
4 →⊢ ⊢→ ?	
10 →⊢ ⊢→ ?	

12.

input	output
12 →⊢ ⊢→ 5	
7 →⊢ ⊢→ 0	
18 →⊢ ⊢→ ?	
? →⊢ ⊢→ 13	

13.

input	output
0 →⊢ ⊢→ 11	
3 →⊢ ⊢→ ?	
12 →⊢ ⊢→ 23	
? →⊢ ⊢→ 31	

14.

input	output
3 →⊢ ⊢→ 1	
9 →⊢ ⊢→ 3	
? →⊢ ⊢→ 4	
15 →⊢ ⊢→ ?	

15.

input	output
0 →⊢ ⊢→ ?	
5 →⊢ ⊢→ 50	
? →⊢ ⊢→ 40	
7 →⊢ ⊢→ 70	

5.5 Using Algebra

Balance puzzles

Many problems in mathematics are easier to solve when symbols or
letters are used instead of numbers.
This is called using *algebra*.
In balance puzzles the scales balance and the symbols ○, △ and □
represent weights.

On the balance ○ and △ represent weights

Find ○ if △ = 5 for this balance puzzle

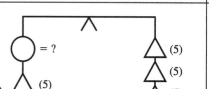

Clearly for these scales to balance exactly, then ○ = 10

Exercise 1

Copy each diagram and find the value of the required symbol.

1. Find □ if △ = 4.

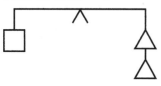

2. Find ○ if △ = 10.

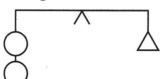

3. Find ○ if □ = 4.

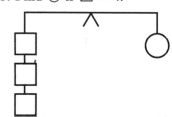

4. Find □ if △ = 12.

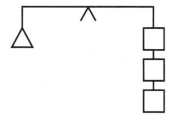

5. Find △ if □ = 2.

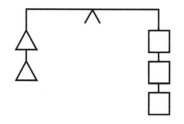

6. Find △ if ○ = 6.

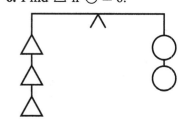

7. Find □ if ○ = 8.

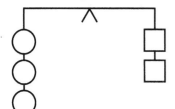

8. Find △ if □ = 15.

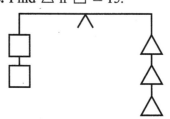

9. Find △ if ○ = 14.

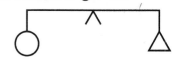

10. Find △ if □ = 7.

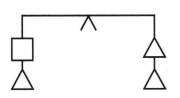

11. Find □ if △ = 8.

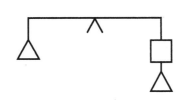

12. Find □ if ○ = 13.

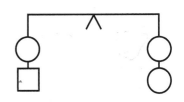

13. Find △ if □ = 14.

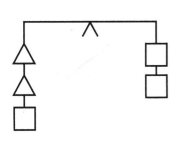

14. Find ○ if △ = 10.

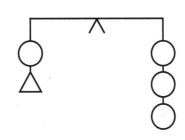

15. Find ○ if □ = 9.

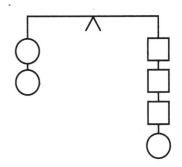

16. Find △ if □ = 11.

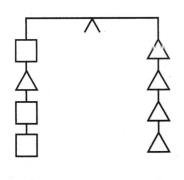

17. Find ○ if □ = 21.

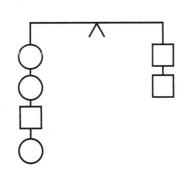

18. Find □ if ○ = 8.

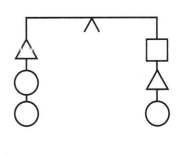

19. Find ○ if △ = 6.

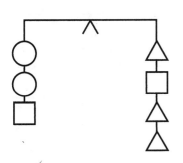

20. Find ○ if □ = 5.

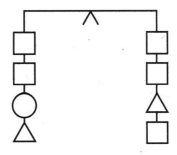

Bigger balance puzzles

In the diagram below, $\triangle = 4$
Find the value of   (a) $\bigcirc$ (b) $\square$

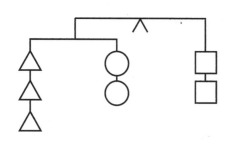

Solution: (a) $3\triangle = 2\bigcirc$
$12 = 2\bigcirc$
$6 = \bigcirc$

(b) $3\triangle + 2\bigcirc = 2\square$
$12 + 12 = 2\square$
$24 = 2\square$
$12 = \square$

Exercise 2

Copy each diagram and find the value of the unknown symbols.

1. $\bigcirc = 10$, find $\triangle$ and $\square$.

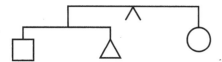

2. $\triangle = 8$, find $\bigcirc$ and $\square$.

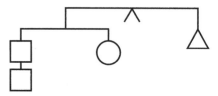

3. $\square = 14$, find $\bigcirc$ and $\triangle$.

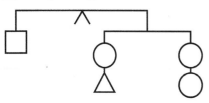

4. $\square = 6$, find $\bigcirc$ and $\triangle$.

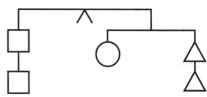

5. $\bigcirc = 8$, find $\square$ and $\triangle$.

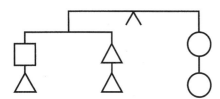

6. $\square = 4$, find $\bigcirc$ and $\triangle$.

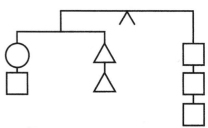

7. △ = 4, find ◯ and □.

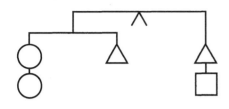

8. ◯ = 10, find △ and □.

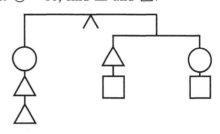

9. △ = 5, find ◯ and □.

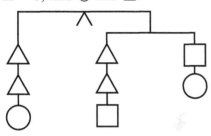

10. □ = 3, find ◯ and △.

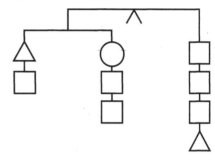

11. □ = 6, find △ and ◯.

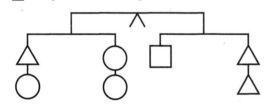

12. ◯ = 5, find □ and △.

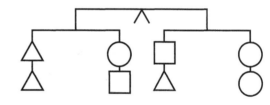

13. ∧ = 4, find ◯ and □.

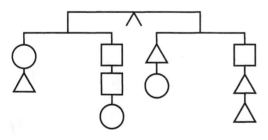

14. ∪ = 8, find □ and △.

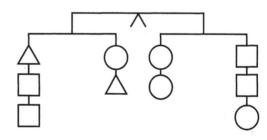

15. □ = 4, find ◯ and △.

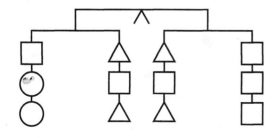

16. ◯ = 5, find △ and □.

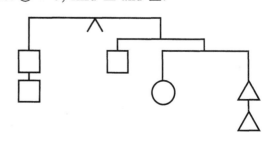

Using letters for numbers

Here is a square with sides of length l cm
The perimeter of the square in cm is $l+l+l+l$.
If we use p cm to stand for the perimeter,
we can write $\qquad p = l+l+l+l$
or $\qquad\qquad p = 4l \qquad$ (This means $4 \times l$)

Exercise 3

1. (a) The perimeter p of the square is
      $$p = x + x + x + x$$
      or $\;\; p = 4x$.

   (b) Find the perimeter, p of this triangle.
      Write '$p = \ldots$'

In Questions **2** to **7** find the perimeter p of the shape.

2.

3.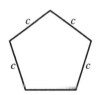

4.

5.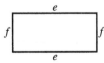

6.

7.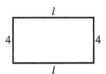

8. Draw and label a rectangle whose perimeter p is given by the formula $\;\; p = 2t + 2m$.

9. Draw and label a triangle whose perimeter is given by the formula $\;\; p = 2y + 7$.

10. Draw and label a pentagon (5 sides) whose perimeter p is given by the formula $\;\; p = 2a + 3b$.

- Suppose there are a number of people in a room. Call this number N. If one more person enters the room there will be $N + 1$ people in the room.

- Suppose there are x cows in a field. After the farmer puts 3 more cows in the field there are $x + 3$ cows in the field.

- Suppose a piece of wood is l centimetres long. If you cut off 5 cm the length left is $l - 5$ cm.

- Suppose there are y people on a bus. At a bus stop n more people get on the bus. Now there are $y + n$ people on the bus.

- If I start with a number N and then double it I will have $2N$. If I then add 7 I will have $2N + 7$.

- When you multiply, write the number before the letter. So write $2N$ *not* $N2$.

Remember: $4p$ means $4 \times p$ or $p \times 4$.

Exercise 4

In Questions **1** to **10** find the number I am left with.

1. I start with M and then double it. $\boxed{M} \rightarrow \boxed{\times 2} \rightarrow ?$

2. I start with N and then add 6.

3. I start with e and then take away 3.

4. I start with d and then add 10.

5. I start with N and then multiply by 3.

6. I start with x, double it and then add 3.

7. I start with y, double it and then take away 7.

8. I start with k, treble it and then add 10.

9. I start with s and multiply by 100.

10. I start with t, multiply it by 6 and then add 11.

11. A piece of wood is 25 cm long. How much remains after I cut off a piece of length x cm?

12. When a man buys a small tree it is h cm tall. During the year it grows a further t cm and then he cuts off 30 cm. How tall is it now?

13. A brick weighs w kg. How much do six bricks weigh?

14. A man shares a sum of N pence equally between four children. How much does each child receive?

15. On Monday there are n people in a cinema. On Friday there are three times as many people plus another 50. How many people are there in the cinema on Friday?

16. A prize of £x is shared equally between you and four others. How much does each person receive?

Finding a rule

- Here is a sequence of shapes made from sticks

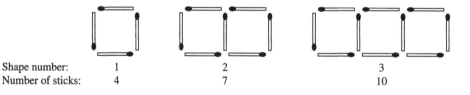

Shape number:	1	2	3
Number of sticks:	4	7	10

- There is a *rule* or *formula* which we can use to calculate the number of sticks for any shape number.

'The number of sticks is three times the shape number add one'.

Check that this rule works for all the shapes above and also for shape number 4 which you can draw.

- We could also write the rule using symbols. Let n stand for the diagram number and let s stand for the number of sticks.

The rule (or formula) is '$s = 3n + 1$'.

Exercise 5

1. Here is a sequence of triangles made from sticks.

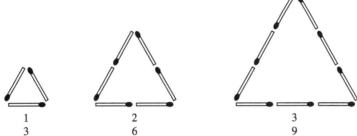

Shape number: 1   2   3
Number of sticks: 3   6   9

    (a) Draw shape number 4 and count the number of sticks.
    (b) Write down and complete the rule for the number of sticks
         in a shape: 'The number of sticks is _____ times the shape
         number'.

2. Here is a sequence of 'steps' made from sticks

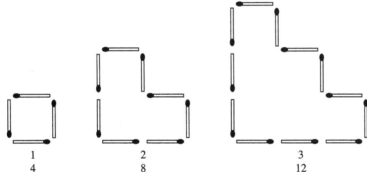

Shape number: 1   2   3
Number of sticks: 4   8   12

    (a) Draw shape number 4 and count the number of sticks.
    (b) Write down the rule for the number of sticks in a shape.
         'The number of sticks is _____ times the shape number'.

3. Louise makes a pattern of triangles from sticks.

Shape number: 1   2   3
Number of sticks: 3   5   7

(a) Draw shape number 4 and shape number 5

(b) Make a table:

shape number	1	2	3	4	5
number of sticks	3	5	7		

(c) Write down the rule for the number of sticks in a shape.
    'The number of sticks is _____ times the shape number and
    then add _____.'

4. Here is a sequence of houses made from sticks

  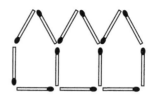

| Shape number: | 1 | 2 | 3 |
| Number of sticks: | 5 | 9 | 13 |

(a) Draw shape number 4.

(b) Make a table:

shape number	1	2	3	4
number of sticks	5	9	13	

(c) Write down the rule.
'The number of sticks is ____ times the shape number and then add ____ .'

5. Paul makes a pattern of squares from dots.

| Shape number: | 1 | 2 | 3 |
| Number of dots: | 4 | 6 | 8 |

(a) Draw shape number 4 and shape number 5.

(b) *Without drawing* the diagram, state the number of dots in shape number 10.

(c) Write the rule:
'The number of dots is ....'

(d) Use the rule to calculate the number of dots in shape number 25.

6. Here is another sequence made from dots.

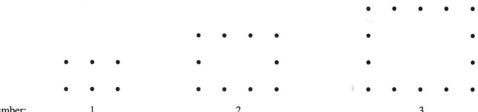

| Shape number: | 1 | 2 | 3 |
| Number of dots: | 6 | 10 | |

(a) Draw shape numbers 4 and 5 and make a table.

shape number	number of dots
1	6
2	10
3	
⋮	

(b) Decide which of the following is the correct rule for the number of dots:
'the shape number times 3 and then add 3'
or 'the shape number times 2 and then add 4'
or 'the shape number times 4 and then add 2'.

7. In this sequence black squares are surrounded by white squares.

      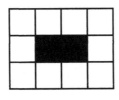   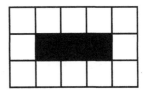

Black squares: $b = 1$ $b = 2$ $b = 3$
White squares: $w = 8$ $w = 10$ $w = 12$

(a) The rule is: 'The number of white squares is two times the number of black squares and then add 6.'

(b) Work out the number of white squares in the diagram which has 20 black squares.

(c) Write the formula, without words, for the number of white squares. Use b for the number of black squares and w for the number of white squares.
Write '$w = $ '.

8. (a) Write in the missing numbers to continue the sequences across the page.

3	4	5	
7	10	13	
1	2	3	

(b) You could write letters in the spaces like this.

e
n
f

The rule is: 'To find n you double e and add on f'

(c) Write the rule without using words.

9. (a) Write the missing numbers in the last cross to continue the patterns.

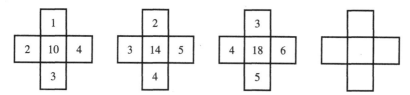

(b) Here is a cross using letters

The rule is: 'To find x you add up a, b, c and d'
(c) Write the rule without using words.

5.6 Long multiplication and division

Long multiplication

- Seventeen 23s is the same as ten 23s plus seven 23s
  17×23 is the same as $10 \times 23 + 7 \times 23$

(a)   23
      $\times 10$
      $\underline{230}$

(b) 23
    $\times 7$
    $\underline{161}$

(c)   230
    $+161$
    $\underline{391}$

(d) Answer : 391

- $16 \times 35 = 10 \times 35 + 6 \times 35$

(a)   35
      $\times 10$
      $\underline{350}$

(b)   35
     $\times 6$
     $\underline{210}$
      $_3$

(c)   350
    $+210$
    $\underline{560}$

(d) Answer : 560

Exercise 1

Work out

1. 23×15 **2.** 31×14 **3.** 32×16 **4.** 17×14

5. 33×18 **6.** 24×19 **7.** 31×17 **8.** 52×13

9. 14×42 **10.** 13×27 **11.** 15×22 **12.** 16×19

13. 12×47 **14.** 18×51 **15.** 19×62 **16.** 17×46

17. 15×56 **18.** 14×81 **19.** 18×29 **20.** 13×73

Exercise 2

Work out

1. 21×24	**2.** 27×32	**3.** 26×28	**4.** 27×21
5. 32×25	**6.** 33×27	**7.** 36×14	**8.** 35×27
9. 34×41	**10.** 42×61	**11.** 31×47	**12.** 53×21
13. 123×32	**14.** 291×42	**15.** 804×61	**16.** 74×243
17. 62×831	**18.** 53×747	**19.** 249×92	**20.** 603×27

Long division

A Use the method for 'short division' with working at the side.

$$24 \text{ remainder } 1$$
$$17\overline{)40^{6}9}$$

$$\begin{array}{r} 17 \\ \times 2 \\ \hline 34 \end{array}$$

$$\begin{array}{r} 17 \\ \times 4 \\ \hline 68 \end{array}$$

B In this method we set it out so that the remainders are easier to find

$$\begin{array}{r} 24 \\ 17\overline{)409} \\ -34 \downarrow \\ \hline 69 \\ -68 \\ \hline 1 \end{array}$$

- 17 into 40 goes 2 times
- $2 \times 17 = 34$
- $40 - 34 = 6$
- 'bring down' 9
- 17 into 69 goes 4 times
- $4 \times 17 = 68$
- $69 - 68 = 1$
- Answer is 24 remainder 1

Exercise 3

Work out

1. $13\overline{)273}$	**2.** $14\overline{)308}$	**3.** $16\overline{)496}$	**4.** $17\overline{)544}$
5. $14\overline{)448}$	**6.** $15\overline{)630}$	**7.** $19\overline{)665}$	**8.** $21\overline{)693}$
9. $17\overline{)459}$	**10.** $15\overline{)510}$	**11.** $14\overline{)672}$	**12.** $17\overline{)544}$
13. $440 \div 22$	**14.** $264 \div 24$	**15.** $506 \div 23$	**16.** $546 \div 26$
17. $317 \div 31$	**18.** $547 \div 25$	**19.** $886 \div 42$	**20.** $963 \div 33$
21. $557 \div 26$	**22.** $528 \div 45$	**23.** $118 \div 52$	**24.** $785 \div 63$
25. $32\overline{)715}$	**26.** $18\overline{)924}$	**27.** $25\overline{)776}$	**28.** $53\overline{)781}$
29. $64\overline{)696}$	**30.** $27\overline{)583}$	**31.** $15\overline{)667}$	**32.** $98\overline{)694}$

Word problems

A minibus can take 16 passengers. How many minibuses are needed for 214 passengers?

(a) Work out 214 ÷ 16

```
      13 remainder 6
16)214
    16
    54
    48
     6
```

(b) You have to think carefully about what the remainder means. If you used 13 minibuses there would be 6 people left over. So you need 14 minibuses altogether.

Exercise 4

To do these questions you have to multiply or divide. Do not use a calculator.

1. Work out the total cost of 45 pens at 22p each. Give your answer in pounds.

2. A box of 15 golf balls costs 975 pence. How much does each ball cost?

3. There are 23 rooms in a school and each room has 33 chairs. How many chairs are there altogether?

4. A shop owner buys 52 tins of paint at 84p each. How much does he spend altogether?

5. Eggs are packed twelve to a box. How many boxes are needed for 444 eggs?

6. Figaro the cat eats one tin of cat food every day. How much will it cost to feed Figaro for 31 days if each tin costs 45p?

7. How many 23-seater coaches will be needed for a school trip for a party of 278?

8. Steve wants to buy as many 24p stamps as possible. He has £5 to spend. How many can he buy and how much change is left?

9. It costs £972 to hire a boat for a day. A trip is organised for 36 people. How much does each person pay?

10. Tins of spaghetti are packed 24 to a box. How many boxes are needed for 868 tins?

11. On average a school needs 87 exercise books a week. How many books are needed for 38 weeks?

12. A prize of 470 chocolate bars is shared equally between 18 winners. How many bars does each winner get and how many are left over?

13. Each class of a school has 31 pupils plus one teacher and there are 15 classes in the school.
The school hall can take 26 rows of chairs with 18 chairs in a row. Is that enough chairs for all the pupils and teachers?

14. When Philip was digging a hole in his garden he struck oil! The oil came out at a rate of £17 for every minute of the day and night. How much does Philip receive in a 24-hour day?

Exercise 5

Copy the cross number pattern shown and complete it using the clues. Do not use a calculator.

1		2		3	4
		5	6		
7	8				
		9		10	
11				12	13
14				15	

Across
1. 14×16
3. $592 \div 16$
5. 31×137
7. $552 \div 23$
12. $756 \div 18$
14. 23×36
15. $870 \div 15$

Down
1. 16×17
2. $308 \div 7$
3. $748 \div 22$
4. 25×31
6. $513 \div 19$
8. $697 \div 17$
9. 28×26
10. 21×45
11. $588 \div 21$
13. $392 \div 14$

Part 6

6.1 Fractions 2

- If a prize of £50 is shared equally between two people, each person receives $\frac{1}{2}$ of £50.

  This is £50 ÷ 2 = £25 each

  > To find one *half* of a quantity, divide the quantity by *two*

- 'Jet', 'Charlie' and 'Trigger' are three horses with a bag of carrots. The bag contains 216 carrots. How many carrots does each horse get if they are shared out equally?

  We need to find $\frac{1}{3}$ of 216

  This is 216 ÷ 3 = 72 carrots each

  > To find $\frac{1}{3}$ of a quantity, divide the quantity by 3

Exercise 1

1. Copy and complete this table.

No.	Fraction of quantity required	Divide the quantity by ...
(a)	$\frac{1}{2}$	2
(b)	$\frac{1}{3}$	
(c)	one quarter	
(d)		10
(e)	$\frac{1}{5}$	
(f)	$\frac{1}{8}$	
(g)		16
(h)	one twelfth	
(i)		100

In Question **2** to **19** copy and complete.

2. $\frac{1}{2}$ of £8 = ?

3. $\frac{1}{4}$ of 28 litres = ?

4. $\frac{1}{3}$ of 60 kg = ?

5. $\frac{1}{4}$ of 20 kg = ?

6. $\frac{1}{2}$ of 16 kg = ?

7. $\frac{1}{3}$ of 60 kg = ?

8. $\frac{1}{2}$ of 150 cm = ?

9. $\frac{1}{3}$ of 27 cm = ?

10. $\frac{1}{4}$ of 280 cm = ?

11. $\frac{1}{5}$ of £10 = ?

12. $\frac{1}{10}$ of £100 = ?

13. $\frac{1}{5}$ of 45 litres = ?

14. $\frac{1}{10}$ of 250 cm = ?

15. $\frac{1}{8}$ of £72 = ?

16. $\frac{1}{20}$ of 300 cm = ?

17. $\frac{1}{4}$ of 288 m = ?

18. $\frac{1}{9}$ of 729 kg = ?

19. $\frac{1}{100}$ of £5000 = ?

20. We can write $\frac{1}{5}$ of $70 = 70 \div 5 = \frac{70}{5}$

Copy the following and fill in the missing numbers.

(a) $\frac{1}{4}$ of $28 = \boxed{} \div \boxed{} = \dfrac{\boxed{}}{\boxed{}}$

(b) $\boxed{}$ of $\boxed{} = 45 \div 9 = \dfrac{\boxed{}}{\boxed{}}$

(c) $\boxed{}$ of $\boxed{} = \boxed{} \div \boxed{} = \dfrac{54}{6}$

(d) $\frac{1}{5}$ of $4 = \boxed{} \div \boxed{} = \dfrac{\boxed{}}{\boxed{}}$

Fraction of a number

(a) In a mixed school with 364 pupils, $\frac{3}{7}$ of the pupils are girls.
How many girls are there?

We need to work out $\frac{3}{7}$ of 364.

$\frac{1}{7}$ of $364 = 364 \div 7$
$\qquad = 52$

$\left[\textit{Working:} \quad \begin{array}{r} 5\,2 \\ 7\overline{)3\,6\,^14} \end{array} \right]$

So $\frac{3}{7}$ of $364 = 52 \times 3$
$\qquad\qquad = 156$

$\left[\textit{Because } \frac{3}{7} \textit{ of 364 is 3 times} \right.$
$\left. \textit{as many as } \frac{1}{7} \textit{ of 364.} \right]$

There are 156 girls in the school.

(b) Work out $\frac{2}{5}$ of £560

$\frac{1}{5}$ of $560 = 560 \div 5$
$\qquad = 112$

$\begin{array}{r} 1\,1\,2 \\ 5\overline{)5\,6\,^10} \end{array}$

So $\frac{2}{5}$ of $560 = 112 \times 2$
$\qquad\qquad = 224$

Answer: £224.

Exercise 2

Copy and complete these problems. (Use a calculator if needed)

1. $\frac{3}{8}$ of £24 = ?
2. $\frac{2}{5}$ of £15 = ?
3. $\frac{3}{4}$ of £36 = ?

4. $\frac{4}{7}$ of £84 = ?
5. $\frac{5}{9}$ of £108 = ?
6. $\frac{2}{3}$ of £216 = ?

7. $\frac{3}{4}$ of 20 kg = ?
8. $\frac{2}{3}$ of 30 kg = ?
9. $\frac{7}{10}$ of 30 g = ?

10. $\frac{5}{8}$ of 480 cm = ?
11. $\frac{4}{5}$ of 80 cm = ?
12. $\frac{2}{3}$ of 120 cm = ?

13. $\frac{2}{5}$ of 30 p = ?
14. $\frac{5}{8}$ of 64 p = ?
15. $\frac{3}{10}$ of 150 p = ?

Exercise 3

1. In a maths test full marks were 120. How many marks did Ben get if he got $\frac{7}{10}$ of full marks?

2. A petrol tank in a car holds 56 litres when full. How much petrol is in the tank when it is $\frac{3}{4}$ full?

3. Sally has driven around $\frac{2}{5}$ of the motorcycle circuit. If the circuit is 1750 metres, how far has she travelled?

4. Mario has an order for 600 pizzas. If $\frac{5}{12}$ of his pizzas must be vegetarian, how many will be non-vegetarian?

5. If a book has 440 pages and you have read $\frac{3}{8}$ so far, how many more pages do you still have to read?

6. 'Tommy' the Toucan's beak is $\frac{7}{10}$ his height. If Tommy stands 210 mm high, how long is his beak?

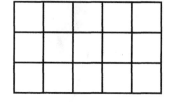

7. Sumitra's fishtank contained 140 fish. If $\frac{3}{5}$ of the fish were females, how many of the fish were males?

8. Draw a copy of the rectangle.
   (a) Shade in $\frac{1}{3}$ of the squares.
   (b) Draw crosses in $\frac{1}{5}$ of the unshaded squares.
   (c) How many squares are neither shaded nor have crosses in them?

6.2 Probability

In probability we ask questions like . . .
'How likely is it?'
'What are the chances of . . . ?'

Here are some questions where we do not know the answer . .
'Will I grow up to be famous?'
'Will I live to be over 100 years old?'
'Who will win the F.A. cup?'

Some events are certain. Some events are impossible.

Some events are in between certain and impossible.

> The probability of an event is a measure of the chance of it happening.
>
> The probability (or chance) of an event occurring is measured on a scale like this . . .
>
> impossible   unlikely   evens   likely   certain

Exercise 1

Draw a probability scale like this . . .

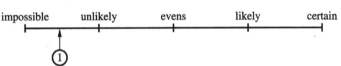

impossible   unlikely   evens   likely   certain

Draw an arrow to show the chance of the events below happening.
The arrow for question ① has been done for you.

1. When a card is selected from a pack it will be an 'ace'.

2. When a coin is tossed it will show a 'head'.

3. Your local vicar will win the national lottery next week.

4. The day after Monday will be Tuesday.

5. There will be a burst pipe in the school heating system next week and the school will have to close for 3 days.

6. You will blink your eyes in the next minute.

7. You will be asked to tidy your room this week.

8. When a slice of toast is dropped, it will land on the floor buttered side down.

9. You will get maths homework this week.

10. England will win the World Cup in 2006.

Probability as a number

Different countries have different words for saying how likely or unlikely any particular event is.
All over the world people use probability as a way of doing this, using numbers on a scale instead of words.
The scale looks like this ...

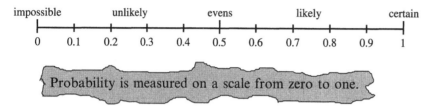

> Probability is measured on a scale from zero to one.

Look at the events in the last exercise and for each one estimate the probability of it occurring using a probability from 0 to 1.

As an example in question $\textcircled{1}$ you might write 'about 0·1'. Copy each question and write your estimate of its probability at the end.

Experimental probability

The chance of certain events occurring can easily be predicted. For example the chance of tossing a head with an ordinary coin. Many events, however, cannot be so easily predicted.

Experiment: To find the experimental probability that a drawing pin will land 'point up' when dropped onto a hard surface.

Step 1.   We will do 50 *trials*. Drop a pin 50 times onto a hard surface.

Step 2.   A *success* is when the pin lands point up.

Step 3.   Make a tally chart like this ...

Number of trials	Number of successes
ЖГ ЖГ ‖	ЖГ ‖

> Experimental probability = $\dfrac{\text{Number of trials in which a success occurs}}{\text{Total number of trials made}}$

Exercise 3

Carry out experiments to work out the experimental probability of some of the following events.

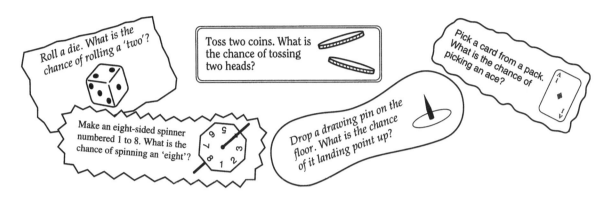

Expected probability

For simple events, like throwing a dice or tossing a coin, we can work out the expected probability of an event occurring.
For a fair dice the *expected probability* of throwing a '3' is $\frac{1}{6}$.
For a normal coin the expected probability of tossing a 'head' is $\frac{1}{2}$

$$\text{Expected probability} = \frac{\text{the number of ways the event can happen}}{\text{the number of possible outcomes}}$$

Random choice: If a card is chosen at random from a pack it means that every card has an equal chance of being chosen.

Nine identical discs numbered 1, 2, 3, 4, 5, 6, 7, 8, 9 are put into a bag. One disc is selected at random.

In this example there are 9 possible equally likely outcomes of a trial.

(a) The probability of selecting a '4' $= \frac{1}{9}$

   This may be written p (selecting a '4') $= \frac{1}{9}$

(b) p (selecting an odd number) $= \frac{5}{9}$

(c) p (selecting a number greater than 5) $= \frac{4}{9}$

Exercise 4

1. A bag contains a red ball, a blue ball and a yellow ball. One ball is chosen at random. Copy and complete these sentences.

   (a) The probability that the red ball is chosen is ... $\dfrac{\Box}{3}$

   (b) The probability that the blue ball is chosen is ... $\dfrac{\Box}{\Box}$

   (c) The probability that the yellow ball is chosen is ... $\dfrac{\Box}{\Box}$

2. One ball is chosen at random from a bag which contains a red ball, a blue ball, a yellow ball and a white ball. Write down the probability that the chosen ball will be

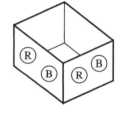

   (a) red   (b) blue   (c) yellow.

3. One ball is chosen at random from a box which contains 2 red balls and 2 blue balls. Write down the probability that the chosen ball will be
   (a) red.
   (b) blue.
   (c) yellow.

4. A hat contains 2 white balls and 1 black ball. One ball is chosen at random. Find the probability that it is
   (a) white.
   (b) black.

5. A pencil case contains pencils of the following colours:- 6 red, 3 black, 1 green and 1 blue. One pencil is selected without looking. Find the probability that the pencil is
   (a) red.
   (b) black.
   (c) green.

6. I roll an ordinary dice.
   Find the probability that I score
   (a) 3
   (b) 1
   (c) less than 5

7. Eight identical discs numbered 1, 2, 3, 4, 5, 6, 7, 8 are put into a bag. One disc is selected at random. Find the probability of selecting an odd number.

8. A bag contains 4 red balls and 7 white balls. One ball is selected at random. Find the probability that it is
(a) red.   (b) white.

9. One card is selected at random from the ten cards shown ...
Find the probability of selecting
(a) the King of spades   (b) a heart
(c) a diamond   (d) a 3

10. I buy a fish at random from a pond containing 3 piranhas, 2 baby sharks and 7 goldfish. Find the probability that the fish I choose is
(a) a goldfish.   (b) a baby shark
(c) dangerous   (d) glad I rescued it!
(e) able to play the piano.

Probability Problems

A pack of playing cards, without Jokers, contains 52 cards.
There is Ace, King, Queen, Jack, 10, 9, 8, 7, 6, 5, 4, 3, 2 of four suits.
The suits are ...

spades hearts diamonds clubs

A pack of cards is shuffled and then one card is chosen at random.
(a) The probability that it is a King of hearts is $\frac{1}{52}$
(b) The probability that it is an ace is $\frac{4}{52}\left(=\frac{1}{13}\right)$
(c) The probability that it is a spade is $\frac{13}{52}\left(=\frac{1}{4}\right)$

Exercise 5

1. Nicole has 3 kings and 1 ace. She
   shuffles the cards and takes one
   without looking.

   Nicole asks two of her friends about
   the probability of getting an ace

Angie says:
'It is $\frac{1}{3}$ because there are
3 kings and 1 ace.'

Syline says
'It is $\frac{1}{4}$ because there are
4 cards and only 1 ace.'

Which of her friends is right?

2. One card is picked at random from a pack of 52.
   Find the probability that it is
   (a) a Queen
   (b) the King of diamonds
   (c) a spade

3. One card is selected at random from a full pack of 52 playing
   cards. Find the probability of selecting
   (a) a heart
   (b) a red card
   (c) a '2'
   (d) any King, Queen or Jack
   (e) the ace of spades

4. A bag contains 3 black balls, 2 green balls, 1 white ball and 5
   orange balls. Find the probability of selecting
   (a) a black ball
   (b) an orange ball
   (c) a white ball

5. Here are two spinners.
   Say whether the following statements are true or false.
   Explain why in each case.
   (a) 'Sarah is more likely to spin a 6 than Ben'.
   (b) 'Sarah and Ben are equally likely to spin an
       even number.'
   (c) 'If Sarah spins her spinner six times,
       she is bound to get at least one 6.'

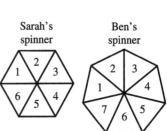

Sarah's   Ben's
spinner   spinner

Two events

- When a 10p coin and a 20p coin are tossed together there are four possible outcomes.

  So, for example, the probability of tossing two tails = $\frac{1}{4}$.

10p	20p
head	head
head	tail
tail	head
tail	tail

- Suppose a red dice and a blue dice are rolled together. This time there are *many* possible outcomes. With the red dice first the outcomes can be listed systematically:

  (1, 1) (1, 2) (1, 3) (1, 4) (1, 5) (1, 6)
  (2, 1) (2, 2) (2, 3) (2, 4) (2, 5) (2, 6)
  (3, 1) (3, 2)   ,   ,   ,   ,
    ,   ,   ,   ,   ,   ,
    ,   ,   ,   ,   ,   ,
    ,   ,   ,   ,   (6, 5) (6, 6)

  There are 36 equally likely outcomes

Exercise 5

1. Look at the table at the top of this page for 2 coins.
   What is the probability of tossing two heads?

2. Look above at the list of outcomes for rolling 2 dice.

   (a) How many ways can you get a total of 12?

   (b) What is the probabilty of getting a total of 12?

3. (a) With 2 dice how many ways can you get a total of 3?

   (b) What is the probability of getting a total of 3?

4. Mrs Rayner would like to have two children.
   Each time she has a baby there is an equal chance of a boy or a girl.
   What is the probability of Mrs Rayner having two girls?

6.3 Percentages

Percentages are fractions with denominator (bottom number) equal
to 100.
So 25% means $\frac{25}{100}$, 67% means $\frac{67}{100}$ and so on.

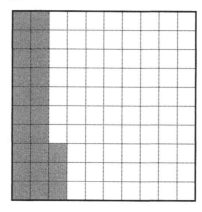

The square contains
100 squares and 23
squares are shaded

Fraction shaded $= \frac{23}{100}$

Percentage shaded $= 23\%$

1. Draw each square and write underneath it

    (a) what fraction is shaded   (b) what percentage is shaded

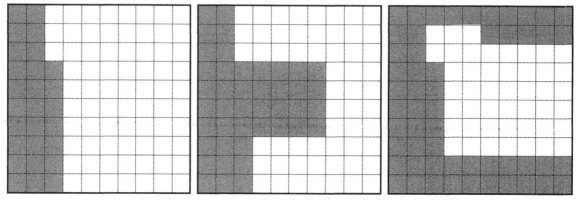

2. If 40% of a square is shaded, what percentage of the square is
not shaded?

3. If 73% of a square is shaded, what percentage of the square is
not shaded?

4. Approximately 67% of the earth's
surface is covered with water.
What percentage of the earth's
surface is land?

5. In this square, 25 out of 100 squares are
shaded to show 25%.
Draw your own numbers (like 17, 21 or 33)
and shade in the correct number of squares to
show the percentage. Try to draw the
numbers the same size.

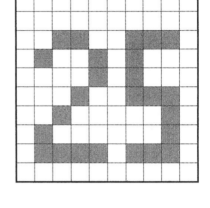

6. Write the following as percentages.

(a) $\frac{7}{100}$ (b) $\frac{15}{100}$

(c) $\frac{99}{100}$ (d) $\frac{3}{100}$

(e) $\frac{100}{100}$ (f) $\frac{130}{100}$

7. Jacques is scuba diving and has used 64%
of his oxygen supply. What percentage of
his oxygen does he still have?

8. On a coach trip 35% of the passengers were
adults and the rest were children. What
percentage of the passengers were children?

9. Goldylocks decided to make porridge for the
3 bears. Father bear got 43% of the porridge
and mother bear got 38% of the porridge.
What percentage of the porridge did baby
bear receive?

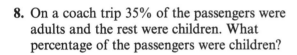

10. (a) What percentage of the 100 squares contain
    (i) ticks?
    (ii) crosses?
    (iii) circles?

  (b) What percentage of the 100 squares are blank?

11.

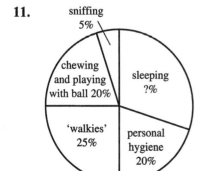

This chart shows how
'Bonzo' the dog spends his
day. What percentage of the
day does Bonzo spend
sleeping?

12. This diagram shows the percentage of 'ingredients' in making concrete patio blocks.

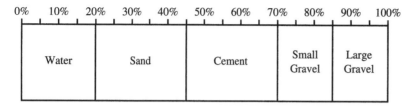

(a) What percentage is sand and cement?
(b) What percentage is gravel?
(c) What percentage is non-liquid?

13. The diagram shows the percentage of people who took part in activities offered at a sports centre on a Friday night.

(a) What percentage went swimming?
(b) What percentage played squash?
(c) What percentage played a racket sport?
(d) What percentage did not play football?
(e) What percentage played activities involving a ball?

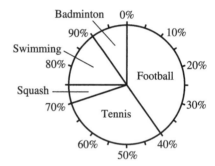

Common percentages

- Some percentages are used a lot and you should learn them.

$$10\% = \frac{10}{100} = \frac{1}{10}, \qquad 30\% = \frac{30}{100} = \frac{3}{10}, \qquad 70\% = \frac{7}{10}, \qquad 90\% = \frac{9}{10}, \qquad 20\% = \frac{20}{100} = \frac{1}{5},$$

$$40\% = \frac{40}{100} = \frac{2}{5}, \qquad 60\% = \frac{3}{5}, \qquad 80\% = \frac{4}{5}, \qquad 25\% = \frac{1}{4}, \qquad 50\% = \frac{1}{2},$$

$$75\% = \frac{3}{4}, \qquad 33\frac{1}{3}\% = \frac{1}{3}, \qquad 66\frac{2}{3}\% = \frac{2}{3}$$

$\frac{1}{4} = 25\%$

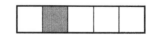

$\frac{1}{5} = 20\%$

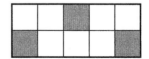

$\frac{3}{10} = 30\%$

Exercise 2

1. For each shape write
   (a) what fraction is shaded
   (b) what percentage is shaded.

 A

B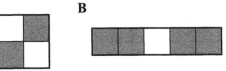

C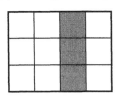

D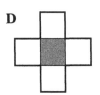

E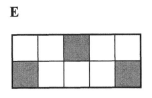

F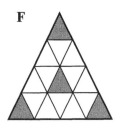

G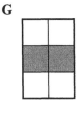

H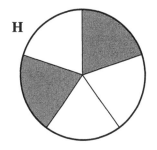

2. Copy these and fill in the spaces.
   (a) $30\% = \frac{}{10}$
   (b) $\frac{3}{4} = \quad \%$
   (c) $\frac{1}{3} = \quad \%$
   (d) $1\% = \frac{}{100}$
   (e) $80\% = -$
   (f) $\frac{1}{10} = \quad \%$

3. These pictures show how much petrol is in a car. E is Empty and F is Full.
   What percentage of a full tank is in each car?

   (a)

   (b)

   (c)

   (d)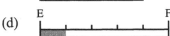

   (e)

4. What percentage could be used in each sentence?
   (a) Three quarters of the pupils at a school had school dinners.
   (b) Three out of five workers voted for a strike.
   (c) Nicki got 15 out of 20 in the spelling test.
   (d) One in three cats prefer 'Whiskas'.
   (e) Half of the customers at a supermarket thought that prices were too high.
   (f) One in four mothers think children are too tidy at home.

5. Draw three diagrams of your own design, like those in Question 1 and shade in:
   (a) 30%
   (b) 75%
   (c) $66\frac{2}{3}\%$

Percentage of a number

(a) Work out 25% of £60.
25% is the same as $\frac{1}{4}$, $\frac{1}{4}$ of £60 is £15.

(b) In a sale, prices are reduced by 20%. Find the 'sale price' of the dress shown.

20% is the same as $\frac{1}{5}$

$\frac{1}{5}$ of £40 = £8.

£40

Sale price = £40 − £8
          = £32.

Exercise 3

1. Work out
(a) 20% of £50   (b) 75% of £12   (c) 10% of £90
(d) 25% of £4000 (e) $33\frac{1}{3}$% of £90   (f) 30% of £40

2. Now do these
(a) 90% of £100   (b) 40% of $30   (c) $66\frac{2}{3}$% of £12
(d) 50% of $1200 (e) 1% of £300   (f) 5% of £100

3. Kate earns £15 for doing a paper round. How much *extra* does she earn when she gets a 20% rise?

4. Full marks in a maths test is 60. How many marks did Tim get if he got 60%?

5. Of the 240 children at a school, 75% walk to school. How many children walk to school?

6. Find the actual cost of the following items in a sale. The normal prices are shown.

(a) £60
25% off
marked price

(b) £15
50% off!

(c) £24
$33\frac{1}{3}$% off
normal
price

(d)

£40
10%
discount
off price

(e)
£80
75% off!

(f) £25
40%
discount
off price

7. In many countries Value Added Tax [V.A.T.] is charged at $17\frac{1}{2}\%$. Here is a method for finding $17\frac{1}{2}\%$ of £4000 without a calculator.

$$
17\tfrac{1}{2}\% \text{ of £4000:} \quad
\begin{aligned}
10\% &= £400 \\
5\% &= £200 \\
2\tfrac{1}{2}\% &= £100 \\
\hline
17\tfrac{1}{2}\% &= £700
\end{aligned}
$$

Use this method to work out:

(a) $17\frac{1}{2}\%$ of £6000   (b) $17\frac{1}{2}\%$ of £440   (c) $17\frac{1}{2}\%$ of £86

8. The price of a car was £6600 but it is increased by 10%. What is the new price?

9. The price of a boat was £36 000 but it is increased by 5%. What is the new price?

10. In a sale the price of a shirt costing £12 is reduced by 25%. Find the reduced price of the shirt.

11. A car is worth £3000. After an accident its value falls by 30%. How much is it worth now?

12. On the first of March a shopkeeper puts all his prices up by 5%. Find the new prices of the following.
(a) a scarf at £10.
(b) a pair of gloves at £12.
(c) a coat at £40.

13. A lizard weighs 500 g. While escaping from a predator it loses its tail and its weight is reduced by 1%. How much does it weigh now?

14. Find the odd one out
(a) 50% of £30   (b) 20% of £50   (c) 25% of £60

15. Find the odd one out
(a) 10% of £70   (b) 25% of £60   (c) 5% of £140

16. A hen weighs 3 kg. After laying an egg her weight is reduced by 2%. How much does she weigh now?

17. A marathon runner weighs 60 kg at the start of a race. During the race his weight is reduced by 5%. How much does he weigh at the end of the race?

6.4 Symmetry

Paper folding activities

1. Take a piece of paper, fold it once and then cut out a shape across the fold.
This will produce a shape with one line of symmetry.

cut along
the broken line ➞

2. Fold another piece of paper twice so that the second fold is at right angles to the first fold. Again cut along the fold to see what shapes you can make.
This will produce a shape with two lines of symmetry.

3. Fold the paper three times and cut.

 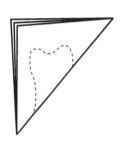

This will produce a shape with four lines of symmetry.

Below are three shapes obtained by folding and cutting as above.
Try to make similar shapes yourself.
Stick the best shapes into your exercise book.

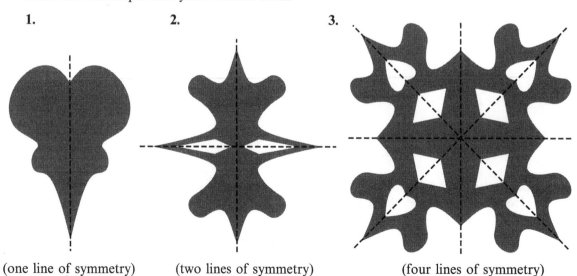

1.	**2.**	**3.**
(one line of symmetry)	(two lines of symmetry)	(four lines of symmetry)

4. More interesting shapes can be obtained as follows:
  (a) Cut out a circle and fold it in half.

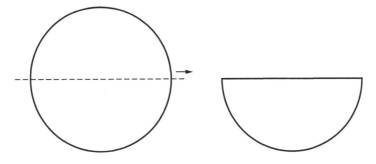

  (b) Fold about the broken line so
      that sectors A and B are equal.

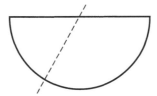

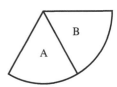

  (c) Fold sector B behind sector A. Now cut
      out a section and see what you obtain.

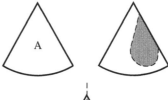

  (d) Even more complicated shapes can be
      obtained by folding once again down the
      middle of the sector.

Here are two shapes obtained by this method of folding.

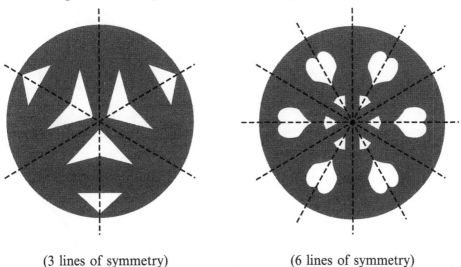

(3 lines of symmetry)   (6 lines of symmetry)

Line symmetry

An object has line symmetry if we can draw a straight line through it (usually dotted) so that it balances perfectly.

To check if a line of symmetry balances perfectly you can:-

(a) Trace over the shape on tracing paper and fold it along the line of symmetry. If the two sections either side of the symmetry line fit onto each other exactly, then it really is a line of symmetry.

(b) Put a small mirror onto the line of symmetry. Look into the mirror and remove it quickly. If there was no difference in what you saw then it must be a line of symmetry.

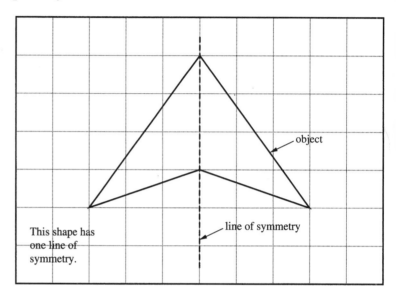

object

line of symmetry

This shape has one line of symmetry.

Exercise 1

Copy each of the following shapes and mark on the diagram all lines of symmetry.

1.

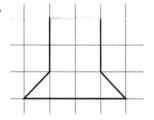

2.

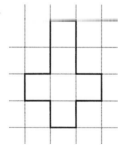

3.

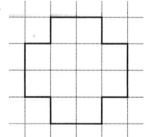

4.

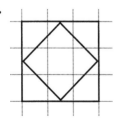

5.

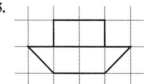

6.

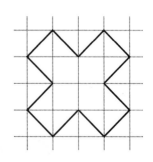

7. 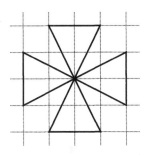   **8.**    **9.**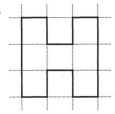

10. 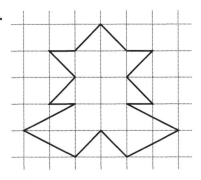   **11.** 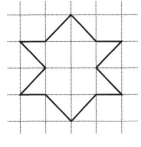   **12.**

13. Design your own pictures with line symmetry.

Line symmetry puzzles

Shade in as many squares as necessary so that the final pattern has lines of symmetry shown by the broken lines.

(a)

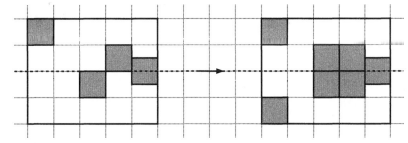

3 squares have been added

(b)

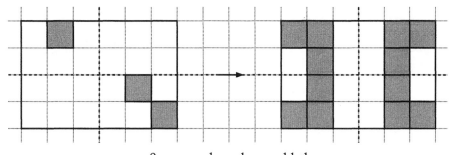

9 squares have been added

Exercise 2

Copy each diagram and, using a different colour, shade in as many squares as necessary so that the final pattern has lines of symmetry shown by the broken lines. For each question write down how many new squares were shaded in.

1.
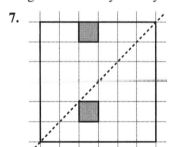

2.
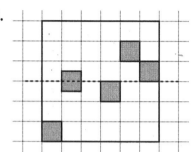

3.
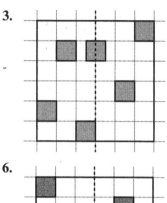

4.
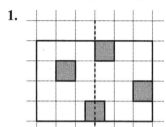

5.
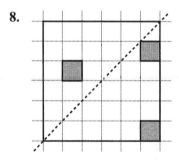

6.
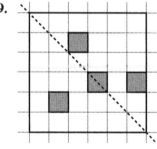

Be careful when the line of symmetry is a diagonal line. You can check your diagram by folding along the line of symmetry.

7.
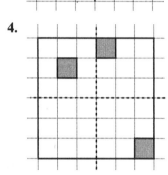

8.
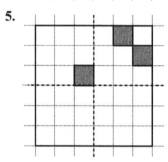

9.
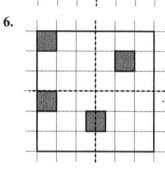

10.
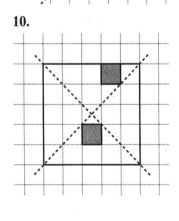

11.*
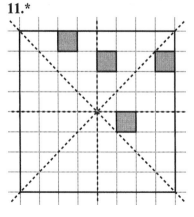

12.*
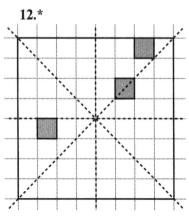

Planes of symmetry

A plane of symmetry divides a 3-D shape into two congruent shapes.
One shape must be a mirror image of the other shape.

Here is one of the
planes of symmetry of
a cuboid

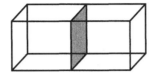

The shaded plane is a plane of
symmetry of the cube.

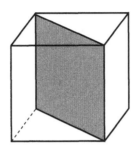

1. How many planes of
   symmetry does this cuboid
   have?

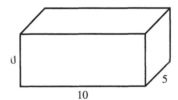

2. How many planes of symmetry do these shapes have?

(a) 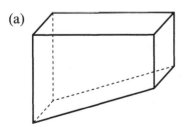   (b) 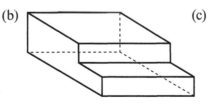   (c)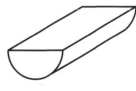

3. Draw a cube and show one of its planes of symmetry.

4. How many planes of symmetry does a sphere have?

The tile factory: an activity

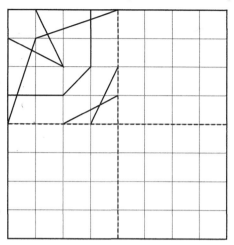

1. Copy this square and pattern onto the top left hand corner of a piece of A4 centimetre squared paper.

2. Lightly mark the reflection lines on the diagram as shown.

3 Use these lines to help you reflect the pattern across ...

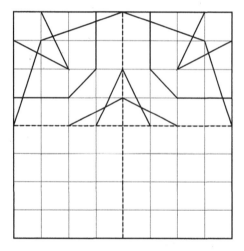

... and then down.

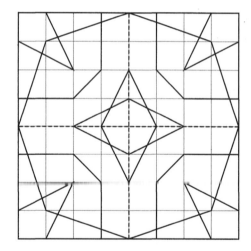

4. Repeat the process with the same tile so that your tile neatly covers the piece of paper →.

5. Now colour or shade in your work as neatly and symmetrically as you can.

Rotational symmetry

We have already seen that many shapes have one or more lines of symmetry. An object like the playing card shown has no lines of symmetry but it does have *rotational symmetry*.

Place a sheet of tracing paper over the drawing of the four of hearts and trace the main features of the card. Turn the tracing paper until the tracing and the card underneath coincide just as they did to start with.

The four of hearts *has* rotational symmetry because the pattern fits onto itself before a complete turn is made. The shape A does not have rotational symmetry because it does not fit onto itself before a complete turn is made. (*Any* shape will always fit onto itself when a complete turn is made.)

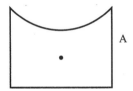

Order of rotational symmetry

The shape B fits onto itself three times when rotated through a complete turn. It has *rotational symmetry of order three*.

The shape C fits onto itself six times when rotated through a complete turn. It has rotational symmetry of order six.

Exercise 4

For each diagram decide whether or not the shape has rotational symmetry. For those diagrams that do have rotational symmetry state the order.

1.

2.

3.

4.

5.

6.

7.

8.

9.

10.

11.

12.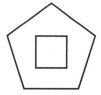

13.

14.

15.

16.

17. Copy and complete the table for the 26 *capital* letters of the alphabet.

Order of rotational symmetry	Capital letters
1	A, B, C, ...
2	
More than 2	

6.5 Handling data

Bar charts and bar-line graphs

When you do a survey the information you collect is called *data*.
This data is usually easier for someone else to understand if you
display it in some sort of chart or graph.

(a) The scores of 35 golfers competing
in a tournament were

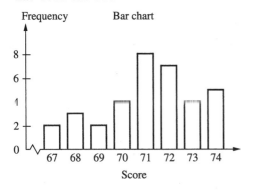

68 74 71 72 71 68 70

74 69 71 70 67 73 71

70 74 69 72 73 74 71

72 74 71 72 72 70 73

67 68 72 73 72 71 71

(b) A tally chart/frequency table is
made for the scores.

score	tally	frequency
67	||	2
68	|||	3
69	||	2
70	||||	4
71	|||| |||	8
72	|||| ||	7
73	||||	4
74	||||	5

(c) This data can be displayed on either a bar chart or on a bar-line
graph. The '$\sim\!\!/\!\!\backslash\!\!\sim$' shows that a section on the horizontal axis
has been cut out.

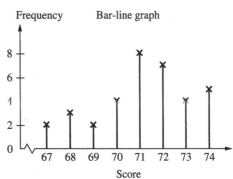

Exercise 1

1. In a survey children were asked to name their
favourite sport.
   (a) What was the most popular sport?
   (b) How many children chose Athletics?
   (c) How many children took part in the survey?

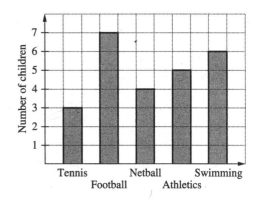

2. Here is a *bar-line graph* showing the number of children in the families of children in a school.

(a) How many families had three children?

(b) How many families were there altogether?

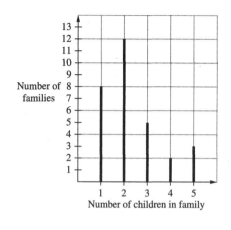

3. Collect your own data for a bar line graph like the one in Question **2**. Ask lots of people to state the number of children in their families.

Draw a graph of the results and use colour to make it more attractive.

4. This table shows the number of different sorts of snacks sold by a shop.

(a) How many snacks were sold on Thursday?

(b) Each Aero costs 22 p. How much was spent on Aeros in the whole week?

(c) Draw a bar chart to show the number of each kind of snack sold in a week.

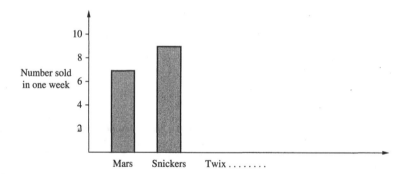

	Mon	Tu	Wed	Th	Fri
Mars	3	1	0	0	3
Snickers	0	4	1	2	2
Twix	2	2	1	3	4
Aero	5	0	0	1	4
Crunchie	2	3	4	1	1
Kit Kat	5	0	2	1	1

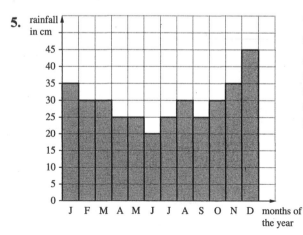

5.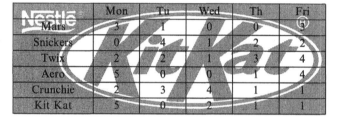

The monthly rainfall in the Lake District is shown left.

(a) How much rain fell in August?

(b) Which was the driest month in the year?

(c) Which was the wettest month in the year?

(d) In which months did 25 cm of rain fall?

(e) In which months did 30 cm of rain fall?

6. Some children were asked to state which was their favourite T.V.
programme from the list below.

Eastenders   E
Top of the Pops   T
Animal Hospital   A
Neighbours   N
Sister Sister   S

The replies were: S N S A N E T T N A E T A E N
                   A S N A T E S E N S E N N E N
                   N A E N N E A A N S E A N A N

Make a tally chart and then draw a bar chart to show the results

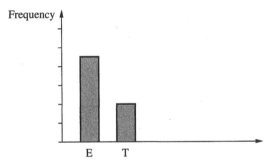

		Tally	Total
EastEnders	E		
ToTP	T		
Animal Hospital	A		
Neighbours	N		
Sister Sister	S		

7. In English some letters occur more frequently than others [e.g.
there are more 'a's than 'z's]. In French different letters are
more common.
Here are two paragraphs: one in English and one in French.
There is the same number of letters in each paragraph.

The England football captain
Alan Shearer walks up an
ordinary suburban garden
path in full kit. He rings the
doorbell and asks, "Is Daniel in?",
Daniel's mum shouts, "It's Alan",
but Daniel is lying on the floor
watching Dennis the Menace on
the TCC (The Children's Channel) network.
"I'm busy," he shouts and his mum
shuts the door. Shearer rings the bell again.
"He promised he'd come out,"
he complains, only to have the door
shut on him again.

Eurogoals Magazine
Les plus beaux buts des
championnats européens
de football Ce magazine
hebdomadaire de cin-
quante-deux minutes pré-
sente une sélection des
meilleures rencontres du
Championnat espagnol,
portugais, belge, néerlan-
dais ou français. L'acent
est mis sur les buts, et les
matchs se soldant par un
0–0 sont systématiquement
écartés. Les grandes
équipes telles que l'Ajax
d'Amsterdam ou le Real

(a) For each paragraph make a tally chart to record how
many times the letters k, i, u appear.
(b) Draw a bar chart for each language and write a
sentence about the main differences in the two charts.

Letter	Tally
k	
i	

Data in groups and line graphs

- Here are the ages of the people at a wedding.

  33 11 45 22 50 38 23 54 18 72   5   58
  37   3 61 51   7 62 24 57 31 27 66   29
  25 39 48 15 52 25 35 18 49 63 13   74

  With so many different numbers over a wide range it is helpful to put the ages into *groups*.

- Here is the start of a tally chart

Ages	Tally	Total (Frequency)
0–9	|||	3
10–19	ⴄ卌	5
20–29	卌 ||	7
30–39		
40–49		
50–59		
60–69		
70–79		

- Here is the start of a frequency chart

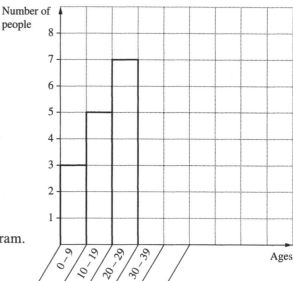

- Finish the tally chart and the frequency diagram. Notice that when the data is in groups the bars are touching.

Exercise 2

1. Shruti started with one frog but it laid eggs and now she has lots! One day she measures all her little pets. Here are the lengths in mm.

   82 63 91 78 27 93 87   48 22 15
   42 28 84 65 87 55 79   66 85 38

   (a) Make a tally chart and then draw the frequency diagram.

Length (mm)	Tally	Frequency
0–20		
21–40		
41–60		
61–80		
81–100		

   (b) How many frogs were more than 60 mm long?

2. Tom has lots of snakes and he likes to weigh
them every week. The weights are shown.
  (a) How many snakes weigh between
      61 and 80 grams?
  (b) How many snakes weigh less
      than 41 grams?
  (c) How many snakes does he
      have altogether?

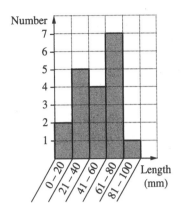

3.  Farmer Gray rears pigs. As an experiment, he decided to feed half of
his pigs with their normal diet and the other half on a new high fibre
diet. The diagrams shows the weight of the pigs in the two groups.

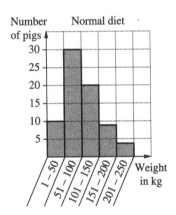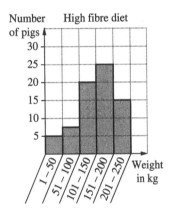

In one sentence describe what effect the new diet had.

4. Here is some information about fireworks.

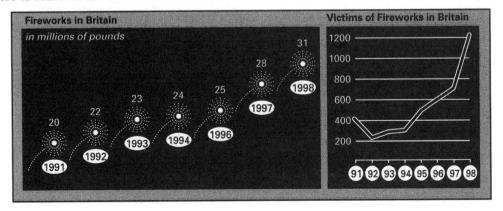

In which year were the lowest number of people injured by
fireworks?

5. The graph shows a car journey from
   A to C via B.
   (a) How far is it from A to C?
   (b) For how long does the car stop
       at B?
   (c) When is the car half way
       between B and C?
   (d) What is the speed of the car
       (i)   between A and B?
       (ii) between B and C?

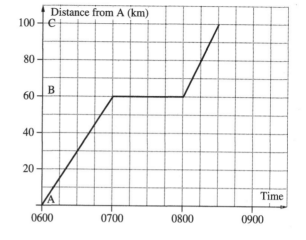

6. The graph shows the motion of a
   train as it goes away from Troon.
   (a) How far from Troon is the train
       at 0900?
   (b) When is the train half way
       between R and S?
   (c) Find the speed of the train
       (i)   from P to Q
       (ii) from Q to R

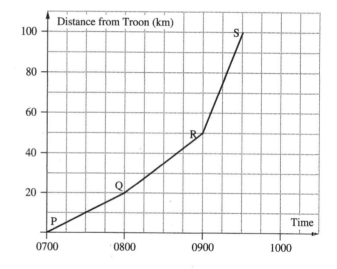

7. The graph converts pounds into
   French francs.
   (a) convert into francs
       (i) £2   (ii) £3·50
   (b) convert into pounds
       (i) 20F   (ii) 12F.
   (c) A mars bar costs 75p. Find
       the equivalent price in France.

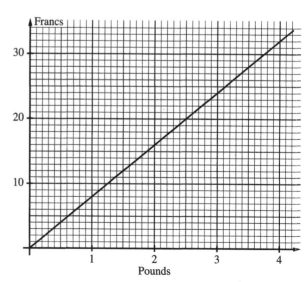

8. A car went on a five hour journey starting at 12.00 with a full tank of petrol. The volume of petrol in the tank was measured after every hour; the results are shown below.

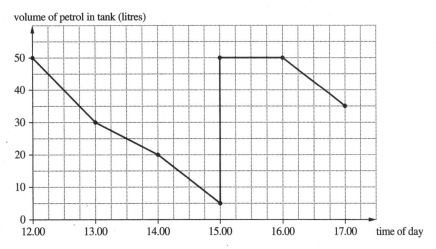

volume of petrol in tank (litres)

(a) How much petrol was in the tank at 13.00?
(b) At what time was there 5 litres in the tank?
(c) How much petrol was used in the first hour of the journey?
(d) What happened at 15.00?
(e) What do you think happened between 15.00 and 16.00?

9. The number of people staying in two different hotels in each month of the year is shown below.

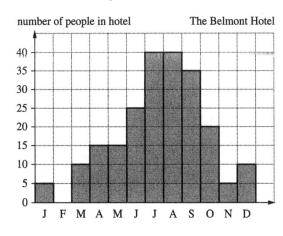

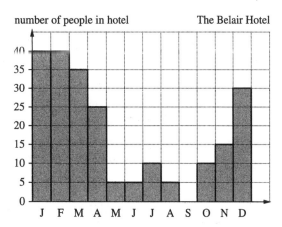

(a) How many people stayed in the 'Belmont' in July?
(b) How many people stayed in the 'Belair' in July?
(c) What was the total number of people staying in the two hotels in April?
(d) One hotel is in a ski resort and the other is by the seaside. Which hotel is in the ski resort?

Pie charts

In a pie chart a circle is divided into sectors to display information.
Pie charts are often used to show the results of a survey. The
sectors of the circle show what *fraction* of the total is in each group.
Here are two pie charts.

● How children go to a school in the Alps.

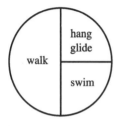

$\frac{1}{2}$ of the children walk to school

$\frac{1}{4}$ of the children swim to school

$\frac{1}{4}$ of the children hang glide to school

● People in a Spanish jail.

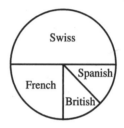

$\frac{1}{8}$ of the people were Spanish

$\frac{1}{8}$ of the people were British

$\frac{1}{4}$ of the people were French

$\frac{1}{2}$ of the people were Swiss

1.   The pie chart shows the contents of a bar
      of chocolate.
      (a) What fraction of the contents is chocolate?
      (b) What fraction of the contents is toffee?
      (c) If the total weight of the packet is 400 g,
          what is the weight of nuts?

2. In a survey children said what pets they
   had at home.
   (a) What fraction of the children had a hamster?
   (b) What fraction of the children had a dog?
   (c) 40 children took part in the survey.
       How many of these children had a pet spider?

3. In another survey children were asked what *pests* they had at
   home. $\frac{1}{3}$ of the children said, 'my sister'.
   What angle would you draw for the 'my sister' sector on a pie
   chart?

4. The pie chart shows the results of a survey in which 80 people were
   asked how they travelled to work. Copy this table and fill it in.

Method	car	walk	train	bus
Number of people				

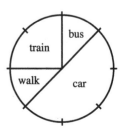

5. In 1997 and 1998 children were asked in a survey to say which country they would most like to go to for a holiday. The pie charts show the results.

100 children answered in each year

Countries in the 'others' section had only one or two votes each.

(a) Which was the most popular country in the 1997 survey?

(b) Which countries were less popular in 1998 than in 1997?

(c) *Roughly* how many children said 'Jamaica' in the 1997 survey?

6. A hidden observer watched Philip in a 40 minute maths lesson.

He spent: 20 minutes talking to a friend,

10 minutes getting ready to work,

5 minutes working,

5 minutes packing up.

Draw and label a pie chart to show Philip's lesson.

7. The children at a school were asked to state their favourite colour. Here are the results.

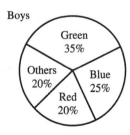

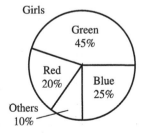

There were 40 boys   There were 25 girls

John says 'The same number of boys and girls chose red.'

Tara says 'More boys than girls chose blue.'

(a) Use both charts to explain whether or not John is right.

(b) Use both charts to explain whether or not Tara is right.

6.6 Averages and range

If you have a set of data, like exam marks or heights, and are asked to find the 'average', just what are you trying to find? The answer is: a single number which can be used to represent the entire set of data. This could be done in three different ways.

- **The mean**
  All the data is added and the total is divided by the number of items. In everyday language the word 'average' usually stands for the mean.

- **The median**
  When the data is arranged in order of size, the median is the one in the middle. If there are two 'middle' numbers, the median is in the middle of these two numbers.

- **The mode** is the number which occurs most often. The mode is the most popular value and comes from the french 'a la mode' meaning 'fashionable'.

- **Range**
  The range is not an average but is the difference between the largest value and the smallest value. The range is a measure of how spread out the data is.

The marks achieved by 10 pupils in a test were:

   8, 5, 7, 4, 5, 6, 9, 7, 5, 10.

(a) Mean mark $= \dfrac{8+5+7+4+5+6+9+7+5+10}{10} = \dfrac{66}{10} = 6.6$

(b) Arrange the marks in order: 4 5 5 5 6 7 7 8 9 10

                                            ↑
                                  the median is here

   Median $= \dfrac{6+7}{2} = 6.5$

(c) Mode $= 5$, since there are more fives than any other number.
(d) Range $= 10 - 4 = 6$

Exercise 1

1. The total weight of seven cars on a transporter is 3360 kg. What is the mean weight of the cars?

2. In four different shops the price of one litre of lemonade is 43p, 37p, 41p, 35p. What is the mean price of the lemonade?

3. In a test the marks were 9, 3, 4, 7, 7. Calculate the mean mark.

4. For each set of numbers find (i) the mean
   (ii) the median

   (a) 8, 5, 9, 8, 7
   (b) 1, 5, 6, 11, 3, 4, 5
   (c) 4, 9, 2, 5.

5. The marks awarded to a skater were
   58, 60, 57, 59, 56.
   Find the mean mark.

6. The shoe sizes of the children in a Year 6 class were

   3, 2, 3, 4, 3, 2, 3, 4, 3, 2, 3, 3
   3, 3, 4, 5, 3, 4, 3, 3, 3, 5, 2, 3.

   What shoe size is the mode?

7. The temperature in a garden was measured at midnight every day for a week. The results (in C) were

   −3, 0, 1, 7, −5, 3, 0.

   What was the range of the temperatures?

Exercise 2

1. The heights of the players who won the Olympic basketball gold medal were (in cm)

   192 218 195 198 201 225 211

   (a) What is the median height of the players?
   (b) What is the range?

2. For each set of numbers find (i) the mode
   (ii) the range

   (a) 1 2 3 4 2 1 2 3 7 1 2 6
   (b) 3 2 3 9 3 4 3 2 3 5
   (c) 2 3 −5 2 2 6 0 2 2

3. (a) Calculate the mean of the numbers 3, 2, 5, 11, 9, 6
   (b) Calculate the new mean when the lowest number is removed.

4. In a maths test the marks for the boys were 9, 3, 5, 7, 4, 8 and
   the marks for the girls were 10, 6, 7, 3.
   (a) Find the mean mark for the boys.
   (b) Find the mean mark for the girls.
   (c) Find the mean mark for the whole class.

5. There were 9 people in the Oxford rowing boat.
   The mean age of the people was 22 and the
   range of their ages was 6.
   Write each sentence below and write next to
   it whether it is *True*, *Possible* or *Impossible*.
   (a) Every person was 22 years old.
   (b) All the people were at least 20 years old
   (c) The oldest person was 6 years older than the
        youngest person.
   (d) The youngest person on the boat was 14 years old

6. There were 5 people living in a tree. The *median* age of the
   people was 11 and the range of their ages was 3.
   Write each sentence below and write next to it whether it is
   True, Possible or *False*.
   (a) Every person was either 10 or 11 years old.
   (b) The oldest person in the tree was 14 years old.
   (c) The mean age of the people was less than 11 years.

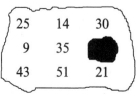

7. Think of five numbers which have a mean of 6 and a median
   of 4. Ask a friend to check your answer.

8. The range for nine numbers on a card is 50. One number is
   covered by an ink stain. What could that number be? [There
   are two possible answers.]

25	14	30
9	35	■
43	51	21

6.7 Mathematical reasoning

Cross numbers without clues

Here are cross number puzzles with a difference. There are no clues, only answers, and you have to find where the answers go.

(a) Copy out the cross number pattern.

(b) Fit all the given numbers into the correct spaces. Work logically and tick off the numbers from lists as you write them in the squares.

1. Ask your teacher if you do not know how to start.

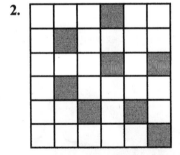

2 digits	3 digits	4 digits	5 digits	6 digits
18	375	1274	37 125	308 513
37	692	1625		
53	828	3742		
74		5181		
87				

2.

2 digits	3 digits	4 digits	5 digits	6 digits
13	382	2630	12 785	375 041
21	582	2725		
45	178	5104		
47		7963		
72				

3.

2 digits	3 digits	4 digits	6 digits
53	182	4483	375 615
63	324	4488	
64	327	6515	**7 digits**
	337		3 745 124
	436		4 253 464
	573		8 253 364
	683		8 764 364
	875		

4.

2 digits	3 digits	4 digits	5 digits	6 digits
27	161	1127	34 462	455 185
36	285	2024	74 562	
54	297	3473	81 072	
63	311	5304	84 762	
64	412	5360		
69	483	5370		
	535	5380		
	536			
	636			
	714			

5.

2 digits	3 digits	4 digits	5 digits	6 digits
21	121	1349	24 561	215 613
22	136	2457	24 681	246 391
22	146	2458	34 581	246 813
23	165	3864		
36	216	4351		
53	217	4462		
55	285	5321		
56	335	5351		
58	473	5557		
61	563	8241		
82	917	8251		
83		9512		
91				

6. *This one is more difficult.*

2 digits	3 digits	4 digits	5 digits	6 digits
16	288	2831	47 185	321 802
37	322	2846	52 314	
56	607	2856	56 324	
69	627	2873	56 337	
72	761	4359		
98	762	5647		
	768	7441		
	769			
	902			
	952			

Puzzles 1

1. The totals for the rows and columns are given. Unfortunately some of the totals are hidden by ink blots. Find the values of the letters.

(a)

A	A	A	A	28
A	B	C	A	27
A	C	D	B	30
D	B	B	B	▓
	25	30	24	

(b)

A	B	A	B	B	18
B	B	E	C	D	21
A	B	B	A	B	18
C	B	C	B	C	19
E	B	D	E	D	26
27	10	25	23	17	

This one is more difficult

(c)

A	A	A	A	24
C	A	C	D	13
A	B	B	A	18
B	B	D	C	12
16	18	15	18	

(d)

A	B	B	A	22
A	A	B	B	22
A	B	A	B	22
B	B	A	B	17
27	17	22	17	

2. In these triangle puzzles the numbers a, b, c, d are connected as follows:

$$a \times b = c$$
$$c \times b = d$$

For example:

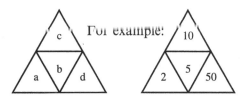

Copy and complete the following triangles:

(a)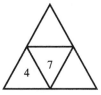

(b)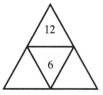

(c)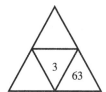

(d)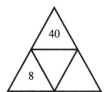

(e)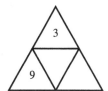

(f)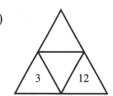

3. Here are some black and white beads in a pattern

(a) What colour is the 20th bead?
(b) What colour is the 71st bead?
(c) What position in the line is the 12th black bead?
(d) What position in the line is the 12th white bead?

Puzzles 2

1. What is the largest possible number of people in a room if no two people have a birthday in the same month?

2. The letters A, B, C, D, E appear once in every row, every column and each main diagonal of the square. Copy the square and fill in the missing letters

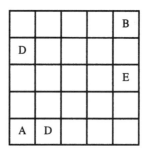

3. Two different numbers on this section of a till receipt are obscured by food stains. What are the two numbers?

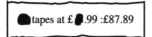

4. Draw four straight lines which pass through all 9 points, without taking your pen from the paper and without going over any line twice.
[Hint: Lines can extend beyond the square].

General statements

In each question below there is a *general statement* about numbers. Think of two examples which illustrate each statement.

For example, here is a general statement:
'The sum of three consecutive numbers is three times the middle number.'
A. $4+5+6=15$; $3 \times 5 = 15$
B. $7+8+9=24$; $3 \times 8 = 24$

1. Any odd number is double a number plus one.

2. A multiple of 9 is also a multiple of 3.

3. The product of two consecutive numbers is even.

4. Dividing a number by 0.1 makes the answer ten times as big.

5. The product of three consecutive numbers is a multiple of 6.

6. The product of four consecutive numbers is 1 less than a square number.

6.7 Mathematical games

Biggest number: a game for the whole class

(a) Draw a rectangle like this with 4 boxes

(b) Your teacher will throw a dice and call out the number which is showing. (eg 'four')

(c) Write this number in one of the boxes.

(d) Your teacher will throw the dice again. (eg 'two')
Write the number in another box.

(e) Your teacher will throw the dice two more times (eg 'three' and then 'two') and again you write the numbers in the boxes.

(f) The object of the game is to get the biggest possible four figure number. The skill (or luck!) is in deciding which box to use for each number.
You score one point if you have written down the largest four digit number which can be made from the digits thrown on the dice. In the example above you score a point if you have 4322 and no points for any other number.
The game can also be played with 5 boxes or 6 boxes for variety.

Wordsearch

The wordsearch below contains keywords associated with Addition, Subtraction, Multiplication and Division.

Your targets are ... 15 words – Good
20 words – Very Good

D	N	O	I	S	I	V	I	D	E	X	B	H	E	A
I	P	Q	M	U	W	X	L	J	P	K	S	L	N	L
F	M	R	U	M	P	G	O	E	S	I	A	O	R	T
F	Y	C	L	S	H	A	R	E	D	N	I	T	R	O
E	B	U	T	J	U	B	L	E	F	T	J	S	K	G
R	D	F	I	O	K	B	H	Y	A	O	D	O	R	E
E	E	D	P	M	X	R	T	C	P	T	R	F	A	T
N	D	H	L	E	S	S	I	R	L	G	E	P	D	H
C	I	T	Y	N	P	L	U	S	A	Z	M	R	D	E
E	V	O	J	T	P	R	O	D	U	C	T	X	I	R
J	I	T	L	I	R	C	F	R	O	M	T	C	T	G
D	D	A	T	M	O	R	E	T	H	A	N	I	I	Z
S	Z	L	D	E	F	E	W	E	R	K	U	V	O	W
U	U	G	T	S	H	X	E	T	Y	E	M	C	N	N
M	I	N	U	S	J	K	R	X	W	T	X	O	P	Z

DIVISION
MULTIPLY
DIFFERENCE
SUM
MINUS
ADDITION
FEWER
PRODUCT
PLUS
LESS
SHARED
DIVIDED
GREATER
TOTAL
SUBTRACTION
TIMES
MORE THAN
ALTOGETHER
MULTIPLICATION
LEFT

Boxes: a game for two players

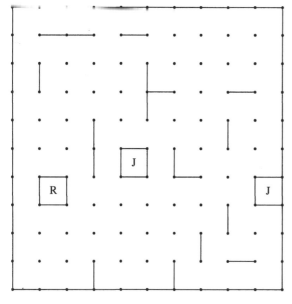

- Draw around the border of a 10 × 10 square on dotty paper (you can also use squared paper).
- Two players take turns to draw horizontal or vertical lines between any two dots on the grid.
- A player wins a square (and writes his initial inside the square) when he draws the fourth side of a square.
- After winning a square a player has one extra turn.
- The winner is the player who has most squares at the end.

In the game above J has
two squares so far and
R has one square.

Distorted grids

- Below the word 'Hi' is shown on an ordinary grid and also on a distorted grid.

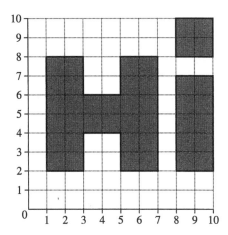

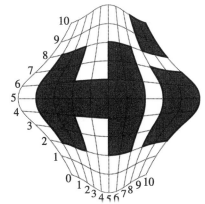

- You can achieve some interesting results by drawing shapes on the grids on the next two pages.

  Ask your teacher for a photocopy of the grids.

- Begin by drawing some or all of theses shapes.

  (a) (1, 1) (1, 5) (3, 5) (3, 3) (5, 3) (5, 9) (7, 9) (7, 1) (1, 1).

  (b) (1, 5) (1, 7) (5, 7) (5, 9) (7, 9) (7, 7) (9, 7) (9, 5) (7, 5) (7, 1) (5, 1) (5, 5) (1, 5).

  (c) (2, 4) (2, 9) (3, 9) (3, 5) (5, 5) (5, 6) (6, 6) (6, 5) (8, 5) (8, 4) (6, 4) (6, 2) (5, 2) (5, 4) (2, 4).

  (d) (4, 1) (8, 5) (8, 6) (7, 7) (5, 7) (4, 6) (3, 7) (4, 6) (3, 7) (4, 8) (7, 8) (9, 6) (9, 5) (6, 2) (9, 2) (9, 1) (4, 1).

- Now draw any shape of your own design. It could be the first letter of your names ... or a bird ... or a box. It's up to you. Colour in your designs.

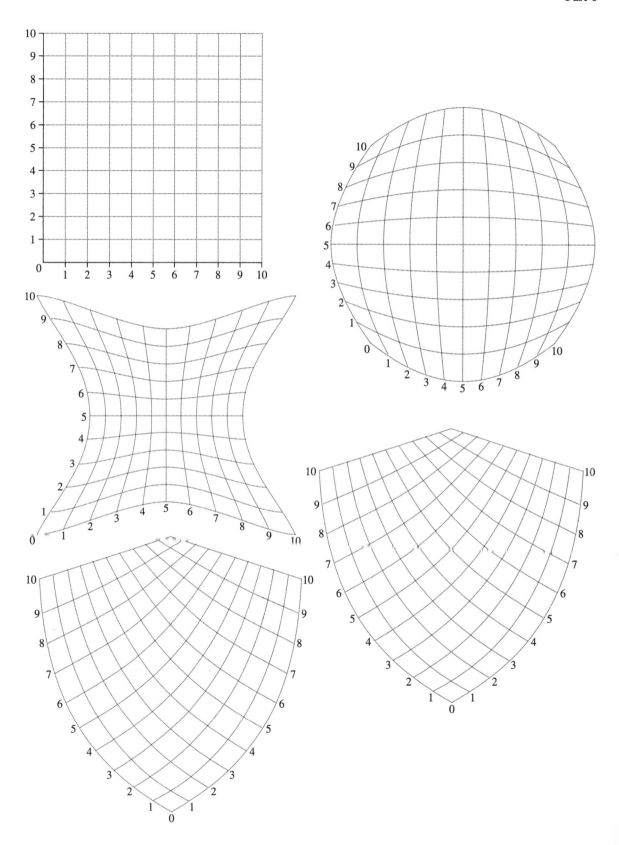

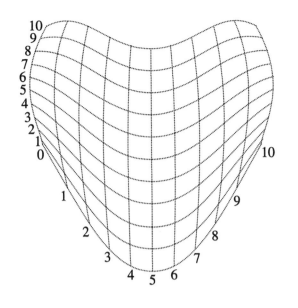

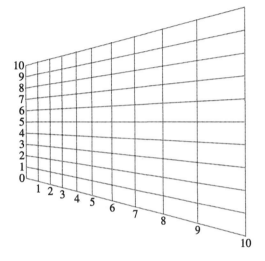

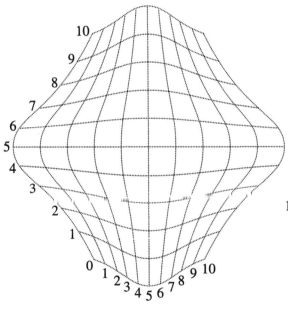

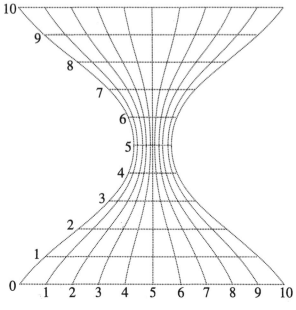

'Lines': a game for two players

- Mark several points on a piece of paper (say 13 points).

- Players take turns to join two of the points with a straight line.

- It is not allowed to draw a line which crosses another line or to draw two lines from one point.

- The winner is the last player to draw a line.

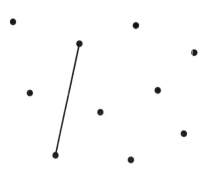

Polyominoes

- The *domino* has only one shape:-

- The *triomino* consists of 3 squares joined along complete edges. Here are both types of triominoes:-

- The *tetromino* consists of 4 squares joined along complete edges

 Draw the five possible shapes for tetrominoes.

- The *pentomino* consists of 5 squares joined along complete edges.

 Draw the twelve different pentominoes.
*Note:- Shapes that can be fitted on top of each other are the same (congruent).

Here are some examples of Pentominoes ...

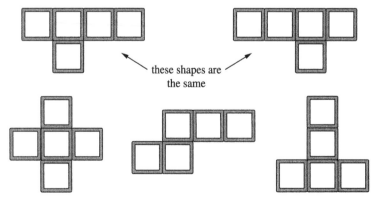

these shapes are the same

... which leaves you just 8 more to find!

Here is a 6 × 5 rectangle which we have started to fill with *different* pentominoes.
Draw your own 6 × 5 rectangle and try to fill it with six different pentominoes.
Colour your design.

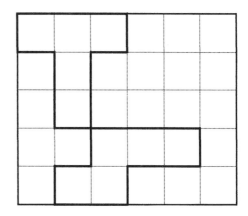

 Draw an 8 × 8 square. Fill up the square with as many *different* pentominoes as you can. You will need a 2 × 2 'filler' somewhere in your design.

It is possible to make a design with all 12 different pentominoes.

 [For enthusiasts!] Try to fit 12 pentominoes into a 12 × 5 rectangle. It is easier if you can draw your pentominoes on cardboard so that you can move them around. Good luck!

Part 7

7.1 Numeracy tests

This section contains four numeracy tests each with 25 questions. A calculator is not allowed.

Numeracy test 1

1. Write 87 in words

2. Write seventy-five in figures.

3. What is the value of the underlined digit in this number: 3$\underline{6}$7?

4. What is $7 + 8 + 9$?

5. What is the sum of 5, 6 and 7?

6. What is 13 subtract 7?

7. What is 39 take away 17?

8. What is 7×8?

9. What are nine elevens?

10. What fraction of this shape is shaded?

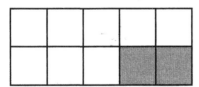

11. What is $24 + 19 - 11$?

12. What number divides 32 into 8 equal parts?

13. Work out $9 + 7 - 5$.

14. Write down the next number in this sequence: 5, 11, 17, 23, ☐

15. Write down the missing number in this sequence: 30, 23, 16, ☐, 2.

16. What fraction of the whole line is AB?

17. What is 50% as a fraction?

18. A pie is cut into four equal parts. What fraction of the whole pie is each piece?

19. Work out $24 \div 3$.

20. Fifty-five per cent of pupils in a school are girls. What percentage are boys?

21. What fraction of this circle is shaded?

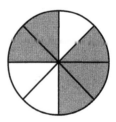

22. What is $2 \cdot 2 + 3 \cdot 6$?

23. What is $1 \cdot 2 + 3 \cdot 5 + 2 \cdot 1$?

24. What is $\frac{3}{10}$ as a decimal?

25. What is the speed in km/hr shown by the pointer?

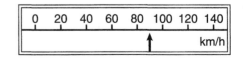

Numeracy test 2

1. What is the value of the underlined digit in this decimal: 0·1̲2?

2. What is the reading on this scale indicated by the arrow?

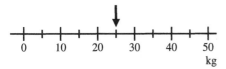

3. Estimate the length of this line in centimetres:

4. How much money is here?

5. What is the cost of 8 pencils at 9 pence each?

6. If I buy 5 cakes for 40 pence, how much does each cake cost?

7. If I buy a portion of chips for 57 pence, how much change will I receive from one pound?

8. How many 50 pence coins should I receive in exchange for 12 one pound coins?

9. A compact disc system costs £320. I am given a discount of £80. What price do I have to pay?

10. Four sisters share 72 pence equally between them. How much does each receive?

11. Each side of a square is 7 cm. What is the area of the square in cm²?

12. How many grams are there in 5 kilograms? (1 kg = 1000 g)

13. If 8 pints = 1 gallon, how many gallons is 24 pints?

14. Jean-Paul skis 7000 metres. How far is this in kilometres? (1000 m = 1 km).

15. How many litres is 3000 millilitres? (1 ℓ = 1000 ml)

16. A piece of wood is 3 metres long. Thirty centimetres is cut off. How much, in centimetres, is left? (1 m = 100 cm).

17. What is the area of this rectangle in m²?

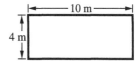

18. If 8 km is about 5 miles, how many miles is 48 km?

19. If there are 60 minutes in an hour, how many minutes is 4 hours?

20. A television programme starts at 18.30 and ends at 19.05. How long is the programme?

21. A 'CD' takes 45 minutes to play. I start the 'CD' at 12.35. At what time does it finish?

22. If I record a 35 minute TV programme on a 2 hour recording tape, how many minutes recording time do I still have on the tape?

23. What is the perimeter of this rectangle?

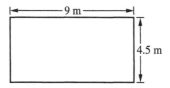

24. If a dog walks an average speed of 4 miles per hour, how far will the dog walk in 3 hours?

25. What is the average of 6 and 10?

Numeracy test 3

1. Write the number six hundred and fifty-seven in figures.

2. Write the number 703 in words.

3. What is the value of the underlined figure in this number: 9<u>8</u>13?

4. What is $537 + 246$?

5. What is $16 + 27 + 48$?

6. What is $78 - 19$?

7. What is $453 - 371$?

8. What is 9×6?

9. Work out 16×8.

10. What is $56 \div 7$?

11. Work out $725 \div 5$.

12. What fraction of the whole figure is shaded in this diagram?

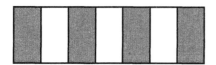

13. Write the next number in this sequence: 1, 3, 6, 10, 15, ☐ .

14. Write the missing number in this sequence: 7, 18, ☐ , 40.

15. Find the missing number: $36 - ☐ = 17$.

16. Find the missing number: $29 + ☐ = 44$.

17. Find the missing number: $☐ - 7 = 61$.

18. If 84% of people wear a wristwatch, what percentage does not?

19. What is 70% as a fraction?

20. What is $36 + 42 - 17$?

21. In which of the following diagrams is $\frac{5}{8}$ of the shape shaded?

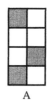  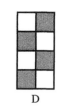 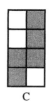

A   B   C   D

22. Write the fraction $\frac{6}{8}$ in its simplest form.

23. What fraction of the whole line is AB?

24. What fraction is 0·75?

25. What is $12·37 + 31·98$?

Numeracy test 4

1. What is $3·14 + 2·52 + 1·31$?

2. What is the reading in kilograms shown in this scale?

3. Estimate the length of this line:

4. Each pace of an Egyptian warrior is 90 cm. How far does he walk, in km, when he walks 100 000 paces?

5. What is the cost of 5 chocolate bars at 32 pence each?

6. If you buy 3 tins of cat food for £2·16, how much did each tin cost?

7. If Ben spends £1·47 on his lunch, how much change will he receive from £2?

8. How many 20 pence coins can I exchange for £3·60?

9. A mountain bicycle costs £500 plus 10% delivery charge. How much extra do you pay for the delivery charge?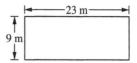

10. A personal computer costs £350. In a sale it is reduced by 20%. What is the reduction in the original price?

11. Trisha, Stella and Vikky have lunch together and agree to share the cost equally. If lunch costs £24.99, how much should each pay?

12. A metal rod is 12 cm long. A piece 1 cm 2 mm is cut off. What length of rod is left in centimetres?

13. What is 4500 grams in kilograms?

14. A cross-country course is 5 km. How far is this in metres?

15. Over a month a man drank 36 pints of beer. How many gallons is this?
(1 gallon = 8 pints)

16. What is the area of this square in square metres?

←—30 m—→

17. A rectangular bowling green is 15 metres long and 12 metres wide. What is its area in square metres?

18. What is the perimeter of this shape?

←——— 23 m ———→

9 m

19. A train leaves St Pancras London at 13.20 and arrives in Sheffield at 15.35. How many minutes did the journey take?

20. A journey by bus takes 35 minutes. If Judith got on the bus at 14.45, at what time does she arrive?

21. A car travels at 60 miles per hour on a motorway. How far has it travelled after $2\frac{1}{2}$ hours?

22. A train covers a journey of 395 miles in 5 hours. What is its average speed in m.p.h?

23. A two hour cassette tape is used to record a radio programme. If the programme lasts 40 minutes, how much recording time is left on the cassette tape?

24. A marathon runner runs on average at 10 m.p.h. How many hours will she take to run 25 miles?

25. Three people are aged 12, 20 and 28. What is their (mean) average age?

7.2 End of book review

Review exercise 1A   Number and algebra

1. In a 'magic square' all rows (←→) columns $\left(\updownarrow\right)$ and diagonals $\left(\times\right)$ add up to the same 'magic number'. Copy and complete this magic square.

6		12	7
	4		
	16	13	2
10			11

2. Harminder has to visit a relative who lives 196 miles away. He stops for lunch after driving 117 miles. How much further does he still have to go?

3. In a new airport terminal, 25 new doors are required.
   (a) If each door is fastened by 3 hinges, how many hinges are needed altogether?
   (b) If each hinge requires 6 screws, what is the total number of screws required to fit all the doors?

4. A multi-storey office block has 104 offices altogether. If there are 8 offices on each floor, how many storeys does the building have?

5. Numbers are missing on four of these calculator buttons. Copy the diagram and write in numbers to make the answer 30.

6. Here are some number cards.   3   4   7   2   9

   (a) Use two cards to make a fraction which is equal to $\frac{1}{2}$. $\frac{\Box}{\Box}$

   (b) Use three of the cards to make the smallest possible fraction. $\frac{\Box}{\Box\Box}$

7. (a) How many 12 centimetre pieces of string can be cut from a piece of string which is 1 metre in length?
   (b) How much string is left over?

8. Look at this group of numbers ...

   $$15, 9, 27, 24, 7$$

   (a) Which of the numbers is a multiple of both 3 and 4?
   (b) Which of the numbers is a prime number?
   (c) Which of the numbers is a square number?

9. Write down these calculations and find the missing digits.

   (a)   3 ☐ 4   (b)   5 ☐ 9   (c)   ☐ 2 ☐
        + 2 6 ☐   + 3 8 ☐   + 3 ☐ 4
        ─────────   ─────────   ─────────
          6 3 9   ☐ 2 5   8 0 0

10. The rule for the number sequences below is '*double and add 2*'. Write down each sequence and fill in the missing numbers.

    (a) 1 → 4 → 10 → 22 → ☐

    (b) ☐ → 6 → 14 → 30

    (c) ☐ → 8 → ☐ → ☐

Review exercise 1B

1. Charlie likes to use number patterns when he selects his lottery numbers.
   (a) Write down the next two numbers in Charlie's pattern:

      1, 3, 6, 10, _?_, _?_,

   (b) Charlie won £10 with this pattern

      1, 4, 9, _?_, 25, 36

   What was the missing number?

2. The numbers on the left have been multiplied either by 10, 100 or 1000. Write the correct number in the boxes. The first one has been done for you. Copy and complete.

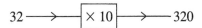

32 ⟶ ×10 ⟶ 320

(a)   20 ⟶ × ⟶ 2000

(b)   1.1 ⟶ × ⟶ 110

(c)   25 ⟶ × ⟶ 25000

3. This shape has $\frac{1}{3}$ shaded.

Copy each diagram and shade the given fraction.

(a)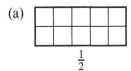
$\frac{1}{2}$

(b)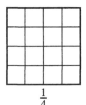
$\frac{1}{4}$

(c)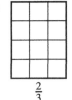
$\frac{2}{3}$

4. Look at the following numbers ...

$$-9, \quad 4, \quad 0, \quad 2, \quad +5$$

(a) Write down the positive numbers.
(b) Write down the negative numbers.
(c) Write the numbers in order, lowest to highest.
(d) Write down the difference between the highest and lowest numbers.

5. Copy and complete this table showing equivalent‑ fractions, decimals and percentages:

Fraction	Decimal	Percentage
	0·5	
$\frac{1}{4}$		
		75%

6. Look at the following input/output machine ...

input ⟶ ×10 ⟶ − 2 ⟶ output

Copy and complete this table using the machine above:

	Input	Output
	3	28
(a)	4	
(b)	7	
(c)	10	
(d)		108
(e)		148

7. Bob the butcher was weighing a turkey ...

KG

0   2   4   6   8

(a) Write down the weight in kilograms of the turkey.
(b) Bob is selling his turkeys at £1·35 a kilogram. What price ticket would Bob put on this turkey?

Bob tells his customers that the cooking time for the turkey is 20 minutes per kilogram plus 20 minutes.

(c) For how long will the turkey on the scales above have to be cooked?
(d) What is the cooking time required for an 8 kg turkey?
(e) Convert your answer to (d) into hours.

8. The diagrams below show three test tubes containing a liquid.

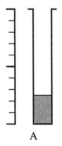
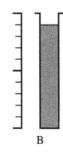
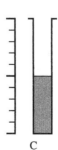

A   B   C

(a) Which of the test tubes above is 0·9 full?
(b) Which of the test tubes is $\frac{1}{4}$ full?
(c) Which of the test tubes is 50% full?

9. Here is a sequence of diagrams showing an arrangement of counters ...

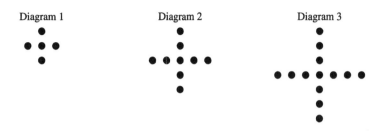

(a) Draw diagram number 4.

(b) Copy and complete this table for the diagrams so far.

Diagram Number	Counters used
1	5
2	
3	
4	

(c) Without drawing, how many counters will be needed for diagram number 5?

(d) Write in words how you found your answer without drawing.

10. Which is larger ...

(a) $\frac{3}{10}$ of £50   or   (b) 25% of £40?

11. Write down the reading from each scale

(a)
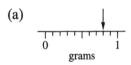

(b)
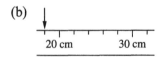

(c)
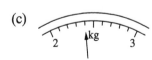

12. Find the number I am thinking of in each part:

(a) If I take away 13 from it, I get 50.

(b) If I double it, I get 250.

(c) If I divide it by 10, I get 6·5.

Review exercise 2   Shape and space

1. Tara and Quentin had these shapes and they were asked to sort the shapes into two groups.

     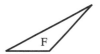

Tara chose shapes A, C and E. She gave Quentin shapes B, D and F.

(a) Who should have this shape, Tara or Quentin?

(b) Give a reason.

2. (a) Sort the shapes below into two groups and label them Group A and Group B.

  Shape 1   Shape 2   Shape 3   Shape 4   Shape 5   Shape 6

(b) Give a reason why you put your shapes into groups 'A' and 'B'.

(c) Write down the correct mathematical name for each of the six shapes.

3. Listed below are various items that can be measured. Copy the list and insert next to each item the most suitable unit of measurement.

(a) The fuel tank of an aircraft.

(b) The mass of a packet of crisps.

(c) The height of your bedroom.

(d) The distance from London to Edinburgh.

(e) The amount of cough mixture on a teaspoon.

(f) The width of a postage stamp.

Units
1. centimetres
2. millilitres
3. grams
4. kilometres
5. litres
6. metres

4. Draw a grid like this ...

(a) Plot these points on the grid and join them up in the order given:
(2, 2), (3, 3), (3, 4),
(2, 5), (5, 5), (4, 4),
(4, 3), (5, 2), (2, 2)

(b) How many lines of symmetry does the shape have?

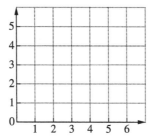

5. The diagram shows a logo
for the 'Ace' sports company.
It represents the letter A in 'Ace'.
If each square is one square
centimetre, work out the area
of the logo in centimetre squares.

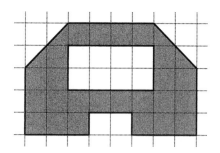

6. Calculate the area of each shape.

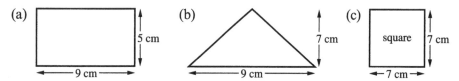

(a) 5 cm, 9 cm   (b) 7 cm, 9 cm   (c) square 7 cm, 7 cm

7. On squared paper draw these shapes:
(a) a quadrilateral with just one right angle
(b) an isosceles triangle
(c) a quadrilateral with no right angles and no parallel sides.

8. A piece of A4 size paper measures 300 mm by 210 mm.
(a) A money spider starts at a corner and decides to
walk around all sides of the paper.
How far will the spider walk in millimetres?
(b) Change your answer in part (a) into centimetres.
(c) Has the spider travelled more or less than one metre?

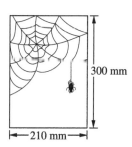

9. A birthday card rests on a horizontal table.
Copy these sentences and fill the space with one of the words:

'vertical;   horizontal;   parallel;   perpendicular'

(a) The edge BC is _____ .

(b) The edge AB is _____ to edge AD.

(c) Edges DE and DC are _____ .

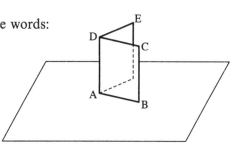

10. In each of the following diagrams, mirror lines are shown as broken lines. Copy each diagram and complete the reflections.

(a)   (b)   (c)

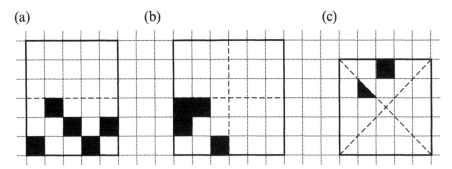

11. Draw the shape on squared paper. Draw the new position after it is turned anti-clockwise through one right angle around the point A.

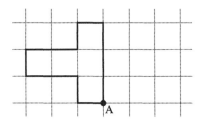

12.

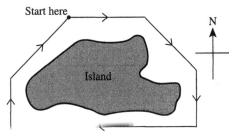

A ship is sailing around an island. Copy and complete the missing compass directions of the ship's journey.

East | then | ☐ | then | ☐ | then | ☐ | then | ☐ | then | ☐

13. On squared paper draw a four-sided shape which has one pair of parallel sides.

14. Draw, as accurately as you can, the triangle shown. Measure the length marked L.

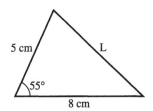

Review exercise 3   Handling data and probability

1. Here is a table showing the percentage of votes for the main political parties in the 1997 General Election predicted by various polling organisations:

Organisation	Labour vote (%)	Conservative vote (%)	Lib Dem vote (%)	Others (%)	Labour lead over Conservative (%)
Harris	48	31	15	6	17
NOP	50	28	14	8	22
ICM	43	33	18	6	10
Gallup	46	33	16	5	13
MORI	47	29	19	5	18
Poll of polls	47	31	16	6	16
Actual result	44	31	17	8	13

(a) Which organisations correctly predicted the Conservative vote?
(b) Which organisation was closest to predicting the Labour vote?
(c) Which organisation correctly predicted the Labour lead over the Conservatives?
(d) Represent the actual result of the election on a bar chart.

2. Eggs are sorted into size by weight. The weight is then converted into an egg size. The sizes range from 1 to 7.
Here are the weights of eggs produced by a farmer's chickens:

65, 56, 62, 69, 64, 51, 53, 57, 60, 59,
45, 59, 50, 57, 54, 58, 53, 59, 55, 58,
56, 46, 55, 44, 61, 55, 52, 70, 60, 56,
70, 66, 62, 42, 49, 63, 50, 57, 64, 72.

Copy and complete this table:

Weight (grams)	Size	Tally	Frequency
Under 45 g	7		
45–49	6		
50–54	5		
55–59	4		
60–64	3		
65–69	2		
70 g or over	1		

3. In a survey, the number of occupants in the cars passing a school was recorded.

(a) How many cars had 4 occupants?

(b) How many cars had more than 3 occupants?

(c) How many cars were in the survey?

(d) What number of occupants was observed most often?

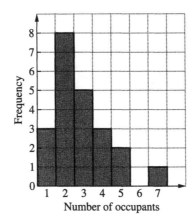

4.

The cards above show the scores awarded by four judges in a diving contest.

(a) Find the mean score.

(b) Find the median score.

(c) Write down the range of scores.

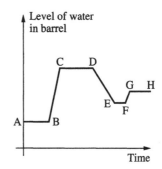

5. This bar line graph shows the number of bedrooms in the houses in one road.

(a) How many houses had 4 bedrooms?

(b) How many houses are in the road?

(c) Why would it not be sensible to join the tops of the bars to make a line graph?

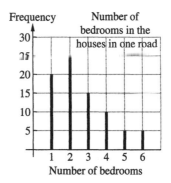

6. Some keen gardeners collect rain water from the roofs of their homes into rain barrels. They use the water from the barrel when the ground is dry to save using tap water.

Look at this graph and write down what you think is happening. Use the labels A, B, C ...

7. This scale shows the probability of events occurring:

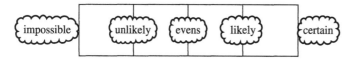

Here are four events:

A. You will have contact with water today.
B. You will not see a red car tomorrow.
C. A coin is tossed and it comes down tails.
D. You will be kidnapped by aliens going home from school in 10 years time.

Copy the scale and mark 4 arrows on it indicating where you would expect A, B, C, and D to be.

8. Karen is going to play a game called 'Lucky Dip.' There are three bags labelled A, B and C. Each bag contains red or white balls. You win if you draw out a red ball from a bag.

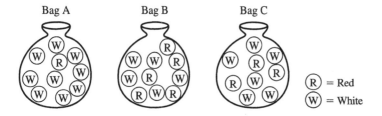

(a) Write down the probability of winning from bag A, from bag B, and from bag C.

(b) Which bag is Karen most likely to win from? Give a reason for your answer.

9. The pie chart shows the most popular colours of cars after a survey.
There were 80 cars in the survey.
(a) How many cars were red?
(b) How many cars were blue or white?
(c) How many cars were not red, white or blue?

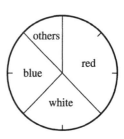

7.3 KS2 Practice Papers

Paper 1

Do not use a calculator in this paper.

1. This chart shows the number of packets of different flavours of crisps sold by a shop.

	M	Tu	W	Th	F
Ready Salted	3	1	2	4	0
Salt'N Vinegar	4	2	5	3	1
Cheese'N Onion	5	1	3	1	4
Roast Beef	3	2	6	4	1
Prawn	1	1	2	4	4

(a) How many packets of crisps were sold on Wednesday?

(b) Each packet of Ready Salted crisps costs 15p. How much was spent on Ready Salted crisps in the whole week?

(c) This is a graph of one flavour of crisps.
Which flavour is it?

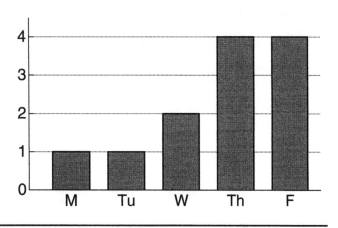

2. (a) Jim has £2. After buying one item from those shown he has £1.20 left. What did he buy?

(b) Jane has two 50p coins and three 20p coins. She buys a Zube and an Ip-Dip. How much has she left?

---

3. Numbers are missing on four of these calculator buttons. Copy the diagram and write in numbers to make the answer 28.

$\boxed{2}\ \boxed{8}\ \boxed{+}\ \boxed{}\ \boxed{}\ \boxed{-}\ \boxed{}\ \boxed{}\ \boxed{=}\ \boxed{2}\ \boxed{8}$

---

4. A painter uses special waterproof paint for fishing rods. The cost for painting different lengths of rods is shown in the table.

Length	Price for 1 rod
0 m up to 1 m	85p
1 m up to $1\frac{1}{2}$ m	£1.20
$1\frac{1}{2}$ m up to 2 m	£1.55
2 m up to $2\frac{1}{2}$ m	£2.20
2 m up to 4 m	£3.25

(a) What is the cost of painting one 75 cm rod?

(b) Find the total cost of painting 10 of the 3 m rods.

5. (a) Points A, D and E are three corners of a square.
    Write down the co-ordinates of the other corner.

  (b) A, B and C are the three corners of a square.
    Write down the co-ordinates of the other corner.

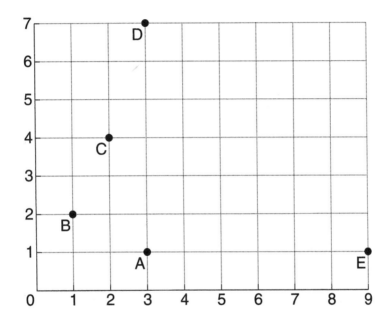

---

6. Write the following with the correct signs inside the circles.

  (a) $4 \times 3 \times 2 \bigcirc 1 = 25$

  (b) $5 \times 2 \times 4 \bigcirc 3 = 37$

  (c) $6 + 5 \bigcirc 4 \bigcirc 1 = 8$

---

7. Estimate the area of each shape. Give your answers as a number of squares.

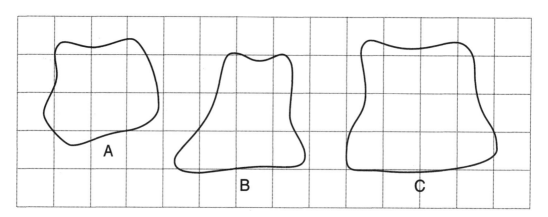

8. (a) Here is a number pattern in which the rule is '3 less than'. Find the missing number.

| 13 | 10 | 7 | 4 | 1 | |

(b) In this number pattern the rule is 'multiply by 2'. Find the missing number.

| | 6 | 12 | 24 | 48 |

9. Draw the shape on squared paper. Draw the new position after it is turned clockwise through one right angle around the point A.

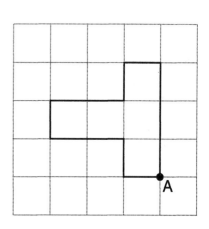

10. Work out the missing digits in each division.

(a) ☐☐ 2   (b)   2 9

4)7 2 ☐   3)☐ 7

---

11. Here is a 5 × 6 grid made of centimetres squares. Some of the grid has been shaded.

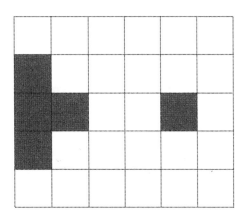

(a) What area has *not* been shaded?

(b) How many squares are there in 20% of the whole grid?

(c) Copy the diagram and shade in 10% of the squares so that your final diagram has reflective symmetry.

---

12. (a) 308 children visit Eurodisney. They go in groups of 13. One group has less than 13. Every group of children has one adult with them. How many adults are there?

(b) Work out the total cost of buying every child a drink at 35p each.

---

13. Here are two spinners.
Say whether the
following statements
are true or false.
Explain why.

Gill's spinner   Nick's spinner

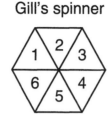

(a) 'Gill is more likely to spin a 4 than Nick'.

(b) 'Gill and Nick are equally likely to spin an even number'.

(c) 'If Nick spins his spinner eight times he is bound to get
at least one 8'.

---

14. Here are some number cards.   ⟨3⟩ ⟨4⟩ ⟨7⟩ ⟨2⟩ ⟨9⟩

(a) Use the two cards to make
a fraction which is equal to $\frac{1}{2}$.

(b) Use three of the cards to make
the smallest possible fraction.

---

15. Reena buys 8 jars of honey.
Each jar costs £1.15.
She works out that it will cost her £42.

(a) Without working out the exact
answer, explain why you know she
must be wrong.

(b) Work out the correct answer.

---

16. There were ten children on a coach journey. The mean age of the children was 11 and the range of their ages was 4. Write each statement below and then write next to it whether it is *True*, *Possible* or *False*.

(a) The youngest child was 9 years old.

(b) Every child was 11 years old.

(c) All the children were at least 10 years old.

---

17. The map has a scale of 1 cm to 8 km.

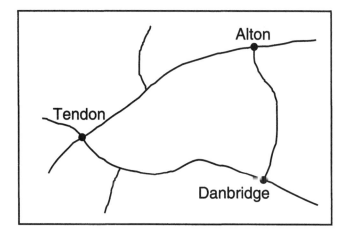

(a) The road from Tendon to Alton, measured on the map, is 4.3 cm long. What is the length of the road in kilometres?

(b) The road from Danbridge to Alton is 24 km long. How long is the road on the map in cm?

Paper 2

You may use a calculator for this paper.

1. Here are three number cards.
   One number that can be made with
   the three cards is 617.

   (a) Use the three cards to make a number which is *more*
   than 617.

   (b) Use the three cards to make a number which is *less* than
   617.

   (c) Use the three cards to make an even number.

2. 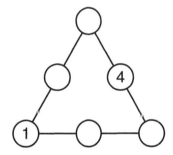 This is a number triangle. The
   numbers along each edge add
   up to 9.
   Copy and complete the triangle.
   The six numbers are 1, 2, 3, 4, 5, 6.

3. A line starts at A and goes along the
   dotted lines to B. It divides the area
   of the square into two halves.

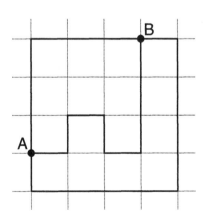

(a) Draw the rectangle shown and draw a line from C to D which divides the area into two halves

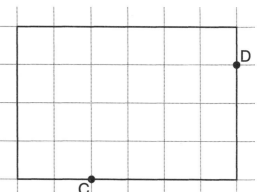

(b) Draw the rectangle again. Draw a new line from C to D which divides the area into two parts so that one part has twice the area of the other part.

---

4. Here is a row of numbers.

1 2 3 4 5 6 7 8 9 10 11 12 13 14 15 16 17

(a) Find *two* numbers next to each other which add up to 29.

(b) Find *three* numbers next to each other which add up to 36.

---

5. Copy the following and find the missing number.

(a) $\boxed{} \div 3 = 50$ (c) $\boxed{} \div 5 = 21$

(b) $\boxed{} \times 6 = 84$ (d) $\boxed{} \times 9 = 180$

---

6. An ice cream and a can of drink
together costs 85p.
Two ice creams and a can of drink
together costs £1.40.

(a) How much does one ice cream
cost?

(b) How much would you pay for three ice creams and two
cans of drink?

---

7. In a survey the children at a
school were asked to state their
favourite sport in the Olympics.

(a) Estimate what fraction of the
children chose gymnastics.

(b) There are 120 children in the
school. Estimate the number of
children who chose athletics.

(c) 15% of the children chose swimming.
How many children was that?

---

8. Write each of the following in the units shown, using
decimals when needed.

(a) 2 m 35 cm = ☐ m   (d) 3.3 kg = ☐ g

(b) 350 g = ☐ kg   (e) 44 cm = ☐ m

(c) 0.62 m = ☐ cm   (f) 27 mm = ☐ cm

9. Here are three patterns.

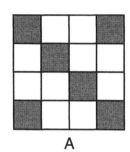
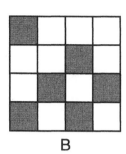
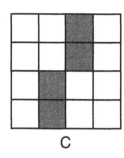

A   B   C

(a) Copy the table and then write 'yes' or 'no' in the spaces to describe each pattern.

	A	B	C
Reflective symmetry	Yes		
Rotational symmetry			

(b) Draw the two patterns on the right and shade in one more square in each so that the final patterns have reflective symmetry.

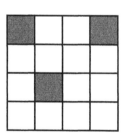
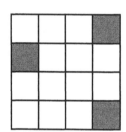

---

10. The rule for the number sequences below is 'double and add 1'.

Write down each sequence and fill in the missing numbers.

(a) $1 \rightarrow 3 \rightarrow 7 \rightarrow 15 \rightarrow \boxed{}$

(b) $\boxed{} \rightarrow 9 \rightarrow 19 \rightarrow 39$

(c) $\boxed{} \rightarrow 11 \rightarrow \boxed{} \rightarrow \boxed{}$

11. Philip has 10 stick insects. These are their lengths in cm.

7.1	6.8	8.5	9.8	4.4
6.5	8.1	5.2	6.6	8.0

What is the mean (average) length of his stick insects?

---

12. On squared paper draw a four-sided shape which has one pair of parallel sides.

---

13. ABCD is a rectangle.

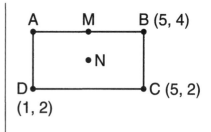

   (a) Write down the co-ordinates of A.

   (b) M is mid-way between A and B.
      What are the co-ordinates of M?

   (c) N is in the middle of the rectangle.
      What are the co-ordinates of N?

---

14. The base of a milk carton is a square 8 cm by 8 cm. The cartons are put on a tray which measures 40 cm by 64 cm. Work out the largest number of cartons which can go on one tray.

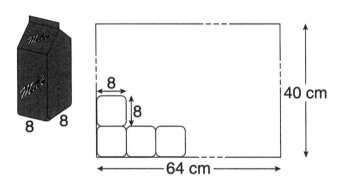

15. Steve spins the two spinners shown.

Draw the missing lines to show how likely these things are.

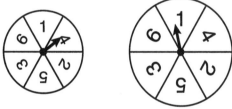

A. The two spinners show '3'

B. The two numbers are different

C. The two numbers add up to 15

D. The two numbers add up to an odd number

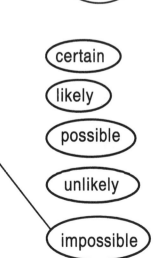

certain

likely

possible

unlikely

impossible

16. This diagram shows the temperature and rainfall readings in one week.

The rainfall is shown as the bar chart.

The temperature is shown as the line graph.

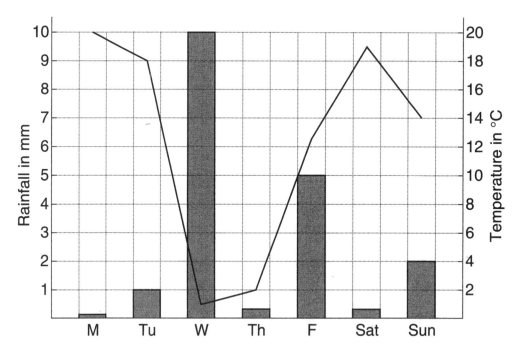

(a) Use both graphs to describe the weather on Monday.

(b) On which day was the weather cold and wet?

(c) Compare the weather on Thursday and Saturday.

---

17. Draw, as accurately as you can, the triangle shown.

Measure the length marked L.

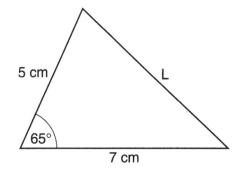

18. A recipe uses 3 eggs and 2 apples for every cake.
A chef has an order for several cakes.
He uses 24 eggs. How many apples does he use?

---

19. Draw the last shape and fill in the missing numbers to continue the patterns.

```
   [2]          [3]          [4]          [ ]
[1][6][3]    [2][9][4]    [3][12][5]   [ ][ ]
```

Here is a shape using letters

```
      [b]
   [a][N][c]
```

The rule is
'To find N you add up a, b and c'.
Write the rule without using words.

Paper 3

You may use a calculator for this paper.

1. Find the number I am thinking of in each part:

   (a) If I take away 13 from it, I get 44.

   (b) If I double it, I get 350.

   (c) If I divide it by 10, I get 3.2.

---

2. (a) Work out the area of the flag shown.

   (b) 40% of the flag is stripes.
   What area of the flag is stripes?

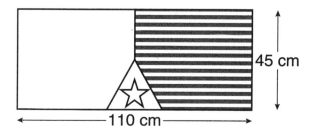

---

3. Here are four number cards.

   Use *all four* cards for the following:

   (a) An add. The answer must be less than 100.

   (b) A take away. The answer must be less than 20.

---

4. Mr and Mrs Baker and their three children are going to a football match.

Work out the cheapest cost for all the tickets.

Ticket prices

Adults	£25.00	Row A
	£21.50	Row B
	£17.00	Row C
Children	£15.00	Row B
	£9.00	Row C

---

5. Karen measures four things with a tape measure.

Her front door	190 cm
Her pet cat	40 cm
Her brother	125 cm
Her bed	214 cm

Draw a line like the one below and put a cross for each of the things she measured.

0   1 m   2 m   3 m

---

6. On squared paper draw these shapes:

(a) a quadrilateral with just one right angle

(b) an isosceles triangle

(c) a quadrilateral with no right angles and no parallel sides.

7. Copy the shape on squared paper and then draw the reflection of the shape in the mirror line (shown by the broken line).

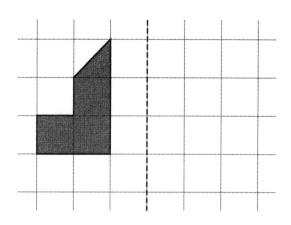

---

8. A hot air balloon will only rise from the ground if the total weight of the people is less than 170 kilograms.

(a) Work out if the balloon can take both Steve and Nick.
Show your working.

Name	John	Steve	Anna	Sue	Nick	Christine
Weight in kg	81.5	75.4	59.8	61.4	93.4	53.4

(b) Could the balloon take Anna, Sue and Christine?

---

9. Copy each line and write $+$, $-$, $\times$ or $\div$ in the circle to make the calculation correct.

(a) $12 \times 5 \bigcirc 3 = 180$

(b) $8 \bigcirc 4 + 5 = 37$

(c) $84 \bigcirc 7 - 5 = 7$

10. Lucy puts 4 pegs in a board.
She turns the board through one right angle.
Draw a picture to show how the board looks
now.

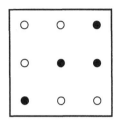

---

11. Here are scales for changing

A   kilograms and pounds

B   litres and gallons

In this question give your
answers to the *nearest
whole number*.

(a) About how many
kilograms are there
in 6 pounds?

(b) About how many litres
are there in 3.3 gallons?

(c) About how many
pounds are there in 1.4
kilograms?

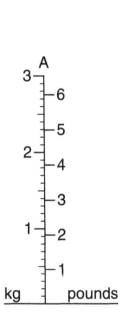

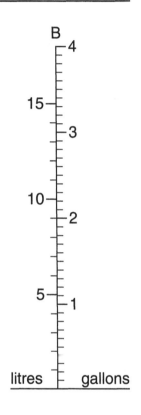

---

12. Do NOT use a calculator for this question.
The tables in a school dining
room are arranged so that 14
children sit together in one
group.

1 group = 14 children

How many groups are there if 322 children are in the room?

13. Sumita has 3 different spinners.

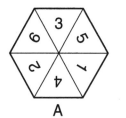 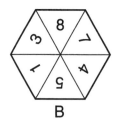 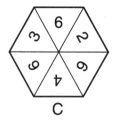

  A   B   C

She spins each spinner 100 times.

(a) Draw a number line and draw arrows labelled A, B and C to show your estimate of how many times each spinner will land on a six.

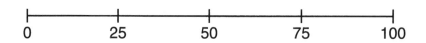

(b) Explain how you worked out your estimate for spinner C.

---

14. Five friends had a swimming race. Their times are shown.

(a) Who came first?

(b) Who came last?

(c) Whose time is nearest to 10 seconds?

Name	Time
Greg	12.94 sec
Ian	9.18 sec
Maya	9.81 sec
Ray	11.22 sec
Rick	10.55 sec

15. Write down each calculation and fill in the missing numbers.

(a) ☐ 6 × 8 = 608

(b) 8 ☐ × 7 = 5 ☐ 1

(c) 7 ☐ × 9 = 6 ☐ 7

---

16. This is a number ring.
Start with any number
and multiply the units
digit by 4 and then add
the tens digit.

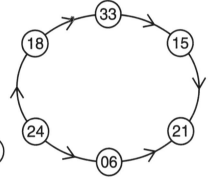

For example ⑮ → 5 × 4 + 1 → ㉑

The rule is then repeated on 21
and so on.

Use the same rule to
complete this number ring.

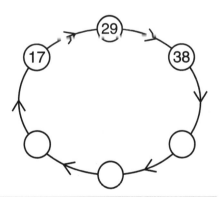

---

17. The graph shows the flights of objects A and B.

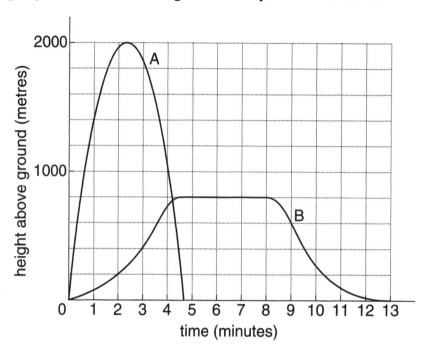

(a) Estimate the time at which they are at the same height.

(b) One of the objects is an aircraft and the other is a rocket.
Which graph do you think represents the flight of the
aircraft? Give reasons for your answer.

---

18. Here is a number puzzle. $\Rightarrow$

First guess: $5 + 4 = 9$

$5 \times 4 = 20$ too big

> Find two numbers which
> add up to 9 and which
> make 17 when
> multiplied together

Second guess $6.5 + 2.5 = 9$
(use a calculator) $6.5 \times 2.5 = 16.25$ too small
Make two more guesses so that you get as close to 17 as you
can.

19. Susie makes a pattern of rectangles from sticks.

  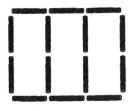

Shape-number	1	2	3
Number of sticks	6	10	14

Susie's rule is   'The number of sticks is four times the shape-number and then add 2'.

(a) Work out the number of sticks in shape-number 8.

(b) One of the shapes needs 50 sticks. What is its shape-number?

(c) Write a formula, without words, to work out the number of sticks for any shape-number. Use *S* for the number of *sticks* and *N* for the shape-number.
Write '*S* = ...'.

INDEX